D1713885

Beyond Belief
True Stories of Civilian Heroes
That Defy Comprehension

Compiled and Edited By
C. Douglas & Pamla M. Sterner
and Dwight Jon Zimmerman

Respectfully Dedicated to the Memory of:
COMEDIAN BOB HOPE
Thanks for the Memories . . .
And for teaching us there are many ways to serve.

Hero
Books
Publishing

COVER: Birlocho

Table of Contents

Introduction

The ability to tell a good story is an art.

World literature is filled with dramatic, sometimes true, but often fictional stories based on real-life characters whose biographies have evolved and been embellished over the years. Many such stories have been passed down from generation to generation, the tales themselves morphing into legendary status with each re-telling. Such legends have altered the history of their characters, often turning even unscrupulous individuals into heroes. I remember a pair of pajamas I had as a young boy with a badge on it that read: *Billy the Kid—Sheriff.*

The evolution of such stories is perhaps best explained in John Ford's 1962 movie *The Man Who Shot Liberty Valance*, adapted from a 1953 short story written by Dorothy M. Johnson. Towards the end of the movie Ransome Foster, a newspaper editor, utters one of the classic lines in entertainment movie history: *"When the truth becomes legend, print the legend."* It is a mantra that has made storytelling more entertaining.

Our goal in publishing the series, *Beyond Belief—True Stories of American Heroes That Defy Comprehension* of which this book about civilian heroes is the fourth, was to tell stories of real heroes, most of them American, and to do so without literary license or embellishment. This book is a compilation of stories that if you heard someone tell them in a bar you would think: *"There is no way this could have happened."*

But each and every story in this book is TRUE.

During my more than two decades of finding and compiling award citations for the *Military Times "Hall of Valor"* database that I curate, time and time again I have stumbled upon a story that, even I find despite my years of transcribing tens of thousands of award citations, strain my own sense of credibility.

Beyond Belief: True Stories of Civilian Heroes

Most of the stories in this book are based on actual award citations, written shortly after the action recounted in them. Such citations were not written by some adept storyteller with a solid grasp of language and drama, but usually by ordinary company/unit clerks and yeomen, based on the signed witness testimony of the men and women who saw the actions. All too often, however, award citations state only a brief synopsis of the actions of a hero in a moment of great danger. When one digs deeper into the witness statements supporting them, fascinating details are discovered.

On Veterans' Day 2020, I published *Beyond Belief—True Stories of American Heroes That Defy Comprehension,* a general military anthology. It was a step I took out of necessity. Over the last decade I have dedicated the vast majority of my working hours to developing the largest and most comprehensive database of military awards ever compiled. In the process I repeatedly read citations that left me shaking my head in wonder and thinking, *"There is a bigger story here that needs to be told."* Reluctant to take needed time away from my database work to write these stories, I thought, *"Why not share these citations with other writers and would-be writers, let them write the stories, and then compile and publish."* It turned out to be both a fun and personally satisfying experience that resulted in one of my favorite books.

After publication of that first book I thought, *"This is great. Let's do it again."* And it was in that vein of thought that I decided to serialize these, leading to: *True Stories of U.S. Navy Heroes that Defy Comprehension,* then *True Stories of Military Chaplains that Defy Comprehension*, and now this book on civilian heroes. My plan is to release two new books in the series every year, released on Memorial Day and Veterans Day.

- - 0 - -

Beyond the sheer incredulity of these stories of ordinary men and women who did amazing things, are the varying styles of our team of talented writers. *New York Times* bestselling author Dwight Jon Zimmerman, with his penchant for history and ability to find and recount little-known stories from history, is always a good read. He also serves as final editor for each volume of *Beyond Belief* stories.

Preface

Jim Fausone contributes as one of the team's finer story tellers, crafting interesting reads with a smooth, personal manner. Each of his three stories in this volume shows the versatility of his writing ability, detailing the stories of heroes from World War I, World War II, and the Vietnam War.

Jim Furlong, a Vietnam War hero (he'll blush in his self-effacing humility when he reads this), writes with a keen sense of military tactics, something he knows well. Jim is himself a recipient of the Distinguished Service Cross, and a brother in the Legion of Valor of the United States of America.

Portrait artist Colin Kimball, who is currently working on a book of his own, often graces his stories with a portrait of the subject of his stories. His well-crafted story in this volume about Vietnam War and later 9/11 hero Rick Rescorla is a carefully composed word portrait.

Adam Ballard, an active duty Marine and son of a Medal of Honor recipient, is a budding young writer who cut his teeth on the second *Beyond Belief* volume and continues to share great stories. Scott Baron, author of 17 military history books of his own, is my go-to-guy for those stories I feel belong in each volume, that no one else has volunteered to cover.

Finally, each *Beyond Belief* volume is graced by the artistic talent of my friend and our cover artist, Mario Birlocho.

The cover story for this volume details the harrowing World War II experience of one of my boyhood heroes, World War I **Ace of Aces** Eddie Rickenbacker. Although I was well-versed in his military exploits, it was not until a few year ago that I became aware of his twenty-four days at sea in a life raft, as a civilian, visiting American pilots early in that war. The harrowing account of how a fifty-two-year-old hero of days gone by survived in that second war, is truly beyond belief.

I have also chosen to dedicate each volume to some of my own personal heroes. For this volume, I chose to make the dedication to the memory of every veteran's favorite non-veteran, entertainer Bob Hope.

Beyond Belief: True Stories of Civilian Heroes

In my high school years I never missed his broadcast of shows in Vietnam. A few years later, on my first Christmas in Vietnam, I opted not to make the long and often dangerous convoy trip from my Fire Support Base to see him. On my second Christmas in Vietnam, however, I said to myself, *"SELF, you simply cannot spend two Christmases in Vietnam and not see Bob Hope."* So I rose early on a morning shortly before Christmas to endure that long convoy to Da Nang, to be one of tens of thousands of G.I.s enjoying the Bob Hope Christmas Show.

Decades later, in 1997, when Pam was preparing a special event in our hometown of Pueblo, I had my first occasion to connect personally with Mr. Hope. On March 25 Pam brought seventeen Medal of Honor recipients to our city to conduct patriotic assemblies in each of Pueblo's fifty-seven public and private schools. That evening we had a large, formal dinner and Pam had invited Las Vegas entertainer Wayne Newton to be our speaker. After Newton accepted our invitation, I contacted Mr. Hope. Within weeks he sent us a very wonderful letter of congratulations to Wayne Newton that was printed on the inside-cover of the dinner program.

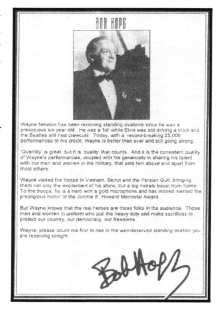

Three years later I was appointed by Colorado Governor Bill Owens to the Colorado State Board of Veterans Affairs, and in 2002 the Board members elected me Chairman. You can imagine my surprise in April of that year to get a letter from Mr. Hope's Director of Public Relations, Ward Grant. In it he wrote, *"(Mr. Hope) commented that as a patriot, speaker, writer, and historian you 'are among the best.' And he continued, 'The fact that Doug laughed*

at my jokes in Da Nang in 1971 has nothing to do with the praise I give him. Okay, it helped a little.'"

I am thankful to Scott Baron for closing this volume with the story of Bob Hope's commitment as a civilian, to America's veterans, activities for which the President of the United States made him an honorary veteran.

I suppose there will be some who will question my decision to include Mr. Hope in this collection. While it is true one cannot pinpoint a single engagement with the enemy in which he demonstrated uncommon valor (he would joke that his draft card classified him "4-Y, as in yellow"), like no other book I've been a part of before, this volume truly reflects that there are many ways to serve, and many ways to become a hero. Some served selflessly for decades like Bob Hope, others like Rick Rescorla who demonstrated valor in combat, went on in post-military life to serve heroically as a civilian. Others, like civilian Joe Galloway, not only performed heroically in a single moment in time but followed it with a lifetime of dedication and service to our nation's veterans.

Some of these heroes are complex individuals. Charles Lindbergh, another of my boyhood heroes, certainly demonstrated bravery in his 1927 trans-Atlantic flight as a civilian. However, military and other historians will long challenge the validity and appropriateness of his award of the Medal of Honor. Few of his detractors are aware of his World War II civilian service that Fifth Air Force commander General George Kenney described as one of the most striking contributions to the Pacific War. Lindbergh's instruction on P-38 performance enabled American pilots to extend their fighter's range, enabling them to escort bombers all the way to distant targets and back, saving many lives.

Another complex individual and personal long-time hero was John Paul Vann. Until reading the excellent story Jim Furlong did for this book, I was unaware of some of the man's personal failures. Not all of our heroes are Boy Scouts.

I sincerely hope the reader will enjoy this collection of stories, including several amazing women heroes, and some rather amazing civilian war correspondents. Heroes come in many uniforms, from many divergent backgrounds.

Beyond Belief: True Stories of Civilian Heroes

Heroes are heroes, not because they did the ordinary or achieved what is expected. Heroes are that because they did something incomprehensible, sometimes seemingly superhuman—an act or lifestyle that defies belief.

To prepare this book we called on some of our friends who have both the ability to tell a good story, and to do it in keeping with the mantra of another fictional entertainment character. Unlike Ransome Foster, *Dragnet* fictional detective Sergeant Joe Friday is remembered for his quote, *"Just the facts, ma'am."* Ironically, in this discussion of fact vs. legend, that well-remembered quote is itself an embellishment. Sergeant Joe Friday never spoke those words in any of the TV shows' eight original seasons from 1951 to 1959. Joe Friday *did* frequently say, while interviewing a woman witness, *"All we want are the facts, ma'am,"* or *"All we know are the facts ma'am."* But the quote as so often remembered reflects another of those alterations in the re-telling of the story of a character, real or fictional.

If you find yourself shaking your head as you read these stories and silently saying to yourself, *"This is unbelievable,"* know that this is the reaction we were seeking to achieve. Each of the authors in this book however, approached their research clinically. Rather than endeavoring to make a good story better through literary license, they have sought to seek and find details behind often abbreviated citations, from credible sources.

Our manta in development is more in keeping with the words that first appeared in Lord Byon's poem *Don Juan* in 1823, *"Tis strange—but true, for truth is always strange,"* or by Margaret Echard in her 1943 novel *Before I Wake*: *"Truth is not only stranger than fiction, but far more interesting."*

C. Douglas & Pamla Sterner

Mr. Eddie Rickenbacker

Time to Play an Ace

By C. Douglas Sterner

War erupted in Europe in 1939, and for two years the United States struggled to remain neutral. By 1941, nine out of ten Americans opposed any American intervention in the crises in Europe and Asia. Prominent spokesmen for the isolationists were the Army Air Service's two living Medal of Honor heroes: Mr. Eddie Rickenbacker and Mr. Charles Lindbergh. Both men had left military service. Rickenbacker resigned his commission as a colonel in the reserves in protest against what he called the *"legalized murder"* of Army pilots ordered to fly the airmail, a duty for which they were not trained. Lindbergh, one of those mail pilots who survived that debacle, resigned his own colonelcy in 1941. He did so in order to avoid political conflicts with the president, as by then he had become a high-profile speaker and leader in the isolationist **America First Committee**, which included Rickenbacker in its membership.

The two men had much in common: both were living icons of American history, both had visited Germany and witnessed that nation's burgeoning *Luftwaffe*. Both had called for an increased and expanded American air force. Though both would earn President Franklin D. Roosevelt's ire for their vocal advocacy of American neutrality, it would be Lindbergh who would suffer the wrath of the president.

1

Beyond Belief: True Stories of Civilian Heroes

Eddie Rickenbacker's loyalty could not be called into question. During World War I the then eighteen-year-old former race car driver had shot down twenty-six enemy aircraft in aerial combat, more than any other American. He was awarded an unprecedented, and unmatched, *eight* awards of the Distinguished Service Cross, and even when one of them was upgraded to the Medal of Honor eighteen years after the war, his seven DSC awards eclipse, even today, those awarded to any other person in history. The second highest number awarded was five, for Captain Douglas Campbell and for First Lieutenant Frank Hunter, both World War I pilots. In the interim between the world wars Rickenbacker was the only surviving World War I Army Air Service Medal of Honor recipient and America's Ace of Aces.

Rickenbacker left military service following World War I, becoming a pioneer in the development of both automobile and airplane transportation, including one of the earliest commercial airlines. He did remain a member of the Reserve Forces, constantly advocating for an independent American Air Force and testifying for the defense in the 1925 court martial of General William "Billy" Mitchell. Rickenbacker was a colonel in the Special Reserve when President Herbert Hoover awarded him the Medal of Honor in 1930. Three years later Franklin Delano Roosevelt became president, and Rickenbacker would find himself often at odds with the new president.

Soon after becoming president, Roosevelt rescinded private air mail contracts, including that of Eastern Air Transport where Rickenbacker was vice president, and transferred air mail delivery to inexperienced and undertrained pilots of the Army Air Corps. After several deadly air crashes, Rickenbacker referred to the policy as "legalized murder." Rickenbacker drew further ire from the President for his opposition to Roosevelt's New Deal policies, prompting FDR's administration to ban NBC Radio from broadcasting Rickenbacker's criticism. When German aggression began in Europe, Rickenbacker was a member of the isolationist **American First Committee**, further alienating him from the president. Their relationship remained strained despite the fact that Rickenbacker left the Committee in 1940 and began advocating American support for Great Britain in its valiant efforts in the **Battle of Britain**.

Rickenbacker's Atlanta Crash
February 27, 1941

In the early morning hours of February 27, 1941, the DC-3 of Eastern Airlines Flight 221, with Eddie Rickenbacker as one of its passengers, crashed just outside of Atlanta, Georgia, killing five and seriously injuring nine others. Among the seriously injured was Rickenbacker. Despite predictions and reports of his death, an irascible Rickenbacker, from his hospital bed, castigated the negative reporting and, four months later, weak but triumphant, walked out of the Atlanta hospital. He and his family moved to a small cottage on Candlewood Lake in Connecticut where he continued to work on rehabilitation.

In early December Rickenbacker and Adelaide were planning for a move to a houseboat in Miami, Florida, where Rickenbacker planned to continue his recovery. Since becoming an executive at Eastern, he had made it a habit of going to the New York office on Sunday, believing he could accomplish more work without distraction. But, that particular Sunday, December 7, 1941, was destined to be full of distraction.

The Japanese attack on Pearl Harbor, followed by Germany's declaration of war against the United States two days later, changed everything. Despite his pre-war isolationist stand, Rickenbacker had an enviable combat record, had advocated for a powerful air force, and, in Washington, had powerful friends, chief among them General Henry Arnold.

"How are you doing Eddie?" Asked Arnold's recognizable voice through the phone lines a few weeks later. *"Are you recovering from that horrible crash in Atlanta okay?"*

Rickenbacker told the general he was doing fine and that the attack on Pearl Harbor was spurring his recovery.

"Eddie, I've got a very important mission for you," Arnold continued. *"I can't tell you over the phone. When can you come to Washington?"*

"I'll be there bright and early Monday morning, Hap," Rickenbacker replied to his old friend who was now Chief of the U.S.

Army Air Forces. When the call ended, Rickenbacker later recalled, *"I had no idea what job he had for me. I knew that it would be an important one, one related to the mission of the Air Forces in our fight for freedom. I thanked God for sparing me to fight again for America. War is hell, but sometimes a necessary hell."*

Monday, March 9, 1942

General Arnold shook hands with his old friend and sized him up to see if indeed Eddie Rickenbacker had sufficiently recovered from the airplane crash. Rickenbacker looked tired, walked with a cane and a noticeable limp, but there was still fire in his eyes.

"I'm concerned about the reports I'm getting from combat groups in training, Eddie," Arnold announced. *"I'm told that they are indifferent, that they haven't got the punch they need to do the job they're being prepared for. I want you to go out and talk to these boys, inspire them, put some fire in them. And while you're there, I want you to look around and see what our problems are."*

After all the roadblocks Rickenbacker had faced from the president due to his prewar sentiments, this was exactly what he wanted to hear. The aging war hero didn't mind at all becoming the cheerleader for a new group of would-be heroes, and the mission directive also gave him opportunity to observe and offer constructive ideas to improve the Army Air Forces. *"I'll be ready to go in ten days,"* he replied.

"Eddie, some of these units will be on their way overseas in ten days," General Arnold remarked. So it was that, on the following day, March 10, Rickenbacker found himself in Florida, this time to visit and motivate young fliers at a unit in Tampa Bay. On Wednesday he was in Savanna, Georgia, to do the same; on Thursday he was in South Carolina; on Friday in Tallahassee, and in New Orleans on Saturday. Rickenbacker took Sunday off to write a report for General Arnold, and then continued his hectic pace in the weeks that followed.

At each of several daily stops over the next month, Rickenbacker spoke to the war-bound airmen, often for more than an hour. It was a tiring pace, but Rickenbacker was dedicated and determined, despite the toll it took on his still-recovering body. He also carefully took note of all he observed, reporting regularly back to General Arnold. In Tallahassee he spoke to a group of Black pilots, all of whom still carried enlisted rank. He wrote a letter to Arnold observing: *"They are a grand bunch of kids and great pilots, but something should be done immediately to commission them. They are deserving of it."* The Black airmen soon received the gold bars of second lieutenants.

In Long Beach, California, Rickenbacker visited with the new pilots of his old 94th Aero Squadron. It was a thrill marred only by a ruling by the adjutant general's office that the famous *Hat in the Ring* insignia could no longer be used by the modern-day 94th Squadron. The young pilots communicated to Rickenbacker that they wished to resurrect the historic trademark, and Rickenbacker went directly to General Arnold.

In an April 12 letter General Arnold thanked Rickenbacker for his efforts over thirty-two days during which he had visited forty-one groups of Army airmen. He wrote: *"Uncle Sam's Hat in the Ring insignia of the 94th Pursuit Squadron which you commanded with such distinction during the first world war is now being returned to that unit."*

When Rickenbacker wrapped up the tour on April 13, he organized his thoughts, wrote his report, and then went to see General Arnold. When he walked into Arnold's office it was not as a military man, but as a successful chairman of a board. Rickenbacker had been out of uniform for more than a decade and had conducted his recent tour as a civilian.

"Cut off the telephones," he asked Arnold when he entered his office, *"I want three hours of your uninterrupted attention."*

"That's impossible, Eddie," the Air Chief replied. *"I want to hear what you have to say, but you've got to be quicker than that."*

Beyond Belief: True Stories of Civilian Heroes

"Hap, you're the head man of this outfit. If you won't listen to me, then there's no sense in my continuing my efforts to be of help to you," Rickenbacker stated. Arnold advised Rickenbacker that all the top generals were on site and encouraged him to go in and talk to them.

"I've been all over the country talking to them," Rickenbacker retorted. *"I want you there, too. Unless you go in with me and listen to what I have to say, then there is no point of my carrying on. I'll walk out right now, and we'll forget the whole thing."*

Thereafter, for seven hours General Arnold and the top brass listened as Eddie Rickenbacker delivered his report and made his recommendations for improvement. Rickenbacker had built a successful airline in the 1930s through hard work, attention to detail, and a frank, direct leadership style. Now he brought it to Washington, D.C., and it was exactly what the fledgling Army Air Service needed most.

Shortly after that, at the direction of Secretary Stimpson, General Arnold called a meeting of all major airline executives. Arnold was speaking to the distinguished assembly when he noticed Rickenbacker walk in and offered him the podium.

Rickenbacker's style remained the forceful, no B.S. approach that had made him an American success story. He said, *"First thing I've got to say is that all of you guys get rid of the chisels that you've got in your pockets. I know. You brought a pocketful of them down here so that you could chisel your way out of doing things that you're going to have to do whether you like it or not. This is the time when you're going to have to think about your country first and your airline second. Because if your country doesn't win this war, you won't have any airline!"*

Rickenbacker's keen mind and frank manner got things done, and he continued to work with General Arnold throughout the summer of 1942, in order to bring necessary changes to the Army Air Forces. His genius, his leadership, and his dedication did not go unnoticed. On September 14, 1942, he received a letter from Secretary of War Henry Stimson himself. It said, in part:

Mr. Eddie Rickenbacker

> Dear Captain Rickenbacker:
>
> This spring you did a magnificent job in evaluating the fighting spirit and training of our men in the Army Forces. I am writing you at this time to ask if you would undertake to go to England and visit the various Army Air Forces stations in the bomber and fighter commands, as a continuation of your tour of inspection in March and April.
>
> I am, of course, fully aware of the high-spirited confidence and efficiency of the AAF air and ground crews. Nevertheless, my interest in our Army airmen overseas is so deep that I would welcome a first-hand report by a non-military observer on how they are getting along.
>
> If you accept this assignment, as I hope you will, I am happy to authorize you to proceed to England and visit the various AAF stations. On your return to this country, you would report to me directly.

Rickenbacker accepted the assignment. *"My personal reason for going on these missions, indeed the foundation of my life,"* he later wrote, *"can be summed up in one sentence: 'Men grow only in proportion to the service they render their fellow men and women.'"*

Following Rickenbacker earlier tour of the stateside installations, he had been offered, and declined, a commission as a brigadier general. Arnold and Stimson upped the ante, offering him the two stars of a major general. Again, the former colonel, who had always preferred the title *"Captain Eddie"*, declined. Rickenbacker felt he could best serve his country as a civilian, unencumbered by military protocol. *"When I return from these missions, I want to be able to pound the table, point to the facts and insist on what I believe to be the most efficient way of doing things,"* he explained.

Rickenbacker went to England, therefore, as a civilian, with unprecedented authority from the Secretary of War to order field commanders to assist him in the completion of his mission. He took with him as his personal aide, Colonel Hans Adamson, a valued personal friend. Adamson had handled the media during Rickenbacker's U.S. tour months earlier.
On Rickenbacker's secret mission to Europe during the fall of 1942, Adamson's job was reversed. To maintain the secrecy of his visit, he was to keep the press away from the American hero.

Beyond Belief: True Stories of Civilian Heroes

For his services, the War Department negotiated a modest salary with Rickenbacker who had asked for nothing at all. He was paid $1, making him a *"Dollar a Day"* man. He even paid his own expenses throughout the mission.

In England Rickenbacker paid particular attention to two key areas: a survey of the conduct of the air war in general, and evaluation of American equipment and personnel in general. Amid his tours of the flying fields he met with key American and British air strategists. He had hoped to meet the famous Air Marshall Sir Hugh Trenchard, but the legendary hero of World War I was abroad. Instead, he left Rickenbacker a copy of his own secret report to the Air Ministry.

Rickenbacker's fifty-first birthday came and went almost without notice on October 8. The man had far more important things to consume his time. Before he departed England three days later, he paid a visit to Lieutenant General Dwight Eisenhower. This was during the period when the European Commander of United States Forces was planning the greatest invasion in history to that point, **Operation Torch**, the landing at North Africa. Three copies of the top-secret plans were to be sent to Washington to ensure that at least one copy arrived. One copy traveled west by Navy cruiser, a second by special courier. When Rickenbacker departed England on October 11, he carried the third copy.

On Tuesday, October 13, Rickenbacker reported directly to Secretary Stimson and received his next assignment. There would be no rest for the American hero. On Wednesday the War Department issued orders authorizing Rickenbacker to make a similar tour of the Pacific, including a visit to the headquarters of General Douglas MacArthur. Secretary Stimson communicated a special, highly sensitive message to Rickenbacker to relay to the Pacific commander. Since it was so highly secret that it could not be written on paper, Rickenbacker memorized it.

On Saturday night, Rickenbacker and Colonel Adamson left New York for the West Coast. Rickenbacker spent Sunday visiting his mother in Los Angeles, then departed the following day on a Pan American *Sikorsky Clipper* for Hawaii, by way of San Francisco. At 10:30 p.m.,

Sgt. Alexander Kaczmarczyk

Tuesday, Rickenbacker and Adamson climbed aboard a B-17D *Flying Fortress* at Hickam Field for the flight from Hawaii to General MacArthur's headquarters at Port Moresby, New Guinea. In addition to the airplane's five-man crew, there was one more passenger, Alexander Kaczmarczyk, whom everyone called *Alex*. Alex was recently discharged from a hospital in Hawaii and was returning to his unit in Australia.

Cpt. William Cherry

Brigadier General William Lynd, commander of Hickam Field, personally drove Rickenbacker and Colonel Adamson to the airfield. As the pilot, Captain William Cherry tried to take off, a tire blew sending the plane out of control. Skillfully he managed to maneuver the big B-17 back on the runway and halt it before it could plunge into the bay beyond the airstrip. The poor start proved a bad omen.

Shortly after midnight, a replacement Flying Fortress taxied off the runway, taking Eddie Rickenbacker and seven American servicemen into the dark clouds of the tropical sky. Three days later the shocking news spread around the world. Rickenbacker was lost, with all aboard.

Lost At Sea

Three small rafts filled with men rose and fell in the twelve-foot swells of the South Pacific, barren but for them and the slowly sinking B-17 **Flying Fortress** that had become lost en route to New Guinea. The first hint of trouble came early that morning, at about 8:30 a.m. when Captain Cherry dropped from cruising altitude to about 1,000 feet to watch for the four-by-eight-mile island of Canton, where the plane was to land for refueling. When the 9:30 a.m. estimated arrival time came and went without sight of the small land speck, concern aboard the B-17 began to grow. At 10:15 a.m., Rickenbacker inquired how much fuel remained as pilot and navigator struggled to find out what had gone wrong. *"A little over four hours,"* Cherry replied.

The crew made radio contact with the American outpost at Palmyra, an atoll located roughly in the center of the Pacific Ocean and about 1,061 miles south-southwest of Hawaii. Captain Cherry climbed to 5,000 feet while the ground crew at Palmyra began firing antiaircraft shells, set to detonate at 7,000 feet, to mark the island's location. From the cockpit Cherry could see nothing. From the windows behind him in the cargo compartment, the anxious crewmen fruitlessly scanned the horizon for any sign of life.

It was obvious that the airplane was lost. With fuel running low, shortly after noon Sergeant James Reynolds, the radio operator, sent out an SOS. By now the airplane was so far off course that the call for help wasn't heard even at Palmyra. Captain Cherry pushed forward on the controls and dropped closer and closer to the waves below, in preparation for the inevitable moment when the fuel was gone and the engines died. Behind him, Rickenbacker and

Sgt. James Reynolds

the crew of the airplane were hastily breaking out rafts and gathering provisions for the anticipated days at sea, mentally steeling themselves for the imminent impact.

Mr. Eddie Rickenbacker

Captain Cherry handled that fateful and dangerous moment skillfully, setting his airplane down in the trough between two waves. Had he been even one or two seconds off in his calculations, the B-17's nose would have plunged into a twelve-foot wave, sending it to the bottom of the ocean. Sergeant Reynolds continued to bang out his SOS in Morris Code until the moment the airplane slammed into the water, tossing provisions and human cargo from wall to wall.

Lt. James Whittaker

Quickly the green-blue water of the ocean began to fill the B-17 as injured and dazed men struggled to release the rafts and exit the doomed airplane. Captain Cherry, Sergeant James Reynolds, and co-pilot Captain John Whittaker got into one of the two larger rafts. Lieutenant John DeAngelis, the crew's navigator, struggled to inflate the smaller two-man raft for himself and Alex. He maneuvered it as close as he could

Lt. John DeAngelis

to the floundering B-17, struggling against the heavy swells, while Alex tried to reach it. When the nearly drowning man tried to climb in, the raft capsized in the twelve-foot swells, forcing both he and DeAngelis to fight even harder for survival. Both men swallowed large amounts of the salty seawater but found within themselves the determination to right their raft and climb back into its cramped but buoyant confines.

Rickenbacker and Sergeant John Bartek, the flight engineer, took the remaining raft. They held it steady next to the slowly sinking B-17 as Colonel Adamson slid out onto the wing of the dying airplane. At age fifty-three, Adamson was the oldest of the eight, and he was in severe pain. His back had been injured in the crash. It was all he could do to slide from the wing and into the waiting arms of Eddie Rickenbacker.

Quickly the eight men took stock of their situation, glancing anxiously at each other across waves that quickly separated them. Despite the efforts to gather water, rations and emergency supplies in the minutes before the crash, when the moment of impact had come, none of the men had managed to transfer these to the rafts.

The big B-17 remained afloat for six minutes, causing the men to later regret the decision not to quickly return for water. Then the end came, the nose dropping and the tail raising heavenward as it plunged to the ocean floor. Rickenbacker looked at his watch. It was 2:36 p.m. Honolulu time, on October 21, 1942.

The heavy seas swamped all three rafts and the men bailed with abandon, at first unmindful of the fact that the current was pushing them further and further away from each other. Quickly Rickenbacker called them all back in, each man paddling furiously to join their comrades. Then the three rafts were lashed together in a line. Rickenbacker later related his sentiment at the time. He said, *"A strong man may last a long time alone, but men together somehow manage to last longer."*

None of the eight men dared guess at how long they might have to survive at sea. The Pacific Ocean was a mighty big place. And, there was a war on.

Day 1

Colonel Adamson was in the worst shape, lying almost motionless in Rickenbacker's raft and struggling against intense pain. All of the men were seasick and went through an initial period of vomiting that eventually faded—all of them that is, except for the young Alex. His body retched for hours into the evening and, although relatively uninjured, he seemed to be suffering nearly as badly as Adamson. The plane's impact had thrown Reynolds, still pounding out his SOS until the last minute, against his radio console cutting a deep gash in his nose. The only other major injury was to Bartek, who shared the second raft with Rickenbacker and Adamson. He had ripped his fingers to the bone on a piece of metal while untangling the ropes to push the rafts out of the forward hatch when the plane crashed.

As the afternoon wore on the eight survivors took stock of their situation. The rafts contained no drinking water, and all the emergency rations now rested on the ocean floor, inside the sunken B-17. Rickenbacker had a chocolate bar in his pocket and Alex had nearly half a dozen, but these had been destroyed when his raft capsized. Captain Cherry had stuffed four oranges in his pockets moments before the crash, and this comprised the full complement of food the men would have available until rescue.

Rickenbacker was still fully dressed in a blue, summer-weight business suit complete with necktie and pocket-handkerchief. Colonel Adamson was in full uniform and the pilot and copilot wore their flight jackets. The other men had stripped down to swim from the sinking plane to the rafts, and their bodies now lay exposed to the elements.

Three men were crammed into each of the two larger, five-man rafts, with DeAngelis and Alex sharing the smaller two-man raft. Rickenbacker wondered who had determined the rafts' rated capacity. Each of the larger ones measured only six feet nine inches long and two feet four inches wide. The three men in each were forced to overlap each other in the pitching seas that threw them from swell to swell.

Almost as soon as the men in the rafts began their odyssey, the eight survivors noticed that they were not alone. From day one until the rescue twenty-four days later, sharks followed the men. When night came, stillness fell across the Pacific, broken only by the agonized groans of Colonel Adamson and the sound of Alex retching in dry heaves as the smaller raft trailed the two larger ones.

Day 2

Throughout the first long, cold night, the men kept up a system of two-hour watches, scanning the darkness for any signs of light from a passing airplane or ship in the distance. During the night the rafts were bumped again and again by the sharks that followed, a grim reminder of the only alternative to the cramped quarters of the small rafts. Rickenbacker suffered in agony, the stiffness and chill of the night leaving him in great pain from injuries now a year old.

Early morning revealed a calming of the high waves, and the three rafts pulled closer together. Rickenbacker was selected custodian of the four oranges that comprised the men's rations. The men determined that they would split one orange every two days, spreading them out to last a week and a day. Rickenbacker carefully cut the first orange in half, then quarters, and finally eighths. Each man thankfully consumed his breakfast. It was the only meal scheduled for the day.

The ocean surface became mirror-calm the second day, and the sun became unbearably hot when it rose into the morning skies. By noon the exposed bodies of the men who had stripped for the swim to the rafts began turning pink — then brilliant red. Blisters rose as flesh baked in the unrelenting heat. Rickenbacker had three large handkerchiefs in his suit pocket and passed these around. The men tied them bandit-fashion below their eyes to protect their faces. A battered hat Adelaide had threatened to burn for years sheltered Rickenbacker's eyes from the blazing sun. He was thankful it had survived not only his fashion-conscious wife, but also the plane crash and its aftermath.

When darkness fell on the second night, Captain Cherry brought out the eighteen flares and Very Gun used for firing them. These, along with two pistols carried by the pilot and copilot, were among the meager lot of survival gear that had reached the raft. Despite the fact that the men were not sure whether or not their errant flight path had taken them into Japanese-controlled waters, it was decided to fire three flares each night for six days in hopes of attracting rescue.

The first flare was shot upward as soon as the darkness was complete. The shell was a dud. Rather than wait the planned interval to release the second flare, Cherry reloaded and fired again. This time the flare burst to burn dimly for a few seconds. Though better than the first, it was not what the men had hoped for.

Days 3–7

Captain Cherry fired the third flare of the night shortly before dawn broke. The seas remained totally calm; the rafts idle on the surface. The sun continued to broil flesh and cause multiple blisters and seeping skin ulcers. Colonel Adamson could barely move from his pain, and Alex continued to retch and shiver. The other men seemed stronger and determined to survive. Even so, death almost seemed preferable to the slow torture. The salty water of the Pacific coated the bodies of the men, then evaporated to leave a white, salty film, further irritating their skin.

Rickenbacker later described the men's first six days at sea as the worst days of his life—far more painful and miserable than the Atlanta plane crash. The fourth night, and each night thereafter until the flares were exhausted, Captain Cherry fired three signals. On the fourth day, Rickenbacker cut the second orange into eighths and the men had their second meal. Most of the men savored their morsel as long as they could, eating even the rind. Rickenbacker and Cherry saved the rinds of theirs for bait. Two hooks and some fishing line had been among the supplies that survived the crash, but the men had no bait. In the clear, calm waters, the men could see hundreds of fish around their rafts. None of the fish, sadly enough, had an appetite for orange peelings.

On their fifth day at sea the men decided to eat the third orange, primarily out of concern for Adamson and Alex, who seemed only to become sicker and weaker. Temperaments began to fray, and discouragement became as pervasive as the hot sun during the day, or the chill at night. Almost to a man, their bodies were blistered, raw, and oozing puss. Conditions in the small rafts were cramped as the men tried to keep from stiffening up. Any time one man moved in the raft to ease his stiffness or find comfort in a new position, his body would brush up against the raw flesh of his comrades, causing pain for all of them.

Lieutenant Whittaker, the forty-one-year-old co-pilot, watched the fruitless efforts of Rickenbacker and Cherry to catch fish. When the orange peelings failed to entice a bite, Rickenbacker fashioned Adamson's key chain into a makeshift spinner. The fish nosed it curiously but refused to take the hook. Whittaker took one of the oars, tearing away the flat paddle with pliers and attempted to sharpen it to a point. The next shark that bumped against the raft felt the point of Whittaker's makeshift spear, but it was far too dull to penetrate the thick skin. After several more jabs Whittaker tossed the useless spear, now equally useless as an oar, into the bottom of the raft.

Adamson, as a colonel, was the ranking member of the group. He was also in great pain, sick, and often delirious. Twenty-seven-year-old Captain Cherry held up reasonably well and continued to command his crew. But it was Eddie Rickenbacker, who became leader, mentor, father-figure, and ultimately villain, for the doomed group. When the weaker men began losing hope and were giving in to the seductive serenity of death, he tried to shock their senses and motivate them to continue on.

At age twenty-two, Alex was the youngest of the eight. He was also in the worst shape, shivering uncontrollably even when the hot sun blistered his body. Unknown to the others, his unquenchable thirst had driven him to drink seawater. Much of the time he was delirious, chanting *"Hail Mary,"* crying out for his mother, or rambling about a girl he called Snooks. During his few lucid moments he would pull a photo of Snooks from his wallet, talk to it, and pray over it. He was now convinced that he would never see his young sweetheart again. It was obvious to the other men that Alex was fading fast and had given up the fight.

Rickenbacker pulled the rope that tethered his own raft to that of DeAngelis and Alex in the rear of the string, drawing them closer until he was face to face with Alex. *"What is wrong with you kid? Why the hell can't you take it?"* Rickenbacker shouted as loud as his weakening voice would allow. It was brutal, but in Rickenbacker's mind, it was also a necessary shock treatment to motivate the young man to fight for his life. The other men looked at Rickenbacker, stunned, and in disdain, unaware that this outburst had been a calculated effort to save the man's life. It was only as a result of the argument that followed that Rickenbacker learned that the young man was recently released from the hospital after contracting a tropical disease of the mouth that left him perpetually thirsty. Alex had been fragile before the crash. Now he was close to death.

On the sixth day at sea Rickenbacker split the fourth and final orange. Already it was drying out and probably wouldn't have survived another day. It quickly vanished along with the last shreds of hope. Up until the last orange was consumed, the men had something to look forward to. Now, nothing remained to anticipate for tomorrow except hot sun, shivering nights, and more doldrums on the surface of the ocean. Tempers continued to flare, bickering was constant, and even the stronger men began totally falling apart.

Rickenbacker had noticed Sergeant Bartek, who shared the middle raft with himself and Adamson, reading daily from the **New Testament** he carried in his jumper pocket. Rickenbacker told the others to pull their rafts closer and instituted twice-daily services of Bible reading and prayer. Two of the men initially objected, both professing a lack of religious conviction. Rickenbacker insisted that all of them contribute, each finding and reading a passage of scripture at each of the twice-daily prayer services.

In the days that followed, some of the men became bitter when they failed to see answers to their prayers, but the practice went on. Rickenbacker later wrote: *"Under the baking sun on the limitless Pacific, I found a new meaning, a new beauty in its familiar words."*

Day 8

Captain Cherry had just finished reading the morning prayer service and each of the eight men had prayed in turn and sung a hymn. Rickenbacker was dozing off as the ceremony gave way to small talk when a light pressure on his head awakened him. At once he guessed it must be a sea gull, and a quick glance at his companions told him he must be right.

All eyes were on Rickenbacker's hat.

Slowly Rickenbacker began moving his arms, reaching his hands alongside his ears and then upward. All the while he resisted the strong urge to grab quickly for the bird, lest it be startled and escape. A deep hush fell across the group of men and all eyes remained riveted on Rickenbacker's every move.

Rickenbacker sensed his hand was near the brim of his hat and continued to move in slow, even, calculated motions. He couldn't see the bird—could only guess at its position on his head. When his hands were close to where he thought the gull must be, he closed his hand and felt the welcome texture of a leg.

In a fraction of a second he wrung the bird's neck and stripped its feathers to reveal moist, dark meat. He divided it equally among the eight men, saving the intestines for bait. When the men had savored the sinewy but delicious sea gull, Cherry dropped his fishing line from his raft with a piece of the bird's intestine. Almost immediately he landed a small mackerel about twelve inches long. This meat was cool and moist, satisfying thirst as well as hunger. Rickenbacker was equally successful when he dropped his own fishing line into the water, landing a small sea bass. It was kept for the following day's meal.

Day 9

His spirits buoyed by the two-course meal on his ninth day at sea, Rickenbacker dozed off when darkness fell. At midnight he woke with a jar. Something was happening, he knew. For the first time in a week he felt movement.

Around the raft the waves were picking up and a wind was whipping through his tattered clothes, illuminated now by flashes of bright lightning. The men could smell rain, and quickly stripped off their clothing to capture the first drops. The storm teased them for two hours and then, as Rickenbacker leaned his head face up over the edge of the raft, he felt the first drop of rain hit him in the face, followed by another, and then another. And then the rain stopped, almost as quickly as it had started.

Lightning still lit the clouds above, and the men could see a squall in the distance. *"It's over there,"* Rickenbacker shouted, as the men picked up oars and paddled with what little strength remained. Somehow, in desperation, they found the strength to continue and were soon being tossed about in the middle of the squall.

In the heavy waves, disaster struck before water could be collected. A rope came loose and the small raft containing DeAngelis and Alex began drifting away into the darkness. The men in the remaining two rafts continued to paddle furiously, searching the dark waters for their comrades and fearing they were lost. Then a white flash off a cresting wave backlit the small craft. The men paddled towards it and re-secured the line.

The rain revived even the quickly fading Adamson enough that he could pitch in to collect water. The men used the first raindrops to rinse out their salt-caked clothes, and then spread them out again to capture the fresh water and wring it out into containers before disaster struck again. The lead raft with Cherry, Whittaker and Reynolds capsized, throwing the men into the now-raging surf. Rickenbacker recalled, *"Determined men who won't give up can do anything."* Somehow, with the help of their comrades, the three men clung to the hand lines along their raft until it could be righted, and they were pushed and pulled back in.

The water collected that night was meager in comparison to the need, but it brought some relief and, more importantly, some new hope. During the morning the men ate the small fish Rickenbacker had caught the previous day, washing it down with each man's ration of water. As the day wore on, Alex's condition worsened, and Rickenbacker increased the dying man's water ration. When evening fell, Rickenbacker transferred Bartek to the tailing raft with DeAngelis, and carefully moved the convulsing, nearly lifeless body of Alex to his own raft.

For two nights and two days Eddie Rickenbacker cradled the quivering body of young Alex next to his own, much like a father cares for his child. It was a gentle side of his nature Rickenbacker had not yet revealed during this dangerous time. For forty-eight hours, he did his best to nurture the quickly fading young sergeant.

On the evening of the twelfth day at sea, during one of his few lucid moments, Alex asked to be placed back in the trailing raft. In the darkness that night Rickenbacker listened to the young man's shallow breathing. Somewhere in the passing of time, Alex gave a long sigh. Then, all was quiet.

Day 13

It was obvious in the early morning darkness that Sergeant Alex Kaczmarczyk had died, but his death was not so easy to accept. At daybreak Bartek paddled up to Rickenbacker's raft while Eddie checked for a pulse, a heartbeat, or a shallow breath. The body was already stiff, but Rickenbacker refused to do what had to be done. Captain Cherry and Lieutenant Whittaker verified Eddie's diagnosis. DeAngelis did the best he could to offer the young man a Catholic burial service, and then the body of the young sergeant was rolled over the edge and into the sea. It didn't sink as they thought it would. Instead, the lifeless body of Alex Kaczmarczyk followed the rafts for some distance, floating face down on the swells of the Pacific.

Days 14–18

The death of Alex dealt a crushing blow to the morale of all seven survivors, reminding them that death was near and forcing them to come to grips with their own mortality. The loss of one man left the smaller raft slightly more spacious, and Bartek asked DeAngelis to change places with him. DeAngelis consented to give up the small raft, but preferred to float with the other officers, generating a series of changes that might have been comical but for the desperate situation of the seven men. Sergeant Reynolds joined Rickenbacker and Adamson in the middle raft, Lieutenant DeAngelis joined Captain Cherry and Lieutenant Whittaker in the lead raft, and Sergeant Bartek floated alone in the trailing smaller raft.

In the early darkness before daybreak, Rickenbacker sensed something wrong. No longer could he feel the tug of a rope behind his own raft. Bartek's small raft was adrift, and Rickenbacker was sure that it hadn't been an accident. When light began streaking across the horizon, Bartek could be seen in the distance. His lone-wolf venture hadn't got him very far, and at the insistent yells of the other men, he paddled back to tether his raft in its proper place. He later admitted honestly that he had untied the raft himself during the night. No one asked him why.

Despite his pain and constant delirium, Colonel Adamson made daily notations on the side of his raft with a pencil. With the water from the storm five days earlier now gone, and with the doldrums returning to the glassy-smooth Pacific, he wrote his last notation of the odyssey: *"Fourteenth day. Rickenbacker and I still alive."* It appeared to be his epitaph. His body burned to a pulp, his back and neck wracked with pain, and his mind fogged by nearly constant delirium, he was close to death. For Rickenbacker it was especially disheartening. Adamson had been a long-time friend and confidant. Now he was wasting away, and there was nothing Rickenbacker could do to stop it.

Sometime during the night Rickenbacker felt the raft lurch violently. His first thought was that a shark had attacked. Then he noticed there was more room in the raft. Adamson was gone.

Reaching over the side, Rickenbacker felt Adamson's shoulder. In despair, his friend had apparently decided to put an end to his misery. Rickenbacker would not let him die, holding tightly to him but finding he was too weak to pull him back into the raft. Only with help from the lead raft was the flaccid body of Colonel Adamson returned to its position at the rear of the raft.

Daylight brought some clarity to Adamson's fogged mind and, realizing what had happened, he tried to force a smile and stuck out a weak hand towards Rickenbacker. Eddie recognized the apology for what it was, and then did what he later claimed was one of the most difficult actions of his life.

"I don't shake hands with your kind," he snarled at his best friend, ignoring the proffered handshake. *"If you want to shake hands, you've got to prove yourself first!"*

Hans Adamson sadly withdrew his hand. Rickenbacker saw it as a decisive moment. Chances were very good that Hans was close to death, and his last memory of Rickenbacker might certainly be a sorrowful one. Rickenbacker honestly believed it was then that Adamson determined to fight . . . to survive . . . to live.

"Rickenbacker, you are the meanest, most cantankerous (expletive) that ever lived," one of the other survivors shouted across the water. Within hearts that had been crushed by too much pain and suffering, anger was arising. Several of the men determined in their hearts that they *"would live for the sheer pleasure of*

burying Rickenbacker at sea," and later admitted the same to Rickenbacker.

In his own mind, Rickenbacker refused to give up or to let anyone else give up. *"It was clear to me,"* he later recalled, *"that God had a purpose in keeping me alive. It was to help the others, to bring them through. I had been saved to serve. It was an awesome responsibility, but I accepted it gladly and proudly . . . I did not forget that I, myself, still had a mission to perform and a message to deliver to General MacArthur."*

Despite the anger and profane words exchanged among the seven men, the twice-daily prayer services continued until about the seventeenth day. That was the day the men finally decided to part ways in hope of rescue. Against Rickenbacker's better judgment, since he had always felt the men had the best chance of rescue by remaining together, the others convinced him it was time to separate. Their hope was that the three healthiest men might be able to break out of the ocean currents that pushed all three rafts southeast, and perhaps find a transport ship or airplane. With most of the remaining water and all of the remaining oars, the three Air Force officers in the lead raft set out in the early afternoon. When darkness fell, little headway had been made. When morning dawned, Rickenbacker looked across the green swells only to find the three rafts still floating nearly side-by-side. It was a great source of disappointment, lessened only by an unexpected rainfall.

The run of good fortune continued into the night when a pack of sharks began feasting upon a school of mackerel all around the rafts. In the frenzy that followed, one mackerel jumped into Rickenbacker's raft, followed by another that jumped into Cherry's raft.

Day 19

The rain that refreshed the seven survivors intermittently became steadier with the dawn. By early afternoon the waves became large, white-capped swells. Water collected the night before, the men knew, might well last for several more days. Suddenly Captain Cherry yelled above the howl of the winds, *"I hear a plane. Listen!"*

Peering intently into the distance, all seven men strained their eyes against the dark clouds. Then they saw it—a single-engine pontoon boat flying low through the squall about five miles away. Bartek stood up in the raft he now shared with Rickenbacker and Adamson, Rickenbacker steadying him against the crash of the ocean swells, to wave his shirt. All seven men, including Adamson, yelled at the top of their voices. Then the dark clouds obscured the small plane in the distance, and it disappeared. The men had gone unseen on the dark waters.

Still, for the first time in nineteen days, the doomed men had seen signs of life beyond the rims of their raft. A new optimism began to grow.

Days 20 and 21

Two similar airplanes appeared in the distant skies the following day. The men had no way of knowing if they were American or Japanese aircraft, but by this time it mattered little. Neither pilot had noticed the three small rafts that floated on the wide expanse of the Pacific Ocean.

Four more airplanes appeared on the distant horizon early the following day, but again the men in the rafts went unseen. During the afternoon the survivors were able to scoop up several minnows that swarmed around the raft. These provided a most welcome meal at a time when hopes once again were beginning to sag. As the day wore on, no more aircraft were spotted. Rickenbacker feared that, perhaps, the rafts had been near an island base, and then floated on past it.

Tempers flared at about six o'clock that evening, and a great argument broke out between Captain Cherry in the lead raft, and DeAngelis in the smaller raft that trailed in the chain. Cherry wanted his navigator to give up the small raft so that he could then set out alone seeking help. *"I'm going to try to make land. Staying together is no good. They'll never see us this way."*

Rickenbacker sided with DeAngelis as tempers grew even hotter, but Cherry remained insistent. He told Rickenbacker, *"I won't go unless you agree it is all right for me to."* Against his better judgment, Rickenbacker finally consented. In the fading twilight, he watched as the B-17's captain floated alone into the distance.

DeAngelis and Whittaker took up the refrain, wanting to strike out on their own as well, along with the nearly dead Sergeant Reynolds. The latter was too ill to add his own preference to the argument. Tempers continued to pit man against man until Rickenbacker was too tired to continue, realizing it was fruitless. When darkness finally fell, three rafts still floated on the dark swells, but now each was separated from the others by miles of water.

Days 22 and 23

Three men floated alone, now, almost too sick to despair their situation. Rickenbacker tried to give Adamson and Bartek their rations of water, but both men were so weak they could hardly lift their heads to drink. During one brief lucid moment Bartek asked, *"Have the planes come back?"*

"No, there haven't been any since day before yesterday," Rickenbacker replied weakly.

"They won't come back," Bartek repeated again and again, fading into delirium.

Day 24

Rickenbacker was awake, but his mind had numbed after days of torment and repeated disappointment. He could see or hear nothing, until he felt Bartek pull feebly on his shirt and whisper weakly through parched lips, *"Listen, Captain—planes! They're back. They're very near."*

Rickenbacker struggled to stand but could only raise his frail body to a seated position as he waved the battered remnant of his old hat at the two passing airplanes. His heart sank when he saw

them fade into the distance. He knew this had been the last chance for any of them. Now the planes had had vanished.

"Half an hour later we heard them again, much closer," he later recalled. *"They came directly out of the sun, straight for us. The first dived right over the raft. We yelled like maniacs. The plane was so low that I could see the pilot's expression. He was smiling and waving. Not until then did I look at the insignia. It was the U.S. Navy and gratitude and happiness filled me. I waved and waved out of a half-crazy notion that the pilot must be made to understand we were not three dead men on a raft."*

Incredibly, and disappointingly, the planes vanished again. Hope washed away with the fear that they would not return. Darkness fell. And then the planes were back, one circling overhead as the other landed on the ocean swells and taxied up to the raft.

Colonel Adamson was so close to death that he had to be hoisted into the cockpit. Lieutenant W. F. Eadie of the rescue aircraft advised Rickenbacker that they were in hostile waters and had to watch for Japanese ships. He told him that an American PT boat was en route to ferry the men to safety, but first the Navy floatplane would have to taxi across the water. With a full cockpit, Rickenbacker had to be strapped in a sitting position on the airplane's left wing. Bartek was similarly tied onto the right wing. For half-an-hour the night wind whipped around the two men as Lieutenant Eadie taxied towards the waiting PT boat.

Throughout the journey Rickenbacker kept shouting: *"This is heaven! Thank God! God bless the Navy!"*

Rickenbacker and Bartek were transferred from the flying boat to the waiting PT boat a short time later; and were rushed to a hospital at the nearby American base on the Ellice Islands (now Tuvalu).

Colonel Adamson, so near death his survival was still uncertain, was flown on to the hospital.

En route, Rickenbacker received the best news he could have hoped for. Two days earlier the raft with Whittaker, DeAngelis and Reynolds had reached a small island after a dangerous brush with violent surf and preying sharks. There, they camped for the night and the following day were surprised by a group of friendly natives. The natives rowed them from the small island to safety, where American rescue forces picked them up. They informed their rescuers to search for the remaining rafts.

That same afternoon a Navy pilot had spotted the raft carrying Captain Cherry. A short time later he, too, was pulled from the waters of the Pacific. All seven survivors had been rescued and were being transported to the hospital. The following morning the men enjoyed their first real meal in twenty-four days: soup and ice cream.

Later, on that Saturday afternoon, five of the seven survivors were flown to a larger hospital in Samoa. Reynolds and Bartek were left behind, too critical to move. Hans Adamson was worse even than those two, but doctors determined that the advantages of the larger, better-equipped hospital, outweighed the dangers of moving him.

The Mission

Despite the ordeal he had just been through, Eddie Rickenbacker hadn't forgotten the reason he had come to the Pacific.

In his first contact to Secretary Stimson he requested, and received, permission to continue that mission. Two weeks later, on December 1, Rickenbacker checked in on his recovering comrades, then boarded a B-24 transport to fly to Australia.

Over the next four days Rickenbacker continued to visit air bases along the route. He maintained his grueling schedule, despite the fact that his body was still weak, and was fifty-five pounds lighter for his ordeal.

General MacArthur refused to allow Rickenbacker to fly to Port Moresby in an unarmed plane and sent a heavily armed B-17 to ferry him. Rickenbacker arrived in time to spend the weekend with the MacArthurs, and to deliver his communiqué from Secretary Stimson. Few secrets of World War II have survived the revealing light of the decades. One that has, is the content of that message.

Ten days later Rickenbacker was back in Samoa after stopping to visit with American airmen at other stations along the way. His stops included a visit to Henderson Field on the island of Guadalcanal, *"A miserable little airstrip"* where *"it was difficult to see how men could even exist under such conditions, much less carry on the highly skilled warfare of the twentieth century,"* he recalled.

Upon his return to Samoa he checked in on his friend Hans, who was improving but still in serious condition. *"I'm going to Upola Island this weekend,"* Rickenbacker advised him. *"I'll be back here on Monday. If you are strong enough, you can fly out with me to Hawaii then."* Rickenbacker's promise was just the motivation Hans needed, and at 5:00 p.m. on December 14, the two men were back in Hawaii.

Rickenbacker left Hawaii on December 15, leaving Hans behind in a hospital to continue his recovery. Eventually it would be complete, and the intrepid colonel who had come so close to death in the Pacific, lived a long and fruitful life. On December 19, Rickenbacker reported to Secretary Stimpson. The following day, from his home in New York, Rickenbacker gave a stirring and patriotic radio address to the Nation.

Beyond Belief: True Stories of Civilian Heroes

He told America, *"You can never approximate the sacrifices our men are making on the battlefront for you and me. If I can only help you understand that, then I will be able to enjoy the first Sunday afternoon I have spent at home in many, many weeks."*

Eddie Rickenbacker was approached by *Life* magazine for the story of his incredible ordeal and survival at sea. Over the next month he wrote it, and it was published in three parts over three consecutive weeks beginning on January 25, 1943. In that story Rickenbacker detailed his *"21 Days Adrift in the Pacific."* The $25,000 fee he received for the story was contributed to the Army Air Forces Aid Society and was presented to the wife of General Hap Arnold who served as that organization's vice president. The printed account of those days at sea was accompanied by black and white drawings.

Later that same year when he published the same account in a book titled *Seven Came Through*, Rickenbacker again referred to his *"twenty-one days at sea."* Only later did he realize that after being lost on October 21, the total time at sea was not twenty-one, but *twenty-four* days. The date of his rescue was Friday the Thirteenth (November 13, 1942).

But Rickenbacker's service to the nation during the war didn't end with his mission to MacArthur. In 1943 he was asked to participate in a fact-finding mission to the Soviet Union. So great was Rickenbacker's reputation that, in the otherwise notoriously secretive country, he was given carte blanche to visit any military post and position he wished by chief of the Red Army, Marshal Georgy Zhukov, himself.

Rickenbacker spent almost two months in the Soviet Union, visited numerous bases, witnessed part of the Battle of Kursk, and came away impressed with how well the Red Army was using Lend-Lease weapons and supplies sent by America. For his service during World War II he was awarded the Medal for Merit, the civilian equivalent to the military's Legion of Merit.

Dr. Mary Edwards Walker

A Woman Ahead of Her Time

By Dwight Jon Zimmerman

Dr. Mary Edwards Walker has a distinction unique in American military history. She is the only woman to be awarded the Medal of Honor; a high point in a life that ran the gamut from great achievement to great injustice.

While many extraordinary women made their mark in nineteenth century America, none garnered more attention or inspired more controversy during their lifetime than the maverick Dr. Mary Edwards Walker. Her rise to the pedestal of international fame and fall into the wilderness of historical footnote was epic. She was the second woman to earn a

An early photographic portrait of Dr. Mary Edwards Walker showing her wearing her Medal of Honor.
Library of Congress

physician's degree in America, a social activist for women's rights and issues that went far beyond suffrage. She was also a temperance advocate, an abolitionist, bestselling author, lecturer, spy, prisoner of war, and, as if that weren't enough, a veterans' advocate as well.

Though all of that contributed to her worldwide fame, it was not so much *what* she did that set her apart from other similarly driven women, it was her status as a fashion pariah that literally made her stand out from her sister suffragettes.

Dr. Walker openly defied the feminine fashion custom of the day of wearing corsets and hoop skirts. Her reason was one of health. Dr. Walker wore pants. While such a fashion statement now is considered acceptable, back then a woman could—and did—go to jail for wearing *"mannish attire"* as it was then called. She stated that corsets and tight skirts were unhealthy (which they were) and that they restricted movement (which they did). Dr. Walker wasn't the only woman to advocate such, but she was the most famous, even more famous than Amelia Bloomer who designed the less restrictive style known as reform dress, also called *"Bloomers."* Throughout her life Dr. Walker would be mocked, arrested, and jailed for wearing pants.

Mary Walker was born on November 26, 1832, in Oswego, New York, the youngest of seven children. Her farmer parents were progressive to the point of revolutionary when it came to the raising of their six daughters and one son. Ignoring the gender norms of the day, they encouraged their daughters to fend for themselves, instilled in them a sense of justice that charged them to be forthright in speaking out, and exercise other traits and behaviors then attributed to men.

When Mary enrolled in Syracuse Medical School in 1853, she found herself confronting a gender-centric prejudice that would dog her medical career: an attitude held by the majority of both men and women of the time who believed that while it was acceptable for a woman to be a nurse, being a doctor was, well, weird, unbecoming, and, most importantly, beyond the intellectual capability of women. Upon graduation in 1855, she divided her time between her medical practice and her women's rights activism, lecturing and writing for dress reform, suffrage, and other social issues.

By the time the Civil War erupted in 1861, Walker was already a rising star on the national scene regarding women's issues, but it was in the Civil War that her fame would skyrocket. In journalism parlance, she was *"good copy."* Early on she had learned how to cultivate reporters, and she maintained a lifelong relationship with the press.

Dr. Mary Edwards Walker

In addition to making powerful and influential friends, she accumulated a number of equally powerful enemies. In the suffragette movement the two most important were Susan B. Anthony and Elisabeth Cady Stanton. The two were rivals who didn't like each other. Though today thought of as united, the suffragette movement actually was rife with rivalries, factions, and differing— even conflicting—agendas.

Even so, these two buried their hatchet in common cause against Dr. Walker. So great became their jealousy and hatred of her (after all, she was something they weren't: an independent career woman, a Civil War hero, and most galling of all, she violated their sense of fashion propriety) that they went so far as to call for her arrest while she was on stage speaking during a women's rights convention. More successfully, they literally wrote Dr. Walker out of the multi-volume post-war official history of the suffragette movement even though she was one of its most influential advocates.

Elizabeth Cady Stanton, seated, and Susan B. Anthony were leaders in the fractious women's suffrage movement of the nineteenth century. Rivals, their hatred and jealousy of Dr. Walker and her prominence in the movement, led them to join in a common cause against her that ultimately saw them all but writing Dr. Walker out of the official history of the movement, even though she was one of its greatest and most famous advocates.

Library of Congress

Dr. Walker's other important adversary was the War Department.

Her battle against the War Department began at the Civil War's outbreak. Dr. Walker was among the many physicians who offered their services to the War Department. But even though the need was acute, she was turned down flat. The reason: she was female and told it was illegal for a woman to be an army officer (doctors were given officer's commissions). But if she wanted to serve, the War Department was willing to accept her as a volunteer nurse.

Dr. Walker dug in her heels. She was a doctor, and she would serve as a doctor, dammit. Thus began a years-long battle between her and the War Department bureaucracy over various issues, the most contentious being her desire to serve as a doctor and concomitant request for an officer's commission. Resolution of the officer's commission sticking point would make history.

In between waging her bureaucratic battle, from 1861 to 1863 she successfully worked as a volunteer physician for the army, going back and forth from Washington hospital to Virginia battlefields treating the wounded and overseeing their transport to Washington, D.C. She also acted as concierge, scribe, lawyer, and War Department red tape cutter for soldiers and their families convalescing and living in Washington, all the while keeping up the pressure to formally serve.

In September 1863, she went west to assist in caring for wounded from the Battle of Chickamauga and the Battle of Chattanooga. Her medical and organizational skills so impressed Army of the Cumberland commander General George Thomas that he signed orders authorizing her appointment as a *"contract civilian physician"* with the equivalent rank of lieutenant. In addition to her medical work for Thomas's army, she also served as a spy, going behind enemy lines in North Georgia to gather intelligence.

Maj Gen. George Thomas, the *"Rock of Chickamauga,"* was a supporter of Dr. Walker's and it was his support that helped Dr. Walker receive the Medal of Honor.

Library of Congress

On April 10, 1864, she was captured and made a prisoner of war at Castle Thunder Prison in Richmond, Virginia, where she became the bane of her jailers. She was released as part of a prisoner exchange on August 12, 1864, and it became a point of pride for her that she was exchanged for a Confederate surgeon with the rank of major. The official notation on the Confederate POW list described her as *"The notorious Miss Dr. Mary E. Walker, Surgeoness of the 52nd Ohio Regulars."*

It was not the first, nor would it be the last time she was called *"notorious."* News of her freedom was reported nationwide, and she met President Abraham Lincoln who asked about her treatment while a prisoner.

Castle Thunder prison in Richmond, Virginia, was a converted tobacco warehouse used to hold political prisoners. Though not as notorious as Andersonville, the Confederate prisoner of war camp in Georgia, it, too, had an unsavory reputation, with its guards noted for their brutality. Library of Congress

After a brief period in recovery she returned to treat soldiers wounded in the Battle of Atlanta, was later a supervisor of a prison in Louisville, Kentucky, and after that director of a refugee house in Clarksville, Tennessee. She was mustered out of the service on June 15, 1865.

She resumed her medical practice in Washington, D.C., once again became active in the women's rights movement (she was always more than just a suffragette), and petitioned President Andrew Johnson to recognize her wartime service retroactively with an officer's commission.

The issue of granting the officer's commission request quickly became an embarrassing political football for the administration. By

Beyond Belief: True Stories of Civilian Heroes

now Dr. Walker was too famous and had too many powerful allies and advocates to be further stonewalled. Judge Advocate General Joseph Holt was assigned Dr. Walker's case and in October 1865 he sent a twelve-page epic of legalistic hemming and hawing to Secretary of War Edwin Stanton that concluded by saying that granting her an army commission would set *"an inconvenient precedent."*

Edwin Stanton succeeded the ineffectual Simon Cameron as Secretary of War in 1862. An able and forceful administrator, he had the unenviable task in the fall of 1865 of navigating the political hot potato of what to do about Dr. Mary Walker. Library of Congress

But, well aware of the political stakes involved, he gave Stanton an out, adding "her sacrifices, her fearless energy under circumstances of peril, her endurance of hardship and imprisonment at the hands of the enemy and especially her active patriotism and eminent loyalty . . . may well be regarded as an almost isolated one in the history of the rebellion; and to signalize and perpetrate it as such would seem to be desirable."

So, it was decided. Instead of an army commission, President Andrew Johnson would award her the Medal of Honor. The unintended consequence of this *"consolation prize"* was that it made history.

Judge Advocate General Joseph Holt was given the assignment of determining what sort of "commendatory acknowledgment" Dr. Walker should receive for her service to the Union army during the war. She had advocated for an officer's commission. Instead, she was awarded the Medal of Honor, and thus made history. Library of Congress

Dr. Mary Edwards Walker

On November 11, 1865, President Johnson signed the citation and on January 24, 1866, Dr. Mary Walker received the decoration, becoming the first woman to be awarded the Medal of Honor. Immensely proud of the decoration, she would wear it every day for the rest of her life. Unfortunately, the story didn't end there.

The President of the United States of America, in the name of Congress, takes pleasure in presenting the Medal of Honor to Assistant Surgeon–Civilian Mary Edwards Walker, United States Civilian, for extraordinary heroism as a Contract Surgeon to the Union Forces. Whereas it appears from official reports that Dr. Mary E. Walker, a graduate of medicine, "has rendered valuable service to the Government, and her efforts have been earnest and untiring in a variety of ways," and that she was assigned to duty and served as an assistant surgeon in charge of female prisoners at Louisville, Kentucky, upon the recommendation of Major Generals Sherman and Thomas, and faithfully served as contract surgeon in the service of the United States, and has devoted herself with much patriotic zeal to the sick and wounded soldiers, both in the field and hospitals, to the detriment of her own health, and has also endured hardships as a prisoner of war four months in a Southern prison while acting as contract surgeon; and Whereas by reason of her not being a commissioned officer in the military service, a brevet or honorary rank cannot, under existing laws, be conferred upon her; and Whereas in the opinion of the President an honorable recognition of her services and sufferings should be made: It is ordered, That a testimonial thereof shall be hereby made and given to the said Dr. Mary E. Walker, and that the usual medal of honor for meritorious services be given her.

Given under my hand in the city of Washington, D.C., this 11th day of November, A.D. 1865.

/s/ Andrew Johnson, President.

Beyond Belief: True Stories of Civilian Heroes

In the Purge of 1917, the U.S. Army's review of Medal of Honor recipients, Dr. Walker's Medal of Honor was one of 911 Army Medals of Honor deemed inappropriately awarded. In her case it was because she was a *"civilian contract surgeon"* and not a soldier (as per the terms of the new criteria). Along with the names of 910 other individuals her name was revoked from the Medal of Honor Roll.

Ordered to return her medal, she refused and defiantly continued to wear it, daring those in power to take it from her. None tried.

But that was not the only late in life indignity she suffered. When she died on February 21, 1919, at age eighty-six, she had also become marginalized as an embarrassing anachronism to the movement she had dedicated most of her life to, a sad conclusion for one who had fought the good fight for women's rights. One year later, on August 26, 1920, the Nineteenth Amendment giving women the right to vote was certified.

Sixty years later, upon the urging of one of Dr. Walker's descendants and after a review and recommendation by the Army Board of Correction of Military Records, on June 19, 1977, Army Secretary Clifford

Dr. Mary Walker circa 1912. At the turn of the twentieth century, Dr. Walker found herself sidelined by the movement she spent most of her life advocating.

Library of Congress

Alexander righted six decades of wrong and restored her decoration.

To date Dr. Mary Edwards Walker remains the only woman to be awarded the Medal of Honor.

Mr. Richard Harding Davis

War Correspondent Extraordinaire

By Dwight Jon Zimmerman

"He was as good an American as ever lived, and his heart flamed against cruelty and injustice. His writings form a text-book of Americanism which all our people would do well to read at the present time."

—Theodore Roosevelt

No one better represented the ideal American male of the **Gilded Age** of the late nineteenth century and **Progressive Era** of the early twentieth century than Richard Harding Davis. He was a polymath: journalist, war correspondent, magazine editor, novelist, playwright, international celebrity, fashion trendsetter, and social activist. His dashing, clean-

"Their First Quarrel," a 1914 illustration by Charles Dana Gibson that depicts his iconic Gibson Girl and her opposite number the Gibson Guy whose likeness was inspired by Richard Harding Davis. Wikipedia

shaven features were the inspiration for the *"Gibson Guy,"* the masculine counterpart to illustrator Charles Dana Gibson's *"Gibson Girl"* that started the beardless fashion in American men.

A close friend of Theodore Roosevelt, it was his reporting as a war correspondent during the Spanish-American War in 1898 that created the legend of the Rough Riders, of which he was made an honorary member. His life and writing influenced writers Sinclair Lewis, Jack London, Theodore Dreiser, H. L. Mencken, and Ernest Hemingway. Dying young, just a week before his fifty-second birthday, his brother Charles wrote that in his short life Richard *"had crowded the work, the pleasures, the kind, chivalrous deeds of many men."*

Davis was born on April 18, 1864, in Philadelphia, Pennsylvania, to Lemuel Clarke Davis, editorial writer for *The Philadelphia Enquirer*, and Rebecca Harding Davis, a novelist who was one of the nation's first social historians and pioneering literary artists, instrumental in creating the American Realist writing style whose practitioners included Horatio Alger, Jr., Stephen Crane, Upton Sinclair, Henry James, Jack London, John Steinbeck, and Edith Wharton, amongst others. After graduating

Richard Harding Davis circa 1890. Library of Congress

from the Episcopal Academy, in the 1880s he attended Lehigh University (where he founded its football team) and John Hopkins University. An indifferent student more interested in participating in every college activity but classroom studies, he never graduated, being asked to leave both institutions because of poor grades.

His newspaper career began when his father helped him get a job as a reporter for the *Philadelphia Record* in 1886. Later that year he joined the *Philadelphia Press* where he made a name for himself through his reporting about a gang of thieves whose ranks he had infiltrated, and the 1889 Johnstown Flood in which more than 2,200

Mr. William Harding Davis

people in Pennsylvania were killed, making it the largest national disaster at the time. That year also saw him working at the *New York Sun* where his flamboyant style and willingness to write about controversial subjects, such as, in 1890, reporting about the first execution of murderer William Kemmler by electric chair, gained him a wider following.

Also in 1890 he achieved major literary success with the publication of *Gallagher and Other Stories*, a collection of short stories whose title character was a copy boy for a Philadelphia newspaper. This was followed by *Van Bibber and Others*, about a New York City bon vivant which followed a similar theme as *Gallagher*. Both were immensely popular and for the next twelve years (a one-year break occurring in 1911 before picking up again until his death), at least one book a year would be released under his name. Subjects ran the gamut, from short story and article collections to novels, biographies (he was one of the first biographers of Winston Churchill), travelogues, plays—works on any and every subject that interested his fertile imagination.

In 1910, the movie *Ransom's Folly*, based on his novel of the same name, was released. In all, forty-seven screen adaptations for movies and television were based on his works (some re-released), with the last being the "Gallagher" ten-episode television series from Disney that aired from 1965-67.

Davis' affiliation with the military began as a war correspondent initially for the Hearst newspaper syndicate in 1896. In 1897 he went to Greece, reporting on the Greco-Turkish War of 1897. Typical of his reporting style was his account of the Battle of Velestino in late April–early May 1897. The following excerpt from that battle concerning the randomness of death in combat serves as an example that set his work apart from typical reporting of the day:

> *"The dead gave dignity to what the other men were doing, and made it noble, and, from another point of view, quite senseless. For their dying had proved nothing. Men who could have been much better spared than they, were still alive in the trenches, and for no reason but through mere dumb chance. There was no selection of the unfittest; it seemed to be ruled*

by unreasoning luck. A certain number of shells and bullets passed through a certain area of space, and men of different bulks blocked that space in different places. If a man happened to be standing in the line of a bullet he was killed and passed into eternity, leaving a wife and children, perhaps, to mourn him. 'Father died,' these children will say, 'doing his duty.' As a matter of fact, father died because he happened to stand up at the wrong moment, or because he turned to ask the man on his right for a match, instead of leaning toward the left, and he projected his bulk of two hundred pounds where a bullet, fired by a man who did not know him and who had not aimed at him, happened to want the right of way. One of the two had to give it, and as the bullet would not, the soldier had his heart torn out. The man who sat next to me happened to stoop to fill his cartridge-box just as the bullet that wanted the space he had occupied passed over his bent shoulder; and so he was not killed, but will live for sixty years, perhaps, and will do much good or much evil . . . . Viewed from that point, and leaving out the fact that God ordered it all, the fortunes of the game of war seemed as capricious as matching pennies, and as impersonal as the wheel at Monte Carlo. In it the brave man did not win because he was brave, but because he was lucky. A fool and a philosopher are equal at a game of dice. And these men who threw dice with death were interesting to watch, because, though they gambled for so great a stake, they did so unconcernedly and without flinching, and without apparently appreciating the seriousness of the game."

When the Spanish-American War broke out Davis, already famous, would reach stratospheric levels of fame thanks to his reporting of that war. In April 1898, armed with a letter of recommendation to the Navy from his friend and former Assistant Secretary of the Navy Theodore Roosevelt to allow him aboard warships, he headed south.

Mr. William Harding Davis

Davis witnessed the U.S. Navy's shelling of the defenses of the Cuban port of Matanzas from the deck of the armored cruiser USS *New York*. His reporting of that action resulted in an edict from the Navy barring war correspondents on warships for the rest of the war.

The armored cruiser USS *New York* on whose deck Richard Harding Davis reported on the bombardment of the Cuban port of Mantanzas in the early days of the Spanish-American War. Naval History and Heritage Command

For the land campaign in Cuba, Davis attached himself to the 1st U.S. Volunteer Cavalry—the Rough Riders—whose second in command was Lieutenant Colonel Theodore Roosevelt. His reporting of their exploits established and burnished the legend of the Rough Riders. In the unit's first engagement, the Battle of Las Guasimas on June 24, 1898, Davis did more than write about the fighting, he participated in it. In a June 26

Theodore Roosevelt (left) and Richard Harding Davis (right) during the Spanish-American War. Library of Congress

Beyond Belief: True Stories of Civilian Heroes

letter to his brother Charles, he recounted the battle and his part in it, writing, *"I borrowed a carbine and joined Capron's troop, a second lieutenant and his Sergeant were in command . . . . The firing was very high and we were in no danger so I told the lieutenant to let us charge across and open place and take a tin shack which was held by the Spaniards' rear guard, for they were in open retreat. Roosevelt ordered his men to do the same thing and we ran forward cheering across the open and then dropped in the grass and fired. I guess I fired about twenty rounds and then formed into a strategy board and went off down the trail to scout."* He concluded the letter writing, *"I ought to tell you more of the charming side of the life—we are all dirty and hungry and sleep on the ground and have grand talks on every subject around the headquarters tent. I was never more happy and content and never so well."*

But as exciting and dramatic as his actions in Cuba were, they paled in comparison to the audacious and near comical one-upmanship stunt Davis executed when he accepted the surrender of the town of Coamo, Puerto Rico, on August 9, 1898.

With the military campaign in Cuba starting to wrap up in late July, the land campaign in the Caribbean shifted to Puerto Rico on July 25, 1898, when American troops landed at Guánica on the island's southwest coast. Taken by surprise, the Spanish Army, which was expecting an American landing on the north shore, immediately rushed down to stop them. A Spanish force arrived at Coamo, a spa town in south-central Puerto Rico of about 5,000 people and famous for its thermal springs. There it began to hastily dig and build defensive fortifications.

American troops arrived at the outskirts of the town on August 8 and at 7:00 a.m. the following morning, American artillery began shelling the Spanish positions. An hour later, the order was given for the infantry to attack.

Davis was one of four war correspondents with the troops. They were standing near a battery of artillery on a hill overlooking the town when the battle began. As it progressed, Davis saw the Second Wisconsin, a battalion of volunteers led by Brigadier General Oswald H. Ernst, about to enter the town well in advance of the main body of troops which was more than a mile behind. Davis later wrote *"it seemed obvious that General Ernst would be the first general officer to enter Coamo, and to receive its surrender. I had never seen five thousand people surrender to one man, and it seemed that, if I were to witness that ceremony, my best plan was to abandon the artillery and, as quickly as possible, pursue the Second Wisconsin. I did not want to share the spectacle of the surrender with my brother correspondents, so I tried to steal away from the three who were present."*

Davis managed to mount his horse and leave without being spotted. But the other war correspondents saw him when he emerged from the forest to cross a clearing. Realizing what he was up to, they immediately mounted their horses and took off in hot pursuit, soon catching up to him.

In their pell-mell dash to get to the town, the war correspondents caught the attention of some American officers and Captain Paget, an observer from the British army. They attached themselves to the quartet, bringing the group's total to eight. When they reached the Spanish defenses outside the town, Davis wrote, *"On either hand was every evidence of hasty and panic-stricken flight. We rejoiced at these evidences of the fact that the Wisconsin Volunteers had swept all before them."*

Then, according to Davis, their horses, which had been confiscated from a Spanish garrison, *"decided this was the race of their lives, and each had made up his mind that, Mexican bit or no Mexican bit, until he had carried his rider first into the town of Coamo, he would not be halted."* Not only that, but in their dash to Coamo, the group's route had taken them around the main body of American soldiers so that, Davis wrote, *"They now were behind us. Instead of a town which had surrendered to a thousand American soldiers, we . . . unarmed men . . . were being swept into a hostile city as fast as the enemy's ponies could take us there."*

The group continued its gallop into town. Though they saw rifle pits and iron barricades, there was no sight of soldiers from either side. They would later learn that the Spanish had retreated north out of the town and that the Wisconsin battalion had rushed through the town in pursuit, not bothering to secure the place.

Beyond Belief: True Stories of Civilian Heroes

Suddenly a man dashed into the middle of the street in front of them and waved a white flag. An instant later the street was filled with townspeople crowding around the group, all waving white flags and shouting, *"Vivan los Americanos!"*

One of the men in the crowd approached Davis and after identifying himself as the mayor, Davis wrote he *"begged to surrender into my hands the town of Coamo. I was afraid that if I did not take him up he would surrender [to one of the others]. I bade him conduct me to his official residence."* There Davis accepted the town's surrender, announcing that he *"was now Military Governor, Mayor, and Chief of Police."* He then requested the seals of office, which the mayor gave him. Davis immediately wrote three letters to himself to three different addresses in the United States, stating what he had done and stamping them with the seals of office. In time he received all three letters, *"documentary proof"* that he had been Military Governor and Mayor of Coamo.

Minutes later Major General James H. Wilson led the main body of troops into town. Davis wrote, *"He looked greatly surprised to see me and asked me what I was doing in his town."* Davis explained, and with that, Davis' rule as military governor and mayor ended, having lasted all of twenty minutes.

When the Boer War broke out in South Africa in 1899, Davis was sent there where he covered it from both the British and Boer sides and where he met Winston Churchill. The future British prime minister was at the time both a journalist and army lieutenant in the conflict. This was followed by him reporting on the Russo-Japanese War (1904–1905), though this time not from the front lines.

When World War I broke out in 1914, he headed over to Europe. That conflict inspired some of his most powerful writing. His short story "The Deserter," predates many of the thoughts and themes presented in Erich Maria Remarque's post-war novel **All Quiet on the Western Front**. And, unlike his reporting of the Rough Riders in which he highlighted individuals and their actions, his "German Army Marching into Brussels" portrays German soldiers as a faceless, almost colorless, monolithic machine.

44

Mr. William Harding Davis

Davis was married twice. The first was to artist Cecil Clark, a childless marriage that ended in divorce in 1912. Later that year he married actress Bessie McCoy and in 1915 they had a daughter, Hope.

Convinced that the United States would eventually have to enter the war on the side of the Allies, upon his return from Europe Davis embarked on a campaign to convince the country of the need to prepare for war. In addition he became a vocal social activist. On April 11, 1916, while on the phone at his desk, he suffered a fatal heart attack at age fifty-one.

Major General Leonard Wood was one of many who wrote tributes. During the Spanish-American War he was a colonel and the commanding officer of the Rough Riders. He wrote, *"The death of Richard Harding Davis was a real loss to the movement for preparedness . . . . Davis was a loyal friend, a thoroughgoing American devoted to the best interests of his country, courageous, sympathetic, and true. His loss has been a very real one to all of us who knew and appreciated him, and in his death the cause of preparedness has lost an able worker and the country a devoted and loyal citizen."*

As Davis predicted, the United States joined the fight, entering the war on April 4, 1917. But, because President Woodrow Wilson's re-election campaign centered on an anti-war platform, the country was ill-prepared and would go into the conflict wearing Allied uniforms, flying British and French aircraft, using French tanks, and other matériel supplied by the Allies.

The Gallant YMCA

Five Distinguished Service Crosses

BY SCOTT BARON

The Young Men's Christian Association (YMCA) is perhaps best known for its athletic and youth programs, a heritage that dates back to its origins in 1844. Its original purpose was to provide wholesome recreation to urban youth at risk from the moral decay of industrialized urban living.

Before long, that mission was extended to caring for members of the military, beginning during the American Civil War. In 1861, a group of local YMCA members joined to voluntarily provide relief services to American soldiers in encampments near the front lines. Within seven months, the movement spread across the country, becoming the first large-scale civilian volunteer service corps, established as the United States Christian Commission. President Abraham Lincoln recognized the Commission for its efforts during the Civil War.

Their work with the military resumed with the Spanish-American War, the border conflict with Mexico, and eventually World War I. The YMCA worked with soldiers in training camps and troop trains in the United States as well as in  Europe, providing recreation, library services, bible study, and religious services, often serving with the troops.

Beyond Belief: True Stories of Civilian Heroes

When World War I began, the YMCA launched a massive program of morale and welfare services for the military, serving 90 percent of American military forces in Europe. Never before had any organization aided so many troops over such a wide geographic area and under such adverse conditions.

Regimental Chaplains partnered with civilian *"camp pastors"* and YMCA Secretaries in providing pastoral and personal counseling, ministering to the wounded and dying, conducting memorial services, and leading troops in worship.

The role the YMCA played in the lives of American soldiers and sailors during the war can be better understood by the following statistics.

- 35,000 volunteers attended to the spiritual and social needs of an armed force of 4.8 million troops.

- The YMCA performed ninety per cent of all welfare work with American Expeditionary Forces in Europe and suffered 286 casualties, including six men and two women working under the YMCA banner killed in action.

- Operated twenty-six R&R leave centers in France that accommodated 1,944,300 American officers and men and managed 4,000 "huts" and tents for recreation and religious services.

- 8000 troop trains were served by YMCA volunteers.

Five Civilian employees of the YMCA, Mandeville J. Barker Jr., Murray Bartlett, William R. Farmer, Mercer Green Johnston and Thomas Whiteside Wilbur were awarded the Distinguished Service Cross, the Army's second-highest award for valor, for their service with the troops under fire during the World War I.

Mandeville J. Barker, Jr.

In September 1918, Mandeville James Barker, Jr. was a civilian Secretary, YMCA attached to the 108th Machine Gun Battalion, 28th Division, American Expeditionary Forces (AEF), near Baslieux-sous-Châtillon, France, near the

Meuse River. Assigned as *"acting chaplain"* he was given the rank of First Lieutenant.

Little is known of Barker's early life. He was born in Rochester, Monroe County, New York, on April 13, 1884, the first of Mandeville Sr.'s six children and the only boy. He earned a Doctor of Divinity degree and was working as rector of the Episcopal Church in Uniontown, Pennsylvania, when he went overseas with the 28th Division, assigned to the 108th Machine Gun Battalion, 55th Infantry Brigade. Once in France, he would be in almost continuous combat until the Armistice in November 1918.

When America entered World War I on April 6, 1917, the 28th Infantry Division was the nation's oldest National Guard division. Organized by Pennsylvania in 1878, it was composed of units that had already earned battle streamers in conflicts from the American Revolution to the Civil War.

The division trained at Camp Hancock from August 19, 1917, to April 20, 1918. Even so, much of their basic training was still incomplete, when orders directed advance elements of the division to depart Camp Hancock on April 21, 1918, for Camp Upton, New York, where final preparations for overseas deployment would be accomplished. After only a short stay at Camp Upton, the division headquarters and its subordinate infantry units departed on May 3–7, 1918, from Hoboken, New Jersey, for England. By May 17 the division was in France, attached to the British for training.

Upon arriving in France, the 28th immediately began developing a reputation for successfully accomplishing difficult tasks. From July 15, 1918, to the end of hostilities on November 11, 1918, the 28th participated in no less than eight major operations.

The 28th was recognized by General John J. Pershing, commander of the AEF, who referred to them in a speech as *"men of iron."* As the 28th continued to take and hold ground against the best the Germans could field against them, Pershing began calling them the *"Iron Division."*

Barker and the 108th would see almost continuous action at Chateau Thierry (July 9–14), the Champagne-Marne defensive (July 15–18), the Aisne-Marne Offensive (July 18–August 10), the Oise-

Beyond Belief: True Stories of Civilian Heroes

Aisne offensive (August 18–September 7), the Meuse-Argonne Offensive (September 26–October 9) and the Thiaucourt Sector (Lorraine) (October 16–November 11).

Barker was popular and endeared himself to officers and men alike by his *"happy combination of buoyant, gallant cheerfulness, sturdy Americanism, deep Christianity, indifference to hardship and the tender care he gave to the wounded."* He was, by many accounts, the most beloved man in the regiment.

The men called Barker *"The Fighting Parson,"* because he frequently went as close to the fighting as possible. On one occasion snipers were firing on the men. Barker borrowed a pair of binoculars, lay flat on the field and, after close observation discovered their location. There were four of them and he notified an artillery observer. Following his information, the artillery fired three rounds and the sniper fire ceased. Two or three days later the regiment went over and took that section of German line and found what was left of the four men. *"The Parson's Boche,"* the men called them.

But it was at Baslieux-sous-Châtillon, a small village about thirteen miles northwest of Epernay, on the night of September 15 that Barker's courage and dedication to *"his boys"* would fully be on display. Baker believed that his job was to look after the men's bodies as well as their souls, and when there was fighting, he liked to be in a position where he could attend to both phases of his work.

That night he went *"over the top"* with troops during a night attack on the heights overlooking the Vesle River. It was not his duty to go, nor was it likely the regimental commander would have granted permission had he known Barker's intention. The purpose of the raid was to neutralize a German machine gun position.

The attacking party wiped out the machine gun nest after an intense fight and then withdrew to its own lines as ordered. In the darkness, some of the wounded went unnoticed. After the battalion returned, cries of the American wounded could be heard out in No Man's Land, calling for help.

Barker, armed only with first aid equipment and canteens of water, slipped out into the dark with only starlight and the voices of the wounded to guide him. Under fire and between the two opposing armies he attended to their wounds as best he could by the light of a small pocket torch, which he had to keep concealed from the enemy snipers.

One after another, Barker located wounded Americans. Those who could walk he sent back to the lines, assisting others, one at a time, back to friendly lines. He administered last rites to a soldier beyond help, remaining until he passed before again returning to his own lines.

Back in the trenches, Barker again heard the cries of a wounded soldier, this time in German, *"Ach Gott! Ach, mein lieber Gott!"* The men of the 110th loved their parson even more for what he did then. He turned right about and went back out, seeking the sobbing man in the darkness.

As Sergeant John Duffy, Company D, 103rd Engineers, later wrote in a letter to his father *"(Barker) found a curly-haired young German, wounded so he could not walk and in mortal terror, not of death or of the dark, but of those 'terrible Americans who torture and kill their prisoners.' Such was the tale with which he and his comrades had been taught to loathe their American enemies. Dr. Barker treated his wounds and carried him back to the American lines. The youngster whimpered with fear when he found where he was going and begged the clergyman not to leave him. When he finally was convinced that he would not be harmed, he kissed the chaplain's hands, crying over them, and insisted on turning over to Dr. Barker everything he owned that could be loosened—helmet, pistol, bayonet, cartridges, buttons, and other odds and ends. All hung over with loot, the parson was, when he came back."*

For his actions, Barker was awarded the Distinguished Service Cross in 1918.

Barker exhibited a different type of courage later, when during the Spanish Flu pandemic of 1918 that continued into 1919, he fearlessly ministered to his flock, risking infection. Little is known of his post-war life. He married Jessie Belle Sykes, a forty-seven-year old widow in 1922. He died in January 1967 at the age of eighty-two in Lexington, Massachusetts and is buried in the Newton Cemetery.

The President of the United States of America, authorized by Act of Congress, July 9, 1918, takes pleasure in presenting the Distinguished Service Cross to Mr. Mandeville James Barker, Jr., Secretary, YMCA., a United States Civilian, for extraordinary heroism in action while attached to the 108th Machine-Gun Battalion, 28th Division, A.E.F., near Baslieux, France, 15 September 1918. Mr. Barker showed a fearless disregard of his own safety by crawling out in front of the line under heavy enemy machine-gun and sniper fire to aid wounded soldiers, whom he carried back to shelter after dressing their wounds. He also administered aid to a wounded German within 20 yards of the enemy lines and brought him in a prisoner.

Murray Bartlett

Murray Bartlett was serving as the first president of the University of the Philippines when war broke out in Europe in 1914. He left that post and returning to the United States in 1915.

When America entered World War I, Bartlett hoped to serve as an Army chaplain, but his application was denied because, at age forty-six, Bartlett was past the maximum age. But because the Army was short of chaplains during World War I, a number of civilian agencies such as the Red Cross and Salvation Army responded to the need by arranging for volunteer civilian clergymen to provide religious support to soldiers and sailors, primarily at stateside posts and in hospitals.

In January 1918, Bartlett was posted to France as a YMCA Overseas Secretary assisting the Army with religious and morale-support activities. He worked closely with the 1st Division and was eventually made Acting Chaplain of the 18th Infantry Regiment. His moment of military glory came at the Battle of Soissons (July 18–22, 1918) where he would earn the Distinguished Service Cross.

Murray Bartlett was born in Poughkeepsie, New York, on March 29, 1871. He graduated from Harvard in 1892 with his A.B. (Bachelors) and in 1893 with his A.M (Masters). He then attended the General Theological Seminary in New York City, graduating in 1896. Bartlett was ordained a deacon in the Protestant Episcopal Church in 1895, and a priest in 1897.

From 1897–1908 he was rector of St. Paul's Church in Rochester, New York. In 1903 he married Blanchard Howard of Buffalo, and in 1908 received the honorary Doctor of Divinity degree from the University of Rochester. In 1911 Murray Bartlett moved to the Philippines and served as the Dean of the American Cathedral of St. Mary and St. John, Manilla. He was a member of the Board of Regents of the University of the Philippines during 1909–1911 and in 1911 was elected the first president of the university. When he resigned the presidency in 1915, he was made President Emeritus.

In 1917 Bartlett enlisted in Red Cross Ambulance Company No. 1, Pasadena, California, and was appointed sergeant. However, when the company was taken into the U.S. Army he was rejected on physical examination because of his age. In October of 1917 he was appointed representative of the Protestant Episcopal Church War Commission at Camp Kearney, California.

Upon becoming YMCA Overseas Secretary, Bartlett was assigned to the 18th Infantry, 1st Division. The first units sailed to Europe from New York City and Hoboken, New Jersey, on June 14, 1917 and throughout the remainder of the year, the rest of the division followed, landing at St. Nazaire, France, and  Liverpool, England. After a brief stay in rest camps, the troops in England proceeded to France, landing at Le Havre. The last unit arrived in St. Nazaire on December 22, 1917. Once fully assembled, the regiment was assigned a section of the Toul front near the Moselle River. At the request of the brigade commander, Bartlett was made the 18th Infantry's acting chaplain.

Bartlett's regiment was already seasoned veterans when they fought in the Battle of Soissons (July 18–22, 1918) part of the much larger Allied Aisne-Marne counter-offensive. His actions earned him a Distinguished Service Cross, which was presented in 1923, as well as a Citation Star (Silver Star).

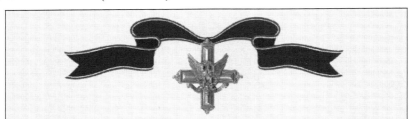

The President of the United States of America, authorized by Act of Congress, July 9, 1918, takes pleasure in presenting the Distinguished Service Cross to Acting Chaplain Murray Bartlett, Secretary, Y.M.C.A., a United States Civilian, for extraordinary heroism in action while serving as acting assistant chaplain in Villers-Tournelle, France, May 1918 and in the Chazelle Ravine, south of Soissons, France, 22 July 1918. Voluntarily assuming the duties of Chaplain, 18th Infantry, Mr. Murray displayed conspicuous bravery in caring for the wounded and burying the dead of his regiment under intense enemy fire, working constantly with the advanced elements of the command until 22 July 1918, when he was seriously wounded while in close proximity to the front line. His cheerful, heroic energy and indifference to personal danger exerted a profound effect upon the morale of the men of his regiment and inspired them to many deeds of gallantry and supreme devotion to duty.

He served with the 18th Infantry until November when he was transferred to headquarters as assistant to the division chaplain. Murray's application to become a full-fledged army chaplain was finally approved in November 1918, but the Armistice occurred before his status could become official.

Bartlett returned to the United States in March 1919 and was honorably discharged. He later recalled, *"I consider by all odds the best thing I ever did was trying to enlist in the Army. The only really unpleasant feature was my inability to enter the service in the regular way. I tried every possible way of getting a Chaplaincy, and finally when I succeeded, the armistice intervened. I lost out by one week."*

Upon his return from Europe in 1919 Bartlett was elected president of Hobart and William Smith Colleges and was made Charles Startin Professor of Religion and Ethics. In 1922, Bartlett finally achieved his goal when he was appointed Division Chaplain of the 98th Division, headquartered in Syracuse, New York. In 1936, he was placed on the inactive list with the rank of lieutenant colonel.

He retired in 1936 and was awarded an honorary degree in 1937. Murray Bartlett passed away at Rochester, New York on November 13, 1949, and was taken to Mt. Hope Cemetery and his remains were cremated.

Finishing the war with a Distinguished Service Cross, the French Croix de Guerre, a Silver Star and Purple Heart, and Chevalier of the French Légion d'honneur, Bartlett Murray is arguably the most decorated civilian in American history.

William R. Farmer

From October 3 to October 27, 1918, Marines of the Third Battalion, 5th Regiment (3/5 Marines) attached to the US Army's 2nd Infantry Division, along with troops of the 36th Infantry Division opposed the Imperial German Army's 200th and 213th divisions, along with elements of six additional German divisions northeast of Reims, in Champagne, France.

During what came to be called the **Battle of Blanc Mont Ridge,** the Marines attacked fearlessly while exposing themselves to enemy fire on the sloping limestone rock. The victory belongs in large part to the Second Division Marines, serving as a unit of the Fourth French Army. Through the Marines' heroic efforts, the Germans were forced to retreat from the Champagne region.

Beyond Belief: True Stories of Civilian Heroes

Among those advancing Americans was Dr. William R. Farmer, a native of New York City who was raised in Pittsburgh, Pennsylvania, and was serving as a civilian YMCA secretary attached to the Marines. He had shared all the dangers and exposures to which the regiment was subjected during their campaign in Champagne, the Saint Mihiel drive, and fighting on the Meuse.

On that October morning, Farmer came under fire as he advanced with the Marines. The fighting was fierce and the number of casualties high as they advanced. His actions would earn him the Distinguished Service Cross.

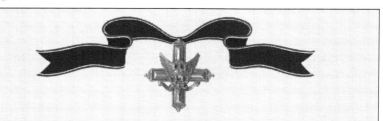

The President of the United States of America, authorized by Act of Congress, July 9, 1918, takes pleasure in presenting the Distinguished Service Cross to Reverend William Robertson Farmer, a United States Civilian, for extraordinary heroism in action while a member of the Y.M.C.A., while serving as a chaplain attached to the Third Battalion, 5th Regiment (Marines), 2d Division, American Expeditionary Forces, near Blanc Mont Ridge, France, 4 October 1918. Reverend Farmer voluntarily established an advanced dressing station under enemy machine-gun and artillery fire. He continued to render first aid until forced back by a threatened counterattack, at which time her personally assisted two seriously wounded men to the first-aid station, then returning to the line and remaining with the unit until it was relieved.

He was also cited by the Commanding General of the 2nd Division with the Silver Star.

Dr. Farmer returned to the United States in January 1919 and had been expected to resume his work as professor of religion at the Western Theology Seminary at Holland, Michigan, the following month. But an attack of bronchitis, possibly after-effects from exposure to both the Spanish flu and poison gas, prevented him from returning.

On May 15, 1919, Farmer traveled to the French Embassy in Washington D.C., where the French ambassador presented him with the Croix de Guerre. He died on April 11, 1958, and was buried at Homewood Cemetery, in Pittsburgh, Pennsylvania.

Thomas Whiteside Wilbor

Born in New Britain, Connecticut, Thomas Wilbor graduated from New Britain High School, before attending and graduating from Yale University. Little is known of his life beyond the fact that he served in France as YMCA Overseas Secretary attached to the 6th Machine Gun Battalion of the 2nd Division. There he worked with the medical detachment, earning a Distinguished Service Cross, and was also cited by the division's commanding general. He died on December 5, 1963 and was buried at Fairview Cemetery in his hometown of New Britain, Connecticut.

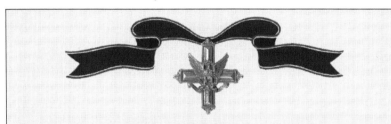

The President of the United States of America, authorized by Act of Congress, July 9, 1918, takes pleasure in presenting the Distinguished Service Cross to Mr. Thomas Whiteside Wilbor, a United States Civilian, for extraordinary heroism in action as a member of the YMCA, attached to the 6th Machine Gun Battalion, 2d Division, American Expeditionary Forces, near Jaulny, France, 13–15 September 1918. Declining to remain in the rear, Mr. Wilbur attached himself to the Medical Department rendering first aid and bringing in wounded, serving at all times in a most valuable manner. He disregarded an order to return to the rear when it seemed that the enemy would launch a counterattack but remained with the wounded until all were safely evacuated.

Mercer Green Johnston

On September 26, 1918, the Allies began the Meuse–Argonne Offensive, a major part of the final Allied campaign of World War I. It ended forty-seven days later with the signing of the armistice on November 11, 1918, ending the war. It was the largest campaign in United States military history, involving 1.2 million American soldiers.

It was also the deadliest in American history, resulting in more than 120,000 casualties including more than 26,000 American dead.

On October 27, near Verdun, France, Reverend Dr. Mercer Green Johnston, a civilian working as a YMCA secretary attached to the AEF went forward through heavy bombardment to render aid to wounded soldiers, and his undaunted courage would result in the award of the Army's highest award for valor.

Mercer Green Johnston was born in Church Hill, Mississippi, on December 3, 1868, the second of five children born to James Steptoe and Mary Mercer Green Johnston. His father was the Episcopal Bishop of the Diocese of West Texas, and the family grew up in San Antonio, Texas.

Johnston initially attended the University of Virginia but transferred to the University of the South at Sewanee, Tennessee, in 1912, where he was active in sport, student government and was editor of *The Purple*, the school newspaper.

He earned both a bachelor's and master's degree in English in 1896, and a Bachelor of Divinity from the seminary in 1898. He later married Katherine Aubrey, the granddaughter of John Forsyth, Secretary of State to both Presidents Andrew Jackson and Martin Van Buren.

After serving as dean of the Manila Cathedral in the Philippine Islands, Johnston returned to the United States in 1912 to take the position of rector of Trinity Church, Newark New Jersey. He became a controversial national figure by his high-profile defense of striking laborers and unions in defiance of church leadership and his subsequent resignation from the Episcopal Church in 1916, stating that he was devoting the rest of his life to working for the underprivileged.

In the summer of 1914, as German troops attacked into France, the expatriate American colony in Paris established a volunteer ambulance service to transport the wounded from the front lines to the American Hospital on the outskirts of Paris.

In January 1915, Abram Piatt Andrew, former Harvard professor and future Congressman, arrived in France as a volunteer ambulance driver. He soon began to transform the service from a subsidiary of the American Hospital to an independent organization, the American Ambulance Field Service, to transport wounded soldiers from the front lines to aid stations in the rear. The American Ambulance Field Service operated as an independent volunteer agency until America's entrance into the war in 1917 when it was absorbed by the American Army.

Volunteers paid for their own transportation to Europe and for their meals while there. At its height, the Field Service numbered 2,000 volunteers and operated not only on the Western Front in France but also in the battlefields of Italy, Greece, Serbia, and Albania. Ernest Hemingway's experiences as an ambulance driver on the Italian front formed the basis of his novel *A Farewell to Arms*.

Johnston volunteered as a chaplain with the American Ambulance Field Service. On August 8, 1917, Johnston, accompanied by his wife, a graduate nurse from John Hopkins Hospital, departed New York for France, the story appearing in national newspapers titled *"Fighting Parson Goes to France."*

After serving with the French Army, and upon America's entry into the war, Johnston took a position as a secretary with the YMCA, attached to the AEF. On the afternoon of October 27 at Verdun, Johnston volunteered to go forward, through heavy bombardment, to gather the dead.

Seriously injured from being gassed, Johnston was awarded the Distinguished Service Cross in 1919, as well as a French Croix de Guerre. He would spend his later years working in the US Rural

Beyond Belief: True Stories of Civilian Heroes

Electrification Administration during President Franklin D. Roosevelt's New Deal program bringing electricity to rural America and as a freelance writer addressing economic, social, and political issues.

Johnston passed away in Washington D.C. on November 20, 1954, at the age of eighty-five, and was interred at Immanuel Episcopal Church Cemetery in Sparks, Maryland.

The President of the United States of America, authorized by Act of Congress, July 9, 1918, takes pleasure in presenting the Distinguished Service Cross to Dr. Mercer Green Johnston, a United States Civilian, for extraordinary heroism in action as a member of the YMCA, attached to the American Expeditionary Forces, near Verdun, France, 27 October 1918. After volunteering and going to the front line through heavy bombardment for the purpose of burying the dead, Dr. Johnston found the litter service of the 101st Infantry, badly disorganized on account of heavy casualties and intense shelling. He immediately took charge of the litter bearers, reorganized the service, took care of the slightly wounded himself, saw to the procuring and loading of ambulances, and, although badly gassed and suffering severely, refused to leave his post until all had been taken care of.

In addition to the five Distinguished Service Crosses, YMCA staff and volunteers were awarded 319 citations and decorations including the French Légion d'honneur, the Order of the British Empire, the French Croix de Guerre, two Distinguished Service Medals and fourteen Silver Stars, including one award of the Silver Star to Miss Dorothy Francis for: *"gallantry in action while serving with Field Hospital No. 12, American Expeditionary Forces, in action near Cheppy, France, 8 October 1918, in voluntarily attending to the wounded for a period of twelve hours under constant shell fire."*

Miss Jane Jeffrey
Red Cross Nurse in World War I

By James G. Fausone

Jane Jeffrey was a Red Cross nurse during World War I. She followed in the footsteps of giants in the profession and proved again that women in war are patriotic and can do their duty in the face of danger. To understand Jane Jeffrey one must understand the context of her life in nursing, women's progress, and world conflict.

JEFFREY'S ENGLISH ROOTS AND THE BEGINNING OF MODERN NURSING

Jane Jeffrey was born on September 28, 1881, in Newmarket, England. Newmarket is a market town in the English county of Suffolk, approximately sixty-five miles north of London.

Little is known of Jane Jeffrey's birth, family, upbringing and early education in Newmarket, England. Her initial voyage to America is not recorded. Records exist of one her trips from England to the United States to nurse a family member in Massachusetts.

Modern nursing is considered to have been founded by Englishwoman Florence Nightingale who, together with thirty-eight

Beyond Belief: True Stories of Civilian Heroes

nurses, traveled to Turkey in 1854 to care for British soldiers wounded in the Crimean War against Russia. Her experience combating the appalling and unsanitary conditions in the military camps where the wounded were housed led her to become a pioneer in nursing care, starting with her establishing the world's first secular nursing school in England upon her return.

The outbreak of the American Civil War in 1861 with its explosive growth of the Union Army opened the doors for women's active participation in nursing care for the military. The War Department hired Dorothea Dix to be Superintendent of U.S. Army Nurses. Together with the volunteer civilian Women's Central Relief Association and the U.S. Sanitary Commission, troops were provided unprecedented nursing care.

The post-Civil War drawdown so depleted the Army's nursing ranks that when the Spanish-American War broke out in 1898, a scandal erupted over the inadequacy of medical care for the troops. Only after a crash-program hiring of civilian nurses was disaster averted. In all, more than 1,500 women nurses worked as contract nurses during that 1898 conflict.

Dr. Anita Newcomb McGee was the Acting Assistant Surgeon in the U.S. Army at the time. Using lessons learned from the debacle in the Spanish-American War, McGee pursued the establishment of a permanent nurse corps. In 1901, the U.S. Army Nursing Corps was established with McGee as its first commanding officer. McGee is now known as the founder of the Army Nurse Corps.

Meanwhile, Jane Jeffrey began carving out a career for herself in nursing. From Red Cross archives, it is known that Jane graduated from Taunton State Hospital School of Nursing in Taunton, Massachusetts in 1905 with extra training at Providence Lying-In Hospital in Rhode Island in 1906, and General Memorial Hospital in New York City in 1909. She worked as head nurse for six years in a small private hospital, Channing Sanitarium in Brookline, Massachusetts, and for nine months in private duty nursing. For some of this time she was also caring for her aunt, Mrs. James

Baldwin of 36 Bellevue Meeting House Hill, Dorchester, Massachusetts. Jane was a registered nurse in good standing in the Massachusetts State Nurses Association.

WORLD WAR

Though Europe had a history of wars dating back to ancient times, when the Great War broke out in 1914, the scope of what came to be called World War I was beyond everyone's comprehension. Originally believed by both sides that it would be short, ending by Christmas, neither side was prepared for the brutal, four-year bloodbath to come.

In short order the Allied military medical services collapsed, overwhelmed by the unanticipated number of casualties. Individually or through organizations, chiefly the YMCA, Salvation Army, and American Red Cross, American women nurses stepped forward to offer their services even though their nation would not officially enter the war until 1917. One such nurse was the naturalized citizen, thirty-seven-year-old Jane Jeffrey.

AMERICAN RED CROSS IN THE GREAT WAR

The Great War also created a period of extraordinary growth for the American Red Cross. Already established as an important branch of the Red Cross before the war, the Nursing Service greatly expanded with the coming of hostilities. Its principal task was to provide trained nurses for the U.S. Army and Navy. The Service enrolled 23,822 Red Cross nurses during the war. Of these, 19,931 were assigned to active duty with the Army, Navy, U.S. Public Health Service, and the Red Cross  overseas. The Red Cross also enrolled and trained nurses' aides to help make up for the shortage of nurses on the home front due to the war effort.

In an *American Journal of Nursing* article in November 1917, Jeffrey was included with a group sent to help in the war effort

Beyond Belief: True Stories of Civilian Heroes

organized by Elizabeth Sullivan of Children's Hospital, Boston. This group was assigned to American Red Cross (ARC) Children's Bureau.

Jeffrey was sent to Bordeaux, France, where she served before being transferred to a military hospital in Jouy-sur-Marne about fifty miles east of Paris along the Grand Morin River. She was assigned to ARC Hospital #107. It had previously been a French staffed military hospital. She found conditions difficult with sanitation conditions primitive to non-existent. Wounded soldiers arrived in large numbers, straining the ability of doctors and nurses to treat them.

Interior of an American Red Cross tent at Jouy-sur-Morin showing the bombing damage cause by German bombers the night of July 15, 1918. Library of Congress

On July 15, 1918, the hospital at Jouy was bombed by German bombers. Two hospital orderlies were killed, and fourteen people injured, of whom one was Jeffrey. An investigation of the raid revealed that it was not an accident due to poor navigation, but a deliberate attack. A large white canvas painted with a large red cross, signifying the complex's identity as a medical facility, had been laid in the courtyard and illuminated at night. Seven witnesses agreed that the German pilots came down to within several hundred feet to make observations before dropping their bombs.

The *Stars and Stripes* newspaper headline of the account read: *"France, Friday July 19, 1918"* and reported: *"Two Hun Planes Drop Bombs on A.R.C. Hospital . . . Four Wounded Men Hit . . . One is Struck in Spot from Which Piece of Shrapnel Had Just Been Removed."* The article goes on to report:

> *"Miss Jane Jeffrey, the only Red Cross nurse who was wounded, was struck near the spine by a piece of metal which traversed the entire length of a ward only a few inches above a long row of mostly surgical cases and penetrated the end wall of the ten outside of which she was standing."*

The "History of American Red Cross Nursing" reported in its book on *The European War* and the attack as Jouy-sur-Morin this way:

> *"At Jouy-sur-Morin, on the night of July 15, Jane Jeffery, an American Red Cross nurse transferred from the Children's Bureau, was severely wounded. A French dispatch contained the following comment:*

> *"Located in a quiet, remote spot, three kilometers from the railroad, the hospital at Jouy-sur-Morin not only bears the distinctive marks of the sanitary service, but on a nearby grass plot there has been spread a huge cross made of white towels, its arms measuring thirty meters. Shortly after the inauguration of the hospital, one of the Allied planes flew over the spot taking photographs to show that the cross was plainly visible from a height of many thousand meters.*

> *"During the night of July 15, two German aviators flew above the American hospital . . . they descended to within a few hundred meters of the buildings and dropped four bombs. It was midnight.*

> *"In the operating-room, the surgeons were at work. At the moment when the first bomb struck, Major*

McCoy held in his forceps the femoral artery of the patient on the table. The lights went out, two more bombs fell, the third failing to explode. In one room, an orderly was killed as he was giving a drink of water to a patient. Nine were wounded . . . one of whom was an American Red Cross nurse.

"We remember that recently sixty German prisoners were treated in this hospital at Jouy-sur-Morin, where they received from perhaps the very nurse whom they have wounded the same care and attention which she was giving our soldiers.

"Miss Jeffery was on night duty attending her patients when a fragment of shell struck her. She showed great spirit and was only concerned because she felt she was causing more trouble to the already overworked staff of doctors and nurses. When I told her the next day we were going to bring her into a hospital here in Paris, she was greatly disappointed. She had hoped to be able to go on duty again in a few days."

Unfortunately, that hope was a vain one. Her injuries were so great that she was unable to return. But Nurse Jeffrey's efforts did not go unnoticed by officials. France awarded her the Légion d'honneur, its highest decoration. And, when she returned to the United States, she was awarded the Distinguished Service Cross.

The President of the United States of America, authorized by Act of Congress, July 9, 1918, takes pleasure in presenting the Distinguished Service Cross to Nurse Jane Jeffrey, a United States Civilian, for extraordinary heroism while she was on duty at American Red Cross Hospital No. 107, at Jouy-sur-Morin (Seine-et-Marne),

Miss Jane Jeffrey

France, 15 July 1918. Miss Jeffrey was severely wounded by an exploding bomb during an air raid. She showed utter disregard for her own safety by refusing to leave her post, though suffering great pain from her wounds. Her courageous attitude and devotion to the task of helping others was inspiring to all of her associates.

Jane Jeffrey's poor health caused by her wounds was such that, after joining the U.S. Public Health Service in New York City, she had to resign for health reasons.

The American Red Cross Historical Program and Collection shared a handwritten note from Jeffrey dated April 1921 talking about the effect of her war injuries and wondering about compensation:

"I am writing to ask you if the American Red Cross made any provision for the Red Cross nurses who were disabled or physically injured during the late war.

I was wounded at Jouy-su-Morin July 15th 1918 while on night duty during an air raid. Unfortunately I was working under the direction of the Red Cross instead of the U.S. Government. Otherwise I would have received compensation or provision made for vocational training as I am incapacitated from continuing my profession.

You may have heard that the U.S. Government conferred the honor of the D.S.C. upon me, which, as you know carries no renumeration & in no way compensates me for me inability to earn my living.

After my return to America & my discharge from the Red Cross which took place immediately after my arrival & without any physical examination, I took treatments for one year for my back at my own expense. In the meantime I tried to do various work because it required less physical exertion but had to give it up.

For the past six months I have been doing dental clinic work in a U.S.P.H.S. Hospital but feel I must give it up."

Beyond Belief: True Stories of Civilian Heroes

There is no record of a response.

While still recovering, Jeffrey was offered a job as a nurse at the Poland Spring House in Poland, Maine, by its proprietor, E.P. Ricker. This offer was 135 miles away from Dorchester and in the Maine countryside. Poland Springs was thirty-seven miles north of Portland, Maine surrounded by hills and lakes. Jeffrey was unmarried, without children and, having experienced war, in need of some peace, pay, and tranquility.

Long before Poland Springs was a national bottled water brand, it was a local inn and resort. The Ricker family built the inn starting back in 1797 and it was a major force in Maine for generations. Over the next 100-plus years, the inn was expanded and became a resort.

Management of the operations passed from one Ricker generation to another. An inn pamphlet explained the history: *"By 1875 . . . Alvan Bolster Ricker, the second son, was taken into the firm, and the same year the Poland Spring House was commenced and opened in 1876. The kitchen was under Alvan Bolster Ricker's supervision. The perfectly*

The Poland Spring House, Poland, ME; from a c. 1920 postcard published by The American Art Post Card Company. Public Domain, Wikimedia Commons

vented department was larger and more convenient than many major hotels. Guests were welcome to watch the food preparation and serving. A.B., as he was called, passed on all food and the dealers in New York and Boston kept the very best for the Rickers."

Family history reports: *"Poland Spring . . . was in need of a year-round nurse and . . . persuaded Miss [Jane] Jeffrey to accept the job and it was there that she met Alvan Bolster Ricker . . . whose wife, Cora Saunders Ricker, had passed away. She married Mr. Ricker September 3, 1925."*

Miss Jane Jeffrey

The celebrity age of Poland Spring's history did not come until the twentieth century. Presidents William Howard Taft, Calvin Coolidge, and Warren Harding also visited the resort. Joseph Kennedy liked to bring his young family of aspiring politicians. Also relaxing at the resort were sports celebrities like Gene Tunney, Babe Ruth, and Sonny Liston, and entertainers like John Barrymore, Joan Crawford, Jimmy Durante and Robert Goulet.

Jeffrey was forty-five years old when she married Alvin Bolster Ricker, who was sixty-five. Ricker passed away in 1933 at eighty-three years of age. The couple had been married for eighteen years.

Jane Jeffrey lived to be seventy-nine years old, passing away in 1960. The unlikely DSC recipient and unexpected heiress honored her husband upon her death by bequeathing funds to establish the library in Poland Spring. The construction allotment for the Alvan Bolster Ricker Memorial Library and Community House was $60,000 plus funds in trust for its perpetual operation and maintenance.

Jane Jeffrey Ricker was posthumously awarded a citation by the editors of *Who's Who in America*, March 30, 1966. The citation was awarded Mrs. Ricker *"as the donor of the most substantial gift in relation to total annual income of an American library."*

She was undoubtedly thinking of the well-being of generations to come when making her bequest, just as you would expect from a nurse. Jane Jeffrey lived a full and unexpected life. The compassion and empathy of a nurse coursed through her veins her entire life.

Mr. Charles Lindbergh

The Lone Eagle's Contribution to World War II

By C. Douglas Sterner

Charles Augustus Lindbergh, who would achieve immortality as the first person to successfully make a trans-Atlantic flight and fall from grace for his isolationist views, was born in Detroit, Michigan, on February 4, 1902, the son of Evangeline and Charles A. Lindbergh, Sr. His father was a successful attorney who lived and practiced law in Little Falls, Minnesota. He was elected to the U.S. Congress when Charles was four years old and served therein for a decade until 1917.

For the next several years young Charles traveled with his family as they commuted from their Minnesota home to Washington, D.C., as well as elsewhere. He later wrote, *"Up to the time I entered the University of Wisconsin (1920) I had never attended for one full school year, and I had received instruction from over a dozen institutions, both public and private, from Washington to California. Through these years I crossed and re-crossed the United States, made one trip to Panama, and had thoroughly developed a desire for travel, which has never been overcome."*

Lindbergh's interest in travel took a new twist at the age of ten when he attended his first air show. It inspired an interest in air travel that was never abated. In 1918 he graduated from Little Falls

Beyond Belief: True Stories of Civilian Heroes

High School in his home state and enrolled as an engineering student in the University of Wisconsin in 1920. During his freshman year he found recreation in shooting matches on the R.O.T.C. team, but aviation became more and more the focus of his dreams for the future.

Motorized aviation which began with the Wright brothers' flight at Kitty Hawk, North Carolina in 1903, seized the world's imagination in the next decade with its aerial combat in World War I, and now, in the 1920s had catapulted itself to the next level of popularity through barnstorming flights, stunt flying, aerial races, and record-setting flights of speed, altitude, and distance—with prestigious trophies and cash awards offered in recognition.

On April 9, 1922, Charles Lindbergh made his first flight as a passenger in the plane-for-hire of Otto Timm in the sky over Lincoln, Nebraska; just another unknown, young, would-be airman. In the weeks that followed he began his own flight training, compiling eight hours of instruction at the cost of $500 by the end of May. Before Lindbergh could make his first solo flight, however, the instruction plane was sold.

Throughout that summer the young man spent a lot of time in the air, but little of it in the cockpit. Throughout Wyoming and Montana Lindbergh dazzled crowds as a wing-walker, parachutist, and performer, completing aerial feats that were popular in the barnstorming era.

In the spring of 1923 the elder Lindbergh, despite his general aversion to the airplane, fronted enough money for his twenty-one-year-old son to purchase his first airplane. It was a war-surplus Curtiss JN-4 Jenny, auctioned to Charles for a price of $500, a fraction of what it had cost the U.S. Government during the war. On April 9, Charles Lindbergh gassed up his first airplane, taxied to the end of the airstrip at Americus, Georgia, where the plane had been sold, and lifted off to make his first solo flight. From there it was on to Alabama, Mississippi, Arkansas, and across the South. For $5 Lindbergh provided the daring and the inquisitive with a five to ten-minute flight. Recalling those early days, he wrote in his 1927 account of the flight that made him famous: *"Some weeks I barely made expenses, and on others I carried passengers all week long at five dollars each. On the whole I was able to make a fair profit in addition to meeting expenses and depreciation."*

In September 1923, Lindbergh submitted forms to Washington, D.C., requesting duty with the United States Army Air Service. The following January he reported to Chanute Field in Illinois to take his entrance examinations. A short time later he received orders to report to Brooks Field in San Antonio, Texas, to join a class of flying cadets scheduled to begin training on March 15. Excitement ran high among the 104 cadets, all of whom were eager to fly the Army's newer and fastest airplanes. None were daunted by reports of a washout rate of forty per cent in the first phase of training.

Classes were tough and demanding, both mentally and physically. Just weeks after the training began, Lindbergh's already stressful situation was compounded by the death of his father. Lindbergh hung in there, survived the dreaded officer review and approval board known as the Benzine Board that sent more than half his classmates home prematurely, and was among the remnant of the original class that was sent to Kelly Field near San Antonio in September.

In 1925, the young man was one of eighteen cadets from the original class of 104 to receive his wings and commission as a second lieutenant in the U.S. Air Service Reserve Corps. Simply surviving to graduation was a considerable accomplishment. Second Lieutenant Charles A. Lindbergh graduated at the head of the class.

Lindbergh returned to the flying circus circuit that summer. In July he spent two weeks instructing other pilots at Richards Field in Missouri as part of his reservist military commitment, then flew passengers for the Missouri National Guard encampment in August. In November he was promoted to First Lieutenant in the 110th Observation Squadron, 35th Division, Missouri National Guard. He also learned that his friends in the Robertson Aircraft Corporation had succeeded in their bid for the government mail contract on the St. Louis/Chicago route. He began flying that route the following spring.

Beyond Belief: True Stories of Civilian Heroes

Flying the mail during this period was a dark, lonely, and dangerous job. The pilot usually flew solo, often at night, and in all manner of weather. The experience that Lindbergh gained flying the mail would prove invaluable for the flight that would make him world famous.

The Great 1927 New York-to-Paris Air Derby

Of the many successes and achievements that made pilots and aircraft designers in the 1920s, the *Holy Grail* was the nonstop trans-Atlantic flight. In 1919, French hotel operator Raymond Orteig offered a prize of $25,000 to the first pilot to fly nonstop between New York and Paris.

At first aviation technology was too primitive to make such a long and demanding journey possible. But by the mid-1920s, engine and aircraft designs had advanced sufficiently to make the dream of a non-stop trans-Atlantic flight a reality.

In 1926, Captain René Fonck, a highly decorated French war hero and the Allies' top ace with 125 claimed (seventy-five official) victories, captured the world's attention when he announced his intention to fly non-stop from New York City to Paris.

On September 26, 1926, together with American Lieutenant Lawrence Curtain as co-pilot/navigator, radio operator Charles Clavies, and mechanic Jacob Islamoff, Fonck powered up the engines of his gigantic Sikorsky S-35 and began roaring down the runway of Roosevelt Field, Long Island.

Suddenly the landing gear on one side collapsed. Instead of flying into the air, the crippled airplane plunged down the steep slope at the end of the runway, crashed, and burst into flames. Only Fonck and Curtain survived.

In 1927, four teams submitted applications to the committee overseeing the Orteig Prize: French war heroes Captain Charles Nungasser and Captain Francis Coli, U.S. Navy Lieutenant Commander Noel Davis and Lt. Stanton Wooster, Arctic explorer and Medal of Honor recipient Commander Richard Byrd whose pilot would be Floyd Bennett, the man who flew his Arctic expedition aircraft, and Columbia Aircraft president Charles Levine. All were famous in their respective fields and the press lauded their announcements and closely followed their preparations.

Lost in the hype was the name of a fifth applicant—someone who mentioned neither team nor crew other than himself, and even then neglecting to provide his first name, signing the application : *C. A. Lindbergh*

The race was on, not to be the first to cross, but the first to make the attempt. It seemed that that person would be Byrd. But, in early spring 1927, his plane, a modified Fokker Trimotor christened *America* crashed, severely injuring Bennett and slightly injuring Byrd.

Levine became the next candidate. But on April 24, his plane, the *Columbia*, also crashed. The next two attempts ended in tragedy. Two days after the *Columbia* crash, Davis and Wooster, flying their airplane the *American Legion*, stalled in the air during a test flight and crashed in a Virginia swamp, killing them both. And on May 8, Nungasser and Coli took off from Paris and pointed their plane, the *White Bird*, west. Last seen over Ireland, the crew and plane were lost somewhere over the Atlantic Ocean, never to be found.

Hope now rested on the shoulders of the fifth applicant about whom almost nothing was known, because unlike the others C. A. Lindbergh made all his preparations without fanfare.

With the help of financial backing from aviation supporting businessmen from St. Louis, Lindbergh contracted with Ryan Aircraft Company based in San Diego to make the *Spirit of St. Louis*, built to his specifications.

Byrd and Levine, meanwhile, were hard at work repairing their aircraft in preparation for making a second attempt.

On the morning of May 20, 1927, Lindbergh in the *Spirit of St. Louis* took off from Roosevelt Field, Long Island, New York. Thirty-three-and-a-half hours later, C. A. Lindbergh touched down at Le Bourget Aerodrome outside Paris, France, in front of a crowd estimated 150,000 strong. Charles Augustus Lindbergh had won the Orteig Prize—and so much more.

Several factors made Lindbergh's achievement even more striking. The other competitors were well known and vaunted aviators, well suited to the challenge, whereas the former airmail pilot from Michigan was a virtual unknown—and certainly an underdog in a very high profile competition. Furthermore, the other competitors were teams, at the least a pilot and navigator and in some cases additional crew, flying large and even multi-engine aircraft. Lindbergh accomplished his grueling and dangerous flight alone—just the man and his single-engine *Spirit of St. Louis*, earning him the moniker *The Lone Eagle*.

On June 13, 1927, Charles Lindbergh returned to New York to a reception like none ever before witnessed. Already he had been feted in Washington, D.C., welcomed by the President, and awarded the Distinguished Flying Cross. A parade in New York City, replete with a snowstorm of ticker tape, was witnessed according to one newspaper, by as many as 4 million Americans. Later the Street Cleaning Commissioner reported that it took 110 trucks and 2,000 *"white wings"* to clean up the streets.

Lindberg's reaction was typical of the atypical hero: *"I wonder if I really deserve all this!"* he said humbly.

Deserved or not, the moment was Lindbergh's. The *Providence Journal* reported that it doubted *"Any man of any age in the world's history has ever been the recipient of such adulation and such honors as have been heaped upon this youth of twenty-five in the last few weeks."*

Perhaps the reasons behind it were more accurately surmised in the *Jersey City Journal*, which wrote: *"Lindbergh's actions in the cockpit of the airplane were heroic, his utterances on land, when he faced adulation unequalled, were the utterances of a hero who is as well-balanced in speech as he is adroit in his manipulations of the airplane."*

The bottom line was simply that Charles Lindbergh was a truly GOOD man, a man of courage and imagination, a man of both dream and determination. When unprecedented honor was heaped upon him in Europe, he did not revel in his own accomplishment, but saw the praise tendered him as a tribute to his country. When he returned to the praise of his own people, he remained the same simple, humble man he had been before his historic flight. President Coolidge perhaps spoke the most accurate summary of Charles Lindbergh when he said, *"The absence of self-acclaim, the refusal to become commercialized, which has marked the conduct of this sincere and genuine exemplar of fine and noble virtues, has endeared him to everyone. He has returned unspoiled."*

In December 1925, millionaire aviation advocate Daniel Guggenheim had created a $2.5 million **Fund for the Promotion of Aeronautics,** to speed development of civil aviation in the United States. On June 4, 1927, Guggenheim opened the Daniel Guggenheim School of Aeronautics at New York University. On July 20, under the auspices and support of the Fund for Promotion of Aeronautics, Lindbergh and the *Spirit of St. Louis* began a tour of the United States – **The Guggenheim Tour.**

Over the next several months America's newest hero visited all 48 states, making 82 stops over 22,000 miles. In cities from coast to coast he gave 147 speeches and rode in parades equaling 1,290 miles. Everywhere he went, Charles Lindbergh was admired and greeted like no American in history. Humbly the young man accepted his new role, not for his own glory, but to promote aviation. His influence paved the way for many new advances. It also had a profound impact on those who saw him. The twelve-year old son of one South Dakota farmer later wrote of his own experience during this time.

<u>Sioux Falls, SD - August 27, 1927</u>

> *"When we learned (Lindbergh) was going to fly into Sioux Falls, Pop and I were like beavers after fresh timber. The whole family dressed up in our finest outfits, and Pop loaded us all into the car and drove us to Renner Field, five miles north of town, to see the new American hero and his airplane. Renner Field was little more than a hay patch, but it offered much more room for the crowd and the cars than did the Sioux Falls airport.*
>
> *"The crowd went wild as soon as the silvery speck appeared*

on the horizon. It came closer and closer, finally settling down at the far end of the field. When the plane taxied to a stop, the crowd mobbed it. A tall, thin figure climbed out and everyone roared and cheered and whistled and applauded, while a band played patriotic and military music. I tried to get as close as possible to the platform draped with red, white, and blue bunting surrounded by hundreds of American flags.

"Moments later an official party escorted Lindbergh up onto the platform, and the noise was enough to drown out the explosions in a dynamite factory. I broke through the edge of the crowd and climbed up to the platform, eager to shake hands with my hero. I was only a few feet away from Lindbergh when several men in military uniform grabbed me and threw me off the platform.

"I was too excited to be disappointed. In fact, I was so excited that I hardly heard a word Lindbergh said as he greeted the crowd and told about his historic flight. Instead of listening, I elbowed my way through the crowd to get over to Lindbergh's plane, which now stood majestically alone, totally ignored by the people crowding around the platform. That silver airship was the most beautiful thing I'd ever seen. I dreamed of climbing inside and flying it away.

"All the way home I chattered excitedly. 'I'm going to be bigger than Lindbergh someday,' I vowed to my father, more determined than ever to become a flier."

"Frank Foss looked at his 12-year-old son Joe and smiled."

(Foss, Joe and Donna, <u>A Proud American</u>, Pocket Books, 1992)

On December 14, 1927, the United States Congress authorized a special award of the Medal of Honor to Army Reserve Captain Charles A. Lindbergh. It was presented by President Coolidge and would remain, perhaps, the most controversial award of our Nation's highest

military Medal in its distinguished history. It was not unlike the Medal of Honor previously presented in peacetime to Richard Byrd for his North Pole mission—the primary difference being that at the time of his New York to Paris flight, though an Army Reservist, Lindbergh was a civilian.

Despite the controversy, which surfaced only in later years and for all the wrong reasons, Charles Lindbergh was indeed a hero. Only three Army airmen to that date had earned Medals of Honor, all during World War I, and all of them posthumously. (Eddie Rickenbacker's Medal of Honor was not presented until 1930.) Thus, Charles Lindbergh became the first living Army airman to receive his nation's highest honor.

The year 1927 was the spectacular highlight of Lindbergh's life. Nations and organizations fell all over themselves in their rush to bestow on him their highest and most prestigious honors. In the United States, in addition to the Medal of Honor from the Army, Congress awarded him the Congressional Gold Medal, and other prestigious organizations joined in giving him their highest awards as well.

But the high point of 1927 was tragically offset by the ultimate low point a parent can have when, five years later in 1932, his son, Charles Jr., was kidnapped and murdered. In 1936 Richard Hauptmann, the accused kidnapper and murder, was executed bringing to an end what the press called the "crime of the century." Wishing to escape the unrelenting publicity that dogged him and his family during the trial and the unrelenting public attention that continued, Lindbergh left the United States for Europe in 1936. There was another reason. He and President Franklin Roosevelt had suffered an irreconcilable breach.

On May 16, 1936, President Roosevelt had delivered a speech calling for a new, increased defense budget in order to secure America's security. It was a stirring speech that Republicans across the board, even former President Herbert Hoover, fell into line in agreement. The honeymoon lasted two days. On May 18, in a nationwide radio address, Lindbergh scathingly attacked the Administration, accusing it of creating with the speech a "defense hysteria" and that America was not threatened by events in Europe and Asia. He claimed that the only reason the country would be in danger "is because there are powerful elements in America who desire us to take part." He echoed George Washington's final speech as president in which he admonished against getting involved in "foreign entanglements."

Isolationists who had remained quiet suddenly had their champion and they exploited the aviator's fame for all it was worth to advance their cause of isolationism. Congressional leaders such as Senator Bennett Clark of Missouri, a Democrat, and Gerald P. Nye of North Dakota, a Republican and Representative John Rankin of Mississippi, another Democrat, immediately led the charge in voicing opposition.

Isolationism would reach its peak in 1940 when the **America First Committee** (AFC) was formed. Membership included future presidents John F. Kennedy and Gerald Ford, and its supporters included both Theodore Roosevelt Jr., and Alice Roosevelt Longworth, the former president's children, and numerous business leaders including powerful newspaper publishers Joseph M. Patterson (*New York Daily News*) and Robert M. McCormick (*Chicago Tribune*), both of whom hated FDR. But the man who became the lightning rod for President Franklin Roosevelt's ire was the AFC's spokesman, Charles Lindbergh.

Lindbergh's series of trips to Nazi Germany between 1936 and 1939 only added to the fire. Ironically, the trips were made at the U.S. Army's request.

"The Albatross"

In 1936 the German government invited Charles Lindbergh to inspect their air establishments. With urging from the American attaché in Berlin Major Truman Smith to comply in order to report back on the condition of German airpower, Lindbergh went. It was the first of five trips, each of which greatly impressed him with the German efforts to build an efficient and powerful air force. During Lindbergh's visit in 1938, Hermann Goering presented Colonel Lindbergh with the Verdienstkreuz der Deutscher Adler (Service Cross of the Order of the German Eagle) for his *services to aviation of the world and particularly his historic 1927 solo flight across the Atlantic.* " In presenting its highest national honor to Lindbergh, the government did no more than any other European nation had already done to honor the man. But because it was Nazi Germany, in the months that followed, Lindbergh's acceptance of the medal became a subject of growing controversy, to the point that his wife Anne Lindbergh referred to the decoration as *"the Albatross."*

Colonel (though he preferred to be called by his active duty rank of captain) Lindbergh, still a member of the Army Air Corps Reserves, was given carte blanch to visit Luftwaffe facilities and factories where its aircraft were manufactured. He came away impressed by the powerful German Luftwaffe. When asked to rate the air forces of the world he spoke what he believed to be the truth: *"Germany number one. Great Britain number two."* It was not a message Americans wanted to hear, or believe, and Lindbergh's frank honesty coupled with *The Albatross* began raising serious questions about his loyalty as an American.

In 1939 as war was brewing in Europe, the Lindberghs moved back to the United States. Lindbergh's inspection tours had impressed him with the efficiency of the German air force, but it had also frightened him. His fear was not for himself, but for his country. He honestly believed that the American Air Corps had been so neglected as to be greatly inferior to the forces being established in Germany. In his journal he wrote: *"There are wars worth fighting, but if we (United States) get in this one, we will bring disaster to the country and possibly our entire civilization. If we get into this war and really fight, nothing but chaos will result . . . it won't be like the last, and God knows what will happen here before we finish it."*

Upon his return and at the behest of Senator Wheeler Lindbergh joined the **America First Committee**, becoming a key spokesman for the group. Because of this, Lindbergh was soon portrayed as anti-Semitic. (He was, in fact, honestly critical of some practices that lent credence to this charge, although he deplored the treatment of the Jews by Nazi Germany, and said so).

Beyond Belief: True Stories of Civilian Heroes

On April 25, 1941, President Franklin D. Roosevelt publicly attacked Lindbergh in a press conference, going so far as to label the man treasonous and questioning his commission in the U.S. Air Service Reserves. Reportedly, there was even talk of stripping Lindbergh of his Medal of Honor. On Sunday, April 27, Lindbergh wrote in his journal: *"(I) have decided to resign. After studying carefully what the President said, I feel it is the only honorable course to take. If I did not tender my resignation, I would lose something in my own character that means more to me than my commission in the Air Corps. No one else might know it, but I would. And if I take this insult from Roosevelt, more, and worse, will probably be forthcoming."*

The following morning Colonel Charles Lindbergh performed one of his most difficult and most courageous acts. He submitted his letters of resignation to the president and to Secretary of War Henry Stimson. In the months that followed, he spoke on behalf of **America First**, always urging his country to avoid the war building in Europe. As a result, he was transformed from hero to polarizing figure.

Now no longer the universally admired iconic Lone Eagle, Lindbergh began the long journey from the top of the mountain of fame and glory down the slope that would end with him dying all but forgotten in Hawaii.

December 7, 1941 – Day of Infamy

The attack Pearl Harbor changed everything. The **America First Committee** disbanded and many of its members, including John Kennedy and Gerald Ford, volunteered for the military. It had been less than a year since Colonel Lindbergh had resigned his commission. Now that the war had come, it was difficult for him to imagine himself not involved in defending the nation he loved. In his journal, he wrote:

DECEMBER 8, 1941
"Now we have been attacked, and attacked in home waters . . . I can see nothing to do under these circumstances except to fight. If I had been in Congress, I certainly would have voted for a declaration of war."

Mr. Charles Lindbergh

> **DECEMBER 11, 1941**
>
> "All that I feared would happen has happened. We are at war all over the world, and we are unprepared for it from either a spiritual or a material standpoint."
>
> **DECEMBER 12, 1941**
>
> "Now that we are at war I want to contribute as best as I can to my country's war effort. It is vital for us to carry on this war as intelligently, as constructively, and as successfully as we can, and I want to do my part."

On December 12 Lindberg added in his journal: *"My first inclination . . . was to write directly to the President, offering my services, and telling him that while I had opposed him in the past and had not changed my convictions, I was ready in time of war to submerge my personal viewpoint in the general welfare and unity of the country."*

In these personal memoirs, unpublished for a quarter-century, Lindbergh went on to explain his concerns: *"The president has the reputation, even among his friends, of being a vindictive man. If I wrote to him at this time, he would probably make what use he could of my offer from a standpoint of politics and publicity and assign me to some position where I would be completely ineffective and out of the way."*

In the end, Lindbergh made his request for a return to military service through Air Corps Chief, General Henry "Hap" Arnold in a letter composed on December 20, less than two weeks after the attack on Pearl Harbor.

On December 30, the press announced that Charles Lindbergh had volunteered for service in the U.S. Army Air Corps. General Arnold had apparently released news of the December 20 letter, and Lindbergh took this as a ray of hope that his request was under consideration. He realized, however, that even Arnold could not act without the acquiescence of the president and had written his letter in such a way that General Arnold could deal with his offer according to the manner he felt most advisable. The two men had worked together in Air Corps business two years earlier, and Lindbergh had a sincere respect for the Air Chief.

Beyond Belief: True Stories of Civilian Heroes

Over the two following weeks Lindbergh waited anxiously for news, hoping that something would break his way. During the period he met with Colonel William "Wild Bill" Donovan, who was heading up an intelligence organization that later became the Office of Strategic Services, the forerunner of the CIA, which needed an aviation expert. The World War I Medal of Honor hero and father of our modern intelligence services was friendly in his efforts to recruit Lindbergh, though he did note that any such move would require the approval of the President. Neither man had much confidence that Roosevelt could put the past animosities between himself and Lindbergh aside.

On January 12 Lindbergh went to Washington, D.C. for a late afternoon meeting with Secretary of War Henry Stimson. The Secretary greeted him warmly, speaking first of a 1930 situation in which Charles Lindbergh had answered a call from the State Department for assistance in a potentially disastrous political situation. To Lindbergh it sounded like the Secretary was saying, *"I owe you one . . . for old time's sake."* Then the conversation seemed to go downhill.

Stimson advised Lindbergh that he was reluctant to put him in a command situation due to his prior antiwar views. He doubted the man's ability to pursue the current war aggressively enough. Lindbergh replied that his views on the war had not been altered but, *"Now that we were in the war my stand was behind my country, as I had always said it would be, and that I wanted to help in whatever way I could be most effective."* At last Secretary Stimson did agree to arrange a meeting between Lindbergh and General Arnold. It took place the following day.

General Arnold met with Lindbergh in the office of Assistant Secretary of War Robert Lovett. Both men assured Lindbergh that there were many ways he could serve the Air Corps, but voiced doubts that the public or the media would respond well to his taking an important position in the command structure. After a half-hour, Lindbergh finally understood, writing: *"In view of the feeling which existed it seemed . . . it would be a mistake . . . to return to the Air Corps."*

Instead, he decided to seek to make his contribution to the war effort through a commercial aviation industry, such as Pan American Airways, Curtiss-Wright, or United Aircraft. *"It goes against my grain to be out of the Air Corps in time of war,"* he wrote in his journal that evening, *"but I am convinced it would be inadvisable for me to push my way back into it.*

"Both Arnold and Lovett seemed friendly personally, but I constantly had the impression that they were thinking of orders from higher up. They were both in a difficult position . . . the situation was loaded with political dynamite and (they) handled themselves accordingly."

Two days after the Stimson–Arnold meeting, Lindbergh had dinner with Eddie Rickenbacker, who had also been a member of the **America First Committee** and had also garnered the wrath of the president. Fortunately for Rickenbacker, he found his role in this new war, thanks in no small part to his combat history in the previous war, and his close friendship with General Arnold.

For Lindbergh, who had never served in time of war or heard a shot fired in anger, his employment situation only got worse. The following Monday he offered his services to Pan American, his first choice among the commercial air lines now turning their efforts towards supporting the war. One week later he received his reply . . . *"obstacles had been put in the way."* Though what kind of obstacles they were remained unstated, Lindbergh knew that those obstacles were insurmountable; almost certainly placed there by President Roosevelt.

His suspicion was confirmed a week later in a meeting with Pan American Airlines boss Juan Trippe who told him that the War Department had been open to Lindbergh working on Pan American's war projects. But, when Trippe had approached the White House for approval of the matter, they were angry with him for even bringing up the subject. They advised Trippe that they did not want Lindbergh *"connected with Pan American in any capacity."*

On February 11, Lindbergh was advised not to pursue work with United, which had recently come under political attack and suspicion for its sale of aviation materials to both Japan and Germany in the pre-war years. Though Lindbergh was not involved in these sales, it was deemed that the hero's own personal baggage would only make matters worse.

Next Lindbergh turned to the Curtiss-Wright Company. On February 25 he was advised that the situation was *"loaded with dynamite"* and that the company's *"officers are afraid of the vindictiveness of the White House, and they have good reason to be."*

Later that night Lindbergh wrote in his journal: *"I am beginning to wonder whether I will be blocked in every attempt I make to take part in this war. I have always stood for what I thought would be to the best interest of this country, and now we are at war I want to take my part in fighting for it, foolish and disastrous as I think the war will prove to be. Our decision has been made, and now we must fight to preserve our national honor and out national future. I have always believed in the past that every American citizen had the right and the duty to state his opinion in peace and to fight for his country in war. But the Roosevelt Administration seems to think otherwise."*

Ultimately, only one man dared to stand up to the president, a man who, briefly, had also been a member of America First. On March 24, Lindbergh met with the owner and officers of a B-24 bomber factory at Willow Run near Detroit. They advised Lindbergh that they could make good use of his knowledge and experience if he would accept a position as a civilian advisor and aeronautical engineer. Lindbergh reminded the men of his previous problems gaining employment with Pan Am, United, and Curtiss-Wright, and advised them to first bring the matter up with the War Department. Henry Ford responded that it *"Annoy(d) him to think he has to ask anyone about what he wants to do in his own factory,"* Lindbergh recorded in his journal.

In Henry Ford, Charles Lindbergh found perhaps the only the man that would give him the opportunity he had struggled to achieve for four months, the opportunity to serve his country in time of war. But, only as a civilian.

A New Ace and American Hero

In the fall of 1942, while Eddie Rickenbacker was lost at sea during his trip to visit airmen in the Pacific, a new hero was emerging at Henderson Field on Guadalcanal. The day before Rickenbacker started his Pacific tour, the young Marine Corps pilot became an ace, having shot down his fifth enemy plane. Three days after Rickenbacker's B-17 went down in the Pacific, he shot down four Japanese airplanes in a single day. On the day Rickenbacker was dividing up the third of his four oranges in a life raft, that Marine pilot was shooting down four more Zeroes. On that same November 7 afternoon, that young pilot himself went down in the Pacific, but was rescued and returned to his unit within forty-eight hours.

For weeks in the Fall of 1942, talk among pilots in the Pacific centered on who would be the first airman of this new war to equal the twenty-six planes shot down record of America's Ace of Aces, Eddie Rickenbacker. Three days after Rickenbacker was pulled from the sea, that same young pilot on Guadalcanal was this new war's undisputed Ace of Aces with twenty-three victories. Less than one month later, he shot down three planes in one day to tie the record of Captain Eddie Rickenbacker of WWI.

Eddie was most gracious, sending both a congratulatory letter and a case of Scotch to the young Marine. For the kid from South Dakota, it was a thrill—Eddie Rickenbacker had been one of his two greatest heroes since his youth, second perhaps only to the one man he admired most—Charles Lindbergh.

Summer, 1943

Major Joseph Jacob Foss was finally back to work, away from what he later called "The Dancing Bear Act" that had followed his earning the title Ace of Aces, his appearance on the cover of *Life* magazine, and the presentation of his Medal of Honor. He was assigned to the Marine base at Santa Barbara, California, where he was building the new Marine Fighting Squadron ONE

HUNDRED-FIFTEEN (VMF-115) and training his pilots in their

Beyond Belief: True Stories of Civilian Heroes

new F4U Corsairs. All of his nearly 100 Marine pilots were young, green, and in need of solid leadership. Authorized to recruit his own top officers, Foss requested several of the men who had served with him on Guadalcanal.

The new Corsairs were supposed to be highly superior to the old Wildcats men like Foss had flown out of Henderson Field a year before, but Major Foss was finding them temperamental. They tended to cut out at altitudes above 21,000 feet, and several crashes had occurred during testing and training, some of them fatal. Foss brought the matter to his commanding officer, who quickly put Foss on the phone to General Bill Wallace, who was in charge of Marine aviation for the West Coast.

"General, I'm having a terrible time with these Corsairs," Foss stated bluntly.

"You'll have an expert tomorrow," the general promised. Foss smiled to himself—military men are quite used to such "promises."

Two days later Foss was working in his cramped office when someone knocked on the door. *"Come in,"* he said routinely, scarcely looking up from his work as a tall, slender man in plain Khakis with no military insignia walked in.

"Major Foss," the gentleman announced, *"It's good to meet you. I'm Charles Lindbergh."*

"The real *Charles Lindbergh?"* Foss asked incredulously looking closely at the new arrival. Lindbergh simply nodded his head.

"Come in, come in!" Foss said, hardly able to contain his excitement. *"When I was a kid, I wanted to meet you in the worst way when you flew into South Dakota, but the cops threw me off the stand. And here you are. Gosh!"*

Lindbergh smiled and, embarrassed, said, *"General Wallace sent me over to see if I can help you solve the Corsair problem."*

Lindbergh spent several weeks with Foss who not only got the handshake he had wanted fifteen years earlier but gained a friend for life. (Foss later served as co-chairman of the nonprofit Lindbergh Foundation.) Foss also learned that the man hated being called

88

Charles or *Lucky Lindy*. *"He wanted to be known either as* Slim *or* Charlie.*"*

To Major Foss's relief, Lindbergh was indeed the expert he needed, and the problems with the Corsairs were soon fixed. When the time came to say good-by. Lindbergh asked Foss if he could address the men. Naturally, Foss consented.

"I just want to thank you for your generous support of my efforts here," Lindbergh told the young Marine pilots who would soon be off to war. *"I've really enjoyed working with you, and there's only one more thing I'd really like to do. I'd like to fly tail-end Charlie with this outfit."*

The applause was long and earnest. Foss announced, *"You've got a job flying with us any time you show up. But if I have anything to do with it, you won't be flying tail-end Charlie. I want you up the line."*

May 25, 1944

It was a somber day as Major Foss returned to his operations office on Emirau Island in the Pacific. He and VMF-115 had been back at war for more than three months, and he was returning from the funeral of one of his pilots who had died the previous day during a test flight. As he got closer to his tent, he noticed a new Corsair on the airfield indicating he had company. A tall, slender man in khakis devoid of military rank or insignia was walking towards him, hand outstretched.

"Hi Joe," he greeted the squadron commander. *"You remember what you said? You promised me I could fly with you."*

Major Foss returned a warm but firm handshake, smiled and said, *"Charlie, Consider yourself on duty right now!"*

Over the weeks that followed, Lindbergh was an observer, flying missions with the men of VMF-115. If he was to understand the problems with the Corsairs, he would need to experience the same problems the young Marine pilots were having When they took to the skies for bombing or strafing missions, one of the Corsairs of

VMF-115 flying formation in the hostile skies was piloted by Lindbergh himself.

> "He flew from morning till night, and he taught us some tricks. Charlie was no coward. I remember one time we were bombing Kavieng, going after an oil dump that had been spotted there . . . The area was heavily fortified, and the hidden entrenchment of antiaircraft fire was intense. The order was to drop our loads and get the hell out of there. I looked back and saw number eight—Charlie—turn around and go back for a second round. When he was coming down the first time, he'd noticed a major dump hidden off to the side, so he made a swing around for a second run by himself with all that AA fire concentrating solely on him. Apparently, he hit something, because there was a big explosion and clouds of smoke billowed.
>
> "When we got back to base, I jumped out of my plane and walked over to chew him out. *"Charlie, you just don't do that. There's no way you're supposed to go back after a target alone. It's a sure way of dying young."*
>
> Joe Foss

Too few Americans knew then, or are aware even today, of the combat courage of Charles Augustus Lindbergh. Lindbergh flew every combat mission with VMF-115 from the date of his arrival until the unit was sent home on June 1. He arrived a celebrity to the young Marines on Emirau, but became an admired friend, not for what he'd done twenty years before, but for his courage and dedication in this new war.

During his visit to Foss and VMF-115, a photographer snapped a photograph of Charlie and Foss, which was promptly printed in *Parade* magazine, disclosing to the world the man's presence in the war zone. (The Navy, without the knowledge or assent of the president, had sanctioned Lindbergh's Pacific mission.)

Major Foss was almost immediately deluged with letters, hundreds of them, from citizens on the home front who had seen that photo. Most of the letters admonished Foss for associating with *"bad company"* and advised him to avoid Charles Lindbergh.

Foss was furious, as were the other men that flew missions with Charlie. As a unit they undertook the task of answering each and every one of more than 700 such letters. Foss pulled no punches in his own replies, stating: *"Lindbergh's out here fighting a war at his own expense while* you're *at home!"*

Lindbergh's Pacific Mission

Lindbergh's Pacific mission had been proposed early in 1944. He was to visit the combat air units as a representative of United Aircraft Corporation, which produced the F4U **Corsair.** His job was to observe the men in the field and help them correct problems with the *"Bent-winged Flying Coffins."* He was to wear a Naval uniform devoid of any rank or other insignia, as his status was that of a civilian.

Though vilified by civilians at home, the Marines welcomed him warmly upon his arrival. In early May, Charlie made a gunnery flight to learn his guns with John L. Smith, one of the Marine Corps' first aces, now a lieutenant colonel. On May 19 he arrived at Henderson Field at Guadalcanal, then traveled to Bougainville before arriving at Emirau in search of Joe Foss on May 25. There he flew with VMF-115 until they went home and continued to fly with VMF-222 after Foss's departure. During the period he also accompanied a PT boat crew on a combat mission.

By the time his work with the Marines was completed, he flew more than a dozen combat air missions in Corsairs, both bombing and strafing from his own fighter airplane. Marine Corps commanders looked the other way when the civilian fired his guns on these missions. Even a civilian *has a right to defend himself,* they said in defense of their actions.

Beyond Belief: True Stories of Civilian Heroes

When the Army Air Forces learned of Lindbergh's presence and his success in helping the Marine pilots solve problems with their Corsairs, they invited Charlie to visit their own airbase and observe their P-38s in action. Lindbergh arrived at New Guinea on June 15, quickly checked out on the P-38 (which was one of the few aircraft he had never piloted), and soon was flying with the Army pilots. In the following two weeks he completed four combat missions with the 475th Fighter Group, commanded by Colonel Charles H. MacDonald, who emerged from World War II as the third-leading American ace in the Pacific with twenty-seven victories. During these missions Lindbergh discovered a way to effectively conserve fuel consumption and extend the airplane's range by 400 miles. Before his concepts could be effectively put into use, however, Charlie got some bad news.

On the evening of July 5 Lindbergh received word that *"a rumor was circulating to the effect that I was flying combat in New Guinea, and that, if true, there should be no more of it."* To answer to these charges, Lindbergh was called to Australia, arriving at Brisbane on July 12 to meet with General George Kenney, commander of the Allied Air Forces in the Southwest Pacific.

Lindbergh didn't care what his status was; he just wanted to be able to do his job. Later in that same afternoon, Charlie echoed this once again in a private meeting with theater commander General Douglas MacArthur, himself. MacArthur was impressed with Lindbergh's ideas that had significantly extended the effective range of the P-38 through his fuel-conservation techniques and was eager to apply Lindbergh's knowledge and experience throughout his air command. He even promised Lindbergh he *"Could have any plane and do any kind of flying"* he wanted to.

> "Kenney told me that a situation had arisen which caused some of the officers at headquarters much concern: that somehow I had managed to get into the forward areas in New Guinea without their knowing about it; that rumors had filtered back to the effect that I was flying combat with the Army squadrons; and that, of course, flying combat as a civilian was against all the regulations there were.

Mr. Charles Lindbergh

Lindbergh spent two days visiting Australia, content to move about at will since the press did not know he was there, and no one recognized him. On July 15 he flew back to New Guinea to resume his work with the three combat squadrons of the 475th Fighter Group.

Throughout the last two weeks of July Lindbergh spent his time teaching the Army Air Force pilots his techniques for extending the range of their flights: cruise control—reduce standard 2,200 rpm to 1,600, set fuel mixtures to auto lean, and slightly increase manifold pressures. Properly applied, it stretched the range of the P-38 *Lightening* by as much as 400 miles—a nine-hour flight.

Lindbergh also continued his flights: bomber protection, reconnaissance, and strafing. He flew with the best. In addition to being under the command of Colonel MacDonald, the 475th Fighter Group was the home to Major Thomas McGuire, well on his way to becoming the nation's second-leading ace with thirty-eight confirmed victories, two behind America's top ace Major Richard Bong.

All the Army pilots quickly gained a great respect for Lindbergh, both for the mechanical genius he brought to aviation, as well as for his courage in the air. He was accorded officer's privileges, but was addressed as Mr. Lindbergh, due his civilian observer status. He was also treated as a member of the squadron, taking the same kudos for a job well done and a good-natured ribbing when he erred. On one mission Lindbergh began dropping behind the rest of the formation after it had taken off, unaware he had forgotten to retract his landing gear. Ahead of him, one of the pilots quipped into the radio, *"Charlie, get your wheels up! You're not flying the Spirit of St. Louis."*

July 28, 1944

Captain Saburo Shimada and Sergeant Saneyoshi Yokogi were flying a rescue mission to locate a downed comrade in their two-seat, armed Mitsubishi 51 Sonias. Both were veterans, well trained and schooled in the crucible of aerial combat. Returning home, the two Japanese pilots had the misfortune to run into the U.S. Army Air Force's 9th Squadron, 49th Group.

In the distance Colonel MacDonald and Charles Lindbergh were returning with their own flights, listening to their American counter-parts bark directions over their radios as the dogfight stretched on.

With great skill and cunning, Captain Shimada and Sergeant Yokogi weaved in and out of cloud cover to escape—much to the frustration of the American pilots. In the distance MacDonald's pilots circled, eager to locate the enemy planes and enter the fray.

As the two Japanese Sonias broke the engagement and dashed for home, two of the pilots from MacDonald's squadron managed to flame Yokogi's aircraft and send it into the sea.

Diving in from 3,000 feet, MacDonald found Captain Shimada's Sonia and stitched a few bursts of machine gun fire across the fuselage. It was at that point that Shimada realized there was no hope in trying to outrun his pursuers, and he turned to fight. Banking sharply, Shimada lined up and dove on the first P-38 he saw. It belonged to the second element leader in MacDonald's formation, Charles Lindbergh, who later recalled that deadly day:

Mr. Charles Lindbergh

"We are spaced 1,000 feet apart. Captain (Danforth) Miller gets in a short deflection burst with no noticeable effect. I start firing as the plane is completing its turn in my direction. I see the tracers and the 20s (20-mm cannon) find their mark, a hail of shells directly on the target. But he straightens out and flies directly toward me.

"I hold the trigger down and my sight on his engine as we approach head on. My tracers and my 20's splatter on his plane. We are close—too close—hurtling at each other at more than 500 miles an hour. I pull back on the controls. His plane zooms suddenly upward with extraordinary sharpness.

"I pull back with all the strength I have. Will we hit? His plane, before a slender toy in my sight, looms huge in size. A second passes—two—three—I can see the finning on his engine cylinders. There is a rough jolt of air as he shoots past behind me.

"By how much did we miss? Ten feet? Probably less than that. There is no time to consider or feel afraid. I am climbing steeply. I bank to the left. No, that will take me into the ack-ack fire above Amahai strip. I reverse to the right. It all has taken seconds.

"My eyes sweep the sky for aircraft. Those are only P-38s and the plane I have just shot down. He is starting down in a wing over--out of control. The nose goes down. The plane turns slightly as it picks up speed—down—toward the sea. A fountain of spray—white foam on the water—waves circling outward as from a stone tossed in a pool—the waves merge into those of the sea—the foam disappears—the surface is as it was before."

Charles Lindbergh in his War Journal

It was Charles Lindbergh's first (and only) aerial combat victory and would never be officially credited to his military record. Three days later the tables were reversed, with Charles Lindbergh almost shot down. He never saw the enemy aircraft, or heard Colonel MacDonald shouting into the radio, *"Zero on your tail!"* The only thing that saved Lindbergh was the Japanese pilot's poor gunnery skills. Lindbergh didn't panic but went into a high-speed turn as MacDonald shouted over the radio, *"Break right! Break right!"* Lindbergh coolly stayed his course, leading the trailing enemy into the range of MacDonald, who intercepted with a series of tracers of his own. The crippled Zero broke and ran, and the American P-38s returned home, now low on fuel.

Word of the flight three days earlier, and Lindbergh's first aerial victory, had reached higher echelons. Colonel MacDonald was reprimanded, and grounded for sixty days. Lindbergh noted, *"I am fully as much to blame for the flight as he; but unfortunately, he must carry the responsibility, as he commands the group."* Ultimately, Colonel MacDonald's grounding was lessened to a sixty-day leave at home. It became a welcomed opportunity for him to see the son that had been born in his absence. Lindbergh continued to fly for ten more days, and then visited other airfields en route to Australia.

On August 22, Charles Lindbergh and Douglas MacArthur met again. But for Lindbergh's detailed war journal, MacArthur's reaction to the controversial flight of July 28 would never have been known. After chewing out the civilian pilot, MacArthur stood to his feet and walked around to perch himself on the edge of his desk, leaning forward as if it were a very private conversation.

"How many Japanese planes have you shot down?" MacArthur asked.

"One," Lindbergh replied frankly and honestly.

"Where was it?"

"Off the south coast of Ceram." Lindbergh said, and MacArthur smiled at that.

"Good! I'm glad you got one."

On September 16 Lindbergh arrived in San Francisco. The man had spent four months in the war zone, flown fifty combat missions with the warriors of a new generation, and proved he was still the hero he had been seventeen years before.

Upon President Roosevelt's death in 1945, Administration anger against him vanished. Lindbergh was free and in the post-war years he served as a consultant to the Chief of Staff of the Air Force and to Pan American Airways. President Dwight Eisenhower recommended he be promoted brigadier general in the Air Force Reserve, which Congress approved. He served on the advisory panel that recommended the site for the Air Force Academy. He also became involved in many environmental causes. He died in Hawaii on August 26, 1974, at age seventy-two.

Beyond Belief: True Stories of Civilian Heroes

Mrs. Amelia Earhart Putnam

Paving the Way for Women in Aviation

By: Adam Ballard

On a warm Friday in July of 1932, words of congratulations and compliment repeated throughout an outdoor awards ceremony in Los Angeles, California. People clapped and grasped hands and spoke of an amazing feat. Amelia Earhart had just become the first woman awarded the Distinguished Flying Cross for her solo trans-Atlantic flight that occurred earlier in the year. Words like "pioneer," "hero," and "championed pilot" were spoken, and although this small-town Kansas woman had difficulty accepting accolades and compliments, she remained poised and humble through the event. As people began to leave the venue, no one could've imagined that in just a few short years the same woman would be at the seat of one of the world's largest aviation mysteries.

The President of the United States of America, authorized by Act of Congress, July 2, 1926, takes pleasure in presenting the Distinguished Flying Cross to Mrs. Amelia Mary Earhart Putnam, a United States Civilian, for heroic courage and skill as a navigator, at the risk of her life, by her nonstop flight in her plane, unnamed, from Harbor Grace, Newfoundland, to Londonderry, Ireland, on 20 May 1932, by which she became the first and only woman, and the second person, to cross the Atlantic Ocean in a plane in solo flight, and also establish new records for speed and elapsed time between two continents.

Beyond Belief: True Stories of Civilian Heroes

Born in Atchison, Kansas on July 24, 1897; to parents Amelia and Samuel Earhart, as she grew up, she began breaking most gender conformities of the time, finding more comfort in small engine repair and physical sports than the more traditional womanly roles of her peers. Upon moving to Des Moines, Iowa, as part of her father's railroad employment, Amelia eyes fell upon the first airplane she had ever seen at the Iowa state fair as part of a traveling display. She was, however, heard to comment to friends and family that she was not overly impressed with the aircraft.

Amelia's father was an alcoholic, which made it difficult for him to hold down a job. It is suspected that this is the reason she often turned her nose against alcohol as an adult. At one point during Samuel's struggle with alcoholism, Amelia, her mother, and sister, Muriel, relocated to Chicago. There, she went graduated from the Hyde Park High School in 1915. Deciding to take a Christmas vacation to Toronto, Canada; Amelia was shocked as she witnessed firsthand the wounded soldiers returning from World War One. She watched as wounded men were shuffled from one place to another on their arrival. She was distraught at the sight of amputees and victims of the German gas attacks whose reports frequented the news.

Amelia remained in Toronto and became a volunteer nurse at the Spadina Military Hospital and continued to work there after the armistice was signed in 1918. Amelia later accredited her views on pacifism as being the direct result of time she spent volunteering there.

While still living in Canada, Amelia and a friend visited a flying exhibition that was hosted by a World War I ace. While standing in an isolated grass lot observing the show; the pilot observed them and dived at them in what was likely an attempt to intimidate or awe the onlookers. With engine roaring and tuffs of grass and foliage flying; her young friend moved from the lot, but Amelia stood her ground. She later stated; *"I am sure he said to himself, 'Watch me make them scamper' . . . I did not understand it at the time,"* she recalled, *"but I believe that little red airplane said something to me as it swished by."*

When her volunteer work was complete, and upon her parents' request; Amelia made a pilgrimage to California to move in with them just outside Long Beach in 1920. In December of that year, knowing that aviation was a growing passion in his daughter, her father brought Amelia to Daughtery Field. There, champion pilot Frank Hawks took her on a $10 aerial tour that changed Amelia's life.

Soaring high in the sky, she felt exhilarated. As the wind streamed over her face, and the sun shone brightly above her, she later recalled; *"By the time I had got two or three hundred feet off the ground . . . I knew I had to fly."*

Amelia set out to make her passion a reality. In order to save the money for pilot's school she began working several jobs, varying from truck driver, to photographer, to stenographer at a local phone company.

Through a combination of work and borrowed money, she got the needed $,1000 (nearly $15,000 dollars today), to pay for flying lessons. Once she began, she was pleased to find her teacher was another female—a self-made pioneer in the world of woman aviators

named Anita Snook. Through Snook's guidance and resolve, Amelia earned her pilot's license in December 1921. She completed all testing requirements in a yellow Kinner Airster biplane she had purchased that Sumer and nicknamed *"The Canary."*

Already eager to make a name for herself and break the stigma surrounding female pilots; on October 22, 1922, Amelia flew *The Canary* to the then record-breaking altitude of 14,000 feet, establishing a world record in the category of female pilots. On May 15, 1923, Amelia earned her international pilot's license, becoming only the sixteenth woman in the United States to do so.

The strain of dealing with her parents' subsequent divorce, and her own financial crisis forced Amelia to temporarily give up aviation. In 1924 she sold her airplane and with her mother drove across the United States to Boston, Massachusetts, with the long-term goal of furthering her education. But once there, Amelia's dreams were quickly diminished when she and her mother could no longer afford the tuition costs. As a result, she found work as a teacher and social worker in Medford, Massachusetts, in 1925.

Believing that this setback would not last indefinitely, Amelia kept her interest in aviation alive by becoming a member of the American Aeronautical Society's Boston chapter. She was eventually elected its vice president and worked her way back into the cockpit. She successfully levied her growing fame and found new work, acting as a sales representative for Kinner Airplane and Motor Corporation, handing out brochures and selling planes throughout the Boston area. She also began promoting flying through the writing of articles for the local newspaper and successfully laying the groundwork for a new organization for female flyers.

In May 1927, Charles Lindbergh's solo flight across the Atlantic brought a new breath of life into the world of aviation, spurring many people to carve out their own slice of aeronautical fame. One such person, Amy Guest, set out to be the first woman to fly or be flown across the Atlantic Ocean. However, when her family objected to the risk involved, she offered to sponsor the project provided *"another girl with the right image"* took her place. Amelia received a phone call in April 1928, from Army Captain Hilton Railey. He asked her the question she'd been waiting for: *"Would you like to fly the Atlantic?"*

She eagerly said *"yes,"* even though she would join two male aviators, one who would be pilot and the other the co-pilot. She would make the trip as a passenger, but even so, she would be the first woman to fly across the Atlantic Ocean.

The project coordinators had selected Wilmer Stultz and co-pilot Louis Gordon for the flight. Although Amelia's primary role was that only of a passenger, she was given the duty of keeping the crew's flight logs during the journey. The crew departed Trepassy Harbor, Newfoundland, on June 17, 1928. Exactly 20 hours and 40 minutes later, their Fokker Trimotor touched down at Pwll, near Burry Port, South Wales. Due to spotty weather conditions, the majority of the flight was done on instruments, something Amelia had no training in. Although she did not pilot the aircraft, after landing she did an interview and was quoted as saying, *"Stultz did all the flying. I was just baggage, like a sack of potatoes."* She continued, *"Maybe someday I'll try it alone."*

When the crew returned to the United States they were feted with the parade through Manhattan, New York. A reception with President Calvin Coolidge at the White House followed.

Continuing to foster and grow her public image, Amelia was affectionately given the nickname *"Queen of the Air"* by some news organizations. Capitalizing on her new fame, in order to raise money for her own attempt, she set out on a cross country lecture and book tour during 1928 and 1929. These efforts further solidified Amelia in the public eye. Celebrity endorsements, product advertising (luggage and magazine covers), and donations poured in. In 1929, she was among the first aviators to promote commercial air travel. Along with Charles Lindbergh, she represented Transcontinental Air Transport (later TWA) in a commercial and other advertisements across the United States.

During this time Amelia fell in love with her publicist, publisher George Putnam. They were married in Noank, Connecticut, on February 7, 1931. Continuing to defy gender conformity, Amelia made her standing clear in a letter written and hand delivered to George on their wedding day. It read, *"I want you to understand I shall not hold you to any medieval code of faithfulness to me nor shall I consider myself bound to you similarly."* She continued, *"I may have to keep some place where I can go to be by myself, now and then, for I cannot guarantee to endure at all times the confinement of even an attractive cage."*

Leaving no time for a honeymoon, Amelia hurriedly began a nine-day cross country tour promoting autogyros and the sponsor company, Beech Nut Chewing gum. When questioned about her desires of flight while on tour, Amelia said, *"I wanted to justify myself to myself. I want to prove that I deserved at least a small fraction of the nice things said about me."*

After collecting enough funds and sponsorship for another record breaking accomplishment, Amelia began preparations for her own solo transatlantic flight. She decided to fly a single engine Lockheed Vega 5B in emulation of Charles Lindbergh's solo flight five years earlier. The aircraft was popular among many aviators for its rugged performance and superior construction. Amelia was assisted in her preparation and modification of the airplane by famed Aviator Bernt Balchen.

On May 20, 1932, five years to the day after Charles Lindberg's famous flight, Amelia Earhart set off. She began at Harbor Grace, Newfoundland. Setting her course for Europe, she later described the flight in great detail: recounting her battle with freezing temperatures that caused an ice build-up on the plane, and fog that brought her visibility to near zero. The majority of her flight was done completely on instruments due to these conditions. She managed to brave the weather for more than fourteen hours and successfully landed on a farm near Londonderry, Northern Ireland. The touchdown was witnessed by two farmhands, and

Crowds gathered to welcome Amelia Earhart and her airplane "Friendship," following her trans-Atlantic solo flight.

when one questioned her as to where she had come from and how far she had flown, Amelia simply stated, *"From America."*

Amelia Earhart went on to be awarded many accolades for her distinguishing flight career. For her solo transatlantic flight she was not only awarded the United States military's Distinguished Flying Cross, but also the Chevalier Légion d'honneur from the French government, and the Gold Medal of the National Geographic Society.

Mrs. Amelia Earhart Putnam

The next great challenge she decided to take up was becoming the first woman to fly around the world. On July 2, 1937, together with her co-pilot Fred Noonan and flying a modified Lockheed Electra, they disappeared somewhere in the Pacific Ocean while en route to a refueling stop at Howland Island in the Central Pacific. Due to her publicly renowned life, and this trip making headlines all over the world; much speculation has been tendered considering her disappearance.

Although we may never know what officially happened to Amelia Earhart, Fred Noonan, and their Lockheed Electra; the astonishing career and reputation of Amelia Earhart is not debatable. Her pioneering aviator skills and tenacity in the face of adversity paved the way for nearly all the female aviators who followed her. Without the mystique that surrounds her death, it is certain that Amelia Earhart would have still been remembered for her skill and courage demonstrated in the 1932 transatlantic solo flight. Her life and achievements inspired women like Jaqueline Cochran, the first woman to fly faster than the speed of sound; Willa Brown, the first African- American woman to earn her commercial pilots license; or Sally Ride, who became the first woman in space just sixty-four years later.

NOTE: Amelia Earhart Putnam is one of only about eight U.S. civilians (including Orville and Wilbur Wright), who have been awarded the Distinguished Flying Cross. Below are the fifteen

Beyond Belief: True Stories of Civilian Heroes

women who have been awarded a total of eighteen Distinguished Flying Crosses in history:

War	Name	Branch		Date of Action
1918-1942	Earhart Putnam, Amelia	Civ		May 20, 1932
WWII	Dial, Kathleen R.	USAAF		Jun. 10, 1944
WWII	Hawkins, Mary Louise	USA*		Sep. 24, 1944
WW II	Lutz, Aleda E.	USA*		Nov. 1, 1944
WWII	Schilbach, Roberta	USA*		World War II
1945-1950	Cochran, Jacqueline	USAF	1st	1947 - 1951
Korean War	Bonham, Jonita Ruth	USAF		Jul 25 – Sep 26, 1950
Vietnam War	Cochran, Jacqueline	USAF	2d	Apr. 1962
Vietnam War	Cochran, Jacqueline	USAF	3d	May – Jun. 1964
Gulf War	Cornum, Rhonda S.	USA*		Feb. 27, 1991
1975-2001	McFetridge, Patricia A.	USCG		Sep. 22, 1990
1975-2001	Collins, Eileen Marie	USAF		Jul. 23 - 27, 1999
GWOT	Bringloe, Julia A.	USA*		Jun. 25 - 27, 2011
GWOT	Stires, Sara A.	USN		Nov. 9, 2001
GWOT	Kniep, Andra V. P.	USAF	1st	Mar. 5, 2002
GWOT	Kniep, Andra V. P.	USAF	2d	Mar. 6, 2002
GWOT	May, Melissa J.	USAF		Mar. 24, 2003
GWOT	Hill, Lori	USA		Mar. 21, 2006

*Indicates Army Nurses/Medical personnel

Mr. Dusko Popov

The James Bond Who Ran Afoul of the FBI

BY DWIGHT JON ZIMMERMAN

His name was Dusko (or Dusan) Popov, a flamboyant son of a wealthy and well-connected Serbian family. Code-named Ivan, he was one of Abwehr's top agents in World War II. Or so the German military intelligence agency thought. In reality Popov, a strong anti-Nazi, was secretly a double agent, codenamed Tricycle working for British MI6. His service for the British during the war was so important that he was awarded the Order of the British Empire. Though not as important, but certainly more famous, was the contribution he made to the genre of spy literature. Popov was the inspiration for the fictional secret agent James Bond.

Dusko Popov in 1941.
Wikipedia

Popov was born into an affluent family on July 10, 1912, in Titel, Austria-Hungary, in what is now Serbia. He grew up in cosmopolitan luxury and when World War II started in Europe in 1939, he was a lawyer with a well-established reputation as an international playboy.

In 1940 British intelligence enrolled him as a double agent. In his autobiography, *Spy/Counterspy* Popov wrote that at the start of his training, MI6 head Stewart Menzies gave Popov this penetrating assessment of the Serb, *"You are honest but without scruples. Your instincts and intuitions are stronger than your intelligence, which is far above average. Your conscience never bothers you, and you are mentally short-sighted and long-sighted at the same time. You are ambitious and ruthless and you can even be cruel. But when you are cruel, it is with an animal cruelty, not a sick cruelty. You like to hit back but you are not in a hurry to do so. When you are frightened, you don't panic. Danger is a stimulant for you. You think more clearly and make better and quicker decisions when pushed by the instinct of self-preservation than by contemplation."* That instinct for self-preservation would serve him well for the six years he would serve on His Majesty's secret service.

Once his training was complete, Popov arranged through Johnny Jebsen, a close friend who was already an Abwehr agent (and would later become a British double agent as well), to become one as well. Thus began the spy career of Ivan/Tricycle. For the rest of the war and using a variety of covers that included import-export business executive and delegate for the Yugoslav Ministry of Information, as well as setting up dummy intelligence networks in England run by MI6, Popov regularly fed disinformation to the Abwehr and gathered real intelligence about German activities which he passed on to his British handlers. Though Popov would score many successes for British intelligence, his one attempt to work with the United States' FBI and help set up a double-agent network in America ended in failure with tragic consequence.

By late spring 1941, the Abwehr had become so impressed with the quality and quantity of the intelligence that he had gathered for them that it wanted Popov to set up an intelligence network in the United States, previous efforts having failed. On August 10, 1941, the Abwehr sent him to the United States to establish a German spy network. Among the intelligence and other material Popov carried with him on his mission was detailed information about Japanese plans for an attack on the American military bases in and around Pearl Harbor. British intelligence's plan called for Popov to hand over to the FBI that intelligence and assist the agency in creating a "hostile" spy network that it would run. Just one problem: FBI Director J. Edgar Hoover.

Mr. Dusko Popov

Upon his arrival in New York City, after meeting the local FBI head and filling him in on his mission and making a point of discussing the Pearl Harbor intelligence, Popov discovered that instead of immediately meeting Hoover to finalize the dummy spy network operation, he'd have to wait for an appointment.

Popov decided if he had to wait, he'd do so in style, renting a Park Avenue apartment, dating and becoming lovers with one beautiful, rich, and, sometimes, famous woman after another. He even took one of them with him on a vacation to Florida. To Popov's surprise, that side trip brought the wrath of the FBI down on him. Agents met him as he was sunning himself on the beach and ordered him to stop his flagrant and illegal activity (taking a woman across state lines for "immoral purposes" a violation of the Mann Act).

Popov's eventual meeting with Hoover, in New York City, was a disaster. The FBI director began by shouting, *"You come here from nowhere and within six weeks install yourself in a Park Avenue penthouse, chase film stars, break a serious law, and try to corrupt my officers. I'm telling you right now I won't stand for it."*

FBI Director J. Edgar Hoover in 1939.
Library of Congress

Stunned, Popov replied, *"I brought a serious warning indicating exactly where, when, how and by whom your country is going to be attacked."* In addition to providing intelligence about the proposed Pearl Harbor raid, he tried to convince Hoover of the value of having an enemy spy ring under FBI control. But Hoover's prejudice against Popov and his lifestyle was manifest. The spy ring offer was rejected.

Popov did eke out some minor FBI assistance that justified his trip to the Germans, but Popov bitterly confessed to Colonel Dick Ellis, his British contact in New York City, that thanks to Hoover's prejudice and short sightedness, the mission was a failure. Then, in December he learned worse news. When he heard of the Imperial Japanese Navy attack on Pearl Harbor, Popov at first thought was that thanks to his information, the American military had successfully repulsed it. But when he discovered that it was a Japanese victory, with the American military on Oahu being completely surprised, he was devastated. For reasons unknown, Hoover had not forwarded that intelligence to the American military.

Most of Popov's intelligence work was done in Spain and Portugal. Thanks to his many contacts in Spain, he played a small but important part in Operation Mincemeat, the disinformation plan to hide the real location of the amphibious landings for Operation Husky. Mincemeat involved the use of a cadaver with a false identity of a British officer carrying a briefcase full of false documents that washed ashore on a Spanish beach. In the days leading up to that part of the operation, Popov aided in the deception by telling the Abwehr that Yugoslav soldiers in England were being ordered to Scotland for parachute training; the idea being that because of the similarities in topography, the Germans would think that it was in preparation for an invasion of Greece. Later, when Mincemeat was executed, Popov was instructed to learn if the Germans had copied the documents in the briefcase and whether or not they believed them (yes, on both counts).

For his services, Popov was awarded the Order of the British Empire. After the war, Popov had a successful business career. He married, had four children, and died in his home in the South of France in 1981 at age sixty-nine.

Though Popov's playboy lifestyle proved offensive to Hoover, it had the opposite effect on fellow MI6 agent Ian Fleming. Prior to the mission that sent Popov to the United States, MI6 gave him eighty thousand dollars in cash for expenses. With time to kill before he left, Popov decided to relax at a local casino in Lisbon. Shortly after entering, he spotted at a baccarat table an acquaintance, an arrogant, wealthy Lithuanian. In his autobiography *Spy/Counterspy*, Popov wrote, *"When holding the bank* [the Lithuanian] *would never set a limit, as was customary. Instead, he'd announce haughtily, 'Banque ouverte,' meaning the others could bet as much as they wished. It was ostentatious and annoying . . . ."*

When the Lithuanian again said, *"Banque ouverte,"* Popov decided to put a stop to the Lithuanian's theatrics. When the croupier called for bets that the Lithuanian, as banker, was obligated to match,

Popov calmly announced, *"Fifty thousand dollars"*—about $1.4 million in today's money. All conversation stopped as Popov counted out the bills. Popov, who knew Fleming was secretly shadowing him because of the cash he was carrying, slyly noticed Fleming's face turn green.

Pointing to the now silent Lithuanian, Popov said, *"I suppose that the casino is backing this man's bet, since you didn't object to his 'Banque ouverte.'"*

"The casino never backs any player's stake, sir," the croupier replied.

Popov then collected his money and huffed, *"I trust you'll call this to the attention of the management and that in the future such irresponsible play will be prohibited. It is a disgrace and an annoyance to the serious players."*

As Popov walked away, he saw Fleming smile with amused comprehension. After he was discharged from MI6, Fleming started a new career as a novelist, creating the famous fictional spy, James Bond. Popov was credited with being the inspiration for Bond, and Popov's casino scene, in its various permutations in Fleming's novels would become the signature scene in the Bond novels and movies.

Dr. Lawton Shank

A Civilian on Wake Island

BY: SCOTT BARON

Most Americans are familiar with the Japanese attack at Pearl Harbor, Hawaii, on December 7, 1941. Fewer know that the Japanese also attacked Singapore, Guam, Midway Island, the Philippines Islands, and Wake Island in the first twenty-four hours on that *"Day of Infamy."*

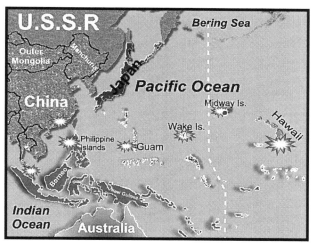

Wake Island (an atoll composed of three small islands) was an isolated American outpost of strategic important to the American presence in the Pacific Ocean. Prior to December 7, it was the only island in the region not under Japanese rule and control. Major James P. S. Devereux commanded the 400 Marines stationed there to defend an outpost that consisted of a newly constructed airfield and a few bunkers.

113

Beyond Belief: True Stories of Civilian Heroes

Four days before the attack on Pearl Harbor, the carrier U.S.S. *Enterprise* had sailed close enough to Wake to dispatch twelve F4F Wildcat fighter airplanes under the command of Major Paul Putnam. Putnam's squadron was expected to fly patrols from the new airfield on Wake. When delivery was accomplished, the big aircraft carrier turned for home. But for the mission to Wake, she would have been a sitting duck in Pearl Harbor on the day of the Japanese attack.

The battle for Wake Island was fought on and around the atoll formed by Wake Island and its minor islets of Peale and Wilkes Islands on the land, air and sea. It was 6:00 a.m. on December 8 at Wake Island (on the other side of the International Date Line), when the first bombs fell on Pearl Harbor and Major Devereaux received word of the attack as he was drinking his morning coffee. He alerted his small shore defenses and Major Putnam and three Marine pilots began flying patrols over the north side of the atoll. A rain squall darkened skies to the south.

It was nearing noon when thirty-six twin-engine Japanese bombers slipped through the storm to surprise Wake's defenders. The four airborne American pilots returned to meet the enemy in the air, but not before the Japanese destroyed seven of the twelve Wildcats on the ground at Wake, and damaged an eighth. The heavy bombardment further destroyed most of the aviation fuel and spare parts needed for the Marine flying squadron that was now reduced to but four aircraft.

Despite the damage, the 400 intrepid Leatherneck riflemen held on, determined to rebuff the enemy bombardment. Unknown to them at the time, even as the first bombs rained down on Wake Island, a large Japanese landing force was departing from Kwajalein to finish the job. They would arrive within three days.

The defense of Wake Island has been compared to the Battle of the Alamo or the Battle of the Little Big Horn. The determined

Dr. Lawton Shank

defenders of Wake Island quickly became well known to the American public back home. The American defenders holding out against all odds provided the American people about the only sliver of good news coming out of the Pacific war.

Captain Henry T. Elrod, one of the pilots from VMF-211, would be awarded the Medal of Honor posthumously for his actions on the island from December 8–23, 1941. His Medal of Honor citation reads, in part, *"Captain Elrod shot down two of a flight of 22 hostile planes and, executing repeated bombing and strafing runs at extremely low altitude and close range, succeeded in inflicting deadly damage upon a large Japanese vessel, thereby sinking the first major warship to be destroyed by small caliber bombs delivered from a fighter-type aircraft. When his plane was disabled by hostile fire and no other ships were operative, Captain Elrod assumed command of one flank of the line set up in defiance of the enemy landing and, conducting a brilliant defense, enabled his men to hold their positions and repulse intense hostile fusillades to provide covering fire for unarmed ammunition carriers. Capturing an automatic weapon during one enemy rush in force, he gave his own firearm to one of his men and fought on vigorously against the Japanese. Responsible in a large measure for the strength of his sector's gallant resistance, on December 23, Captain Elrod led his men with bold aggressiveness until he fell, mortally wounded."*

Major James Patrick Sinnott Devereux was the Commanding Officer of the 1st Marine Defense Battalion, at the Naval Air Station on Wake Island. *"Major Devereux was responsible for directing defenses of that post during the Japanese siege from 7 through 22 December 1941, against impossible odds."* For his *"inspiring leadership and the valiant devotion to duty"* was awarded the Navy Cross in April 1942, an award he was unaware of as he spent the rest of the war as a Japanese prisoner of war.

Beyond Belief: True Stories of Civilian Heroes

Major Paul Albert Putnam, Commanding Officer of Marine Fighting Squadron 211 (VMF-211), Marine Air Group 22 (MAG-22), would also be awarded the Navy Cross. His citation read, *"On 21 December 1941 . . . when the island was subjected to a relentless attack by carrier-based hostile aircraft, Major Putnam proceeded by truck to the airfield and, although severely strafed by enemy planes on the way and forced to abandon his truck on two separate occasions, succeeded in reaching his objective. Then, embarking in a friendly fighter plane, he executed an unsupported flight far out to sea in a desperate attempt to locate the Japanese carrier."* He kept the unit's aircraft aloft to the last plane, and then, like all the pilots, he picked up a rifle and fought as an infantryman.

Lieutenant Colonel Walter Bayler was the only Marine to escape capture or death on Wake Island. He departed the island on a Navy PBY Catalina on December 20, later providing an accurate recounting of the events on Wake Island to the press and people of America, while also providing photos and maps of the island. The reason Bayler was able to leave Wake Island was because he was a radio technician, and his services and abilities were desperately needed elsewhere, and he left in the last plane that was available. Seven months later he was awarded the Legion of Merit with "V" as the chief of all communications during the invasion of Guadalcanal.

After the American surrender on December 23, 1941, the island was held by the Japanese for the duration of the war. The Japanese garrison on the island surrendered to a detachment of United States Marines on September 4, 1945, after the earlier surrender of Japan aboard the battleship U.S.S. *Missouri* in Tokyo Bay on September 2, 1945.

Wake Island

The defense of Wake Island was depicted in the movie "Wake Island," starring Brian Donlevy, Robert Preston, Barbara Britton, and William Bendix, earning four Academy Award nominations. The heroic defense of Wake Island by U.S. Marines, sailors, soldiers, and civilians became a potent rallying point for Americans in the dark days following Pearl Harbor. Released on August 11, 1942, four days after U.S. Marines landed at Guadalcanal, it was the first major war movie of World War II.

In addition to Elrod's Medal of Honor, eleven Navy Crosses and at least six Silver Stars were awarded for action on Wake Island. All but three Navy Crosses were awarded to U.S. Marines, one of them posthumously. Two Navy Crosses were awarded to members of the U.S. Navy, and another Navy Cross was awarded to a civilian physician, Dr. Lawton Shank, the only U.S. civilian in history to receive the that high honor.

Lawton Ely Shank was born on April 29, 1907, in Angola, Indiana, the oldest of three children born to Hudson Lyle and Lulu Ely Shank. He and his brother and sister were raised in Angola, and later San Diego, California. He attended the University of Indiana Medical School, graduating in 1936 with a BS in Medicine. That same year he married Ruby Vlair

Ricker, a surgical nurse he'd met while working in a local hospital. Their only son, Ely, was born in 1937. Shank was also an inactivated member of the U.S. Army Reserve.

It was during the Depression that Shank went to work for Pan American Airways in the Pacific. Ruby remained in Indiana when Shank sailed for Honolulu aboard the S.S. *Lurline* in July 1940, and then flew to Canton, China, via a Pan American Clipper. Canton was a terminus for the Pan American Clipper Service, and Shank served there until early 1941, when he was assigned to Pan American's Wake Island station.

Wake Island was a remote, layover station in the mid-Pacific for the China and Philippine Clippers and boasted a four-star hotel on Peale Island. As a contract physician, Shank was primarily responsible for treating Pan American employees, but also cared for Navy civilian contractors until their own physician, Dr. Thomas Barrett, arrived in March 1941. For reasons lost to history, Shank returned to the mainland in July.

The Pan American Wake Island Hotel on Peale Island, one of three islands that composed the Wake Island atoll.

As tensions with the Japanese increased, and war appeared inevitable, the U.S. Government began fortifying several islands in the Pacific as a first line of defense against Japanese aggression. A construction consortium, the Contractors Pacific Naval Air Bases (CPNAB) was employed to build or fortify the bases, including those on Wake Island.

On August 19, the first elements of the 1st Marine Defense Battalion arrived on Wake Island, with the reminder arriving October 15 under the command of Major P.S. Devereux, bringing the number of Marines to 450 officers and men. The Marine Detachment was supplemented on December 12 by Marine Corps Fighter Squadron VMF-211, consisting of twelve Grumman F-4F *Wildcat* fighters, twelve officers and forty-nine enlisted men, commanded by Marine aviator Major Paul A. Putnam. Also present on the island were sixty-eight U.S. Navy personnel, ten officers and fifty-nine enlisted, five members of the Army Air Corps, and about 1,221 civilian workers, mostly working for the Morrison-Knudsen Civil Engineering Company.

Dr. Lawton Shank

On November 28, naval aviator Commander Winfield S. Cunningham reported to Wake to assume overall command of U.S. forces on the island. Commander Cunningham would himself be decorated with the Navy Cross for *"extraordinary heroism and distinguished service in the line of his profession as Commanding Officer of Commanding Officer,*  *Naval Air Station, Wake Island, where he was responsible for directing defenses of that post during the Japanese siege from 7 through 22 December 1941, against impossible odds."*

Shank took employment as a contract physician with CPNAB and returned to Wake Island aboard a Clipper, arriving on October 12, 1941. He was joined by a Navy doctor, Lieutenant (Junior Grade) Gustave Mason Kahn in November, but Dr. Barrett departed Wake Island on December 4, 1941, leaving Shank as the only civilian doctor. Four days later, the United States was at war.

On the morning of December 8, 1941 (December 7 in Hawaii), Captain Henry Wilson, U.S. Signal Corps was on Wake Island to support the ferrying of B-17 Flying Fortresses to the Philippine Islands, when he monitored message from Hickam Field in Hawaii "ISLAND OF OAHU UNDER ATTACK. THIS IS NO DRILL. THIS IS THE REAL THING."

As Major Devereux assembled his officers and Major Putnam ordered two sections of two Wildcats into the air. As the Marines manned their battle stations, Springfield M1903 rifles were issued to Navy and Air Corps personnel as well as civilian contractor volunteers in order to mount a united defense.

The anticipated attack came at 11:58 a.m. when thirty-six twin-engine Mitsubishi Nell medium bombers appeared overhead. Their primary target appeared to have been the airfield, and bombs destroyed all eight Wildcats on the ground, as well as destroying vital spare parts, supplies and two fuel storage tanks, which started fires, and killing twenty-five. They next bombed the Pan American station, setting the hotel, fuel tanks and auxiliary buildings on fire, killing four Marines, several corpsmen and fifty-five civilians.

Beyond Belief: True Stories of Civilian Heroes

Once the bombs were released, the aircraft strafed the island, killing eighteen and wounding several others. Doctors Shank and Kahn were overwhelmed and ill-prepared for the number of casualties and worked on wounded and injured throughout the night.

The following day, December 9, 1941, twenty-seven *Nells* returned at 11:45 a.m. This time the defenders were prepared, and the remaining Wildcats downed one bomber and antiaircraft fire downed another and damaged twelve others, but the remainder got through to wreak havoc, with direct hits on the hospital and adjoining barracks, destroying warehouses, barracks, machine shops and the headquarters building.

Doctors Shank and Kahn, already exhausted, along with volunteers, entered the burning hospital to carry wounded patients to two ammunition bunkers serving as makeshift hospitals. As Shank's Navy Cross citation later documented: *"while in the camp hospital, during an intensive bombing and strafing attack in the course of which the hospital was completely destroyed and several persons therein killed or wounded, Doctor Shank remained at his post and supervised the evacuation of the patients and equipment. With absolute disregard for his own safety, and displaying great presence of mind, he was thus enabled to save those still living and to establish a new hospital in an empty magazine."*

Marine Gunner, later Captain, John Hamas, witnessed Shank's actions and would recommend Shank, an Army Reservist, for the Medal of Honor.

Daily attacks continued, and on December 11, the defenders successfully repelled an attempted landing by Japanese forces under the command of Rear Admiral Sadamichi Kajioka, consisting of three light cruisers (*Yubri, Tatsuta* and *Tenryu*), six destroyers (*Oite, Hayate, Mutsuki, Kisaragi, Mochizuki* and *Yayoi*) two transports (*Kongo Maru* and *Konyru Maru*) and 450 men of Special Naval Landing Force Five.

In the forty-five minute engagement, Marine guns sank the destroyer *Hayate*, and damaged all three cruisers and three destroyers (*Oite, Mochizuki* and *Yayoi*) and Patrol Boat 33. By 7:00 a.m. Admiral Kajioka ordered the fleet to retire behind a smoke screen.

The *Hayate* was the first Japanese surface ship sunk in the war. Pursuing *Wildcats* sank the destroyer *Kisaragi,* sending it to the bottom of the ocean with 500 Japanese soldiers. The Marine pilots also damaged the *Tenryu* and set the *Kongu Maru* on fire. Such victories aside, the battle damage to Wake Island was heavy and by nightfall Major Putnam commanded what was now only a two-plane air force.

The events of that day would prove to be the only time of the entire war that an amphibious landing party from either side was successfully repelled at the beaches.

The fate of Wake Island was sealed, however. Isolated and vastly outnumbered, the 400 Marines could not survive on guts and determination alone. For two more weeks they provided America with the first good news in the dark days that followed the attack at Pearl Harbor. When commanders at Hawaii radioed Wake Island to inquire what the Leathernecks might need, some accounts say they defiantly responded: *"Send us more Japs!"* Although Devereaux denied ever sending such a message, whether accurately recounted or not, those words seemed to represent the defiant attitude of Wake's defenders.

Over the next six days, Wake Island was attacked eight times. On December 23, Admiral Kajioka returned with two light aircraft carriers, two cruisers, five destroyers, three submarines, a mine layer, a floatplane tender and a 2,000-man landing force which began landing at 4:15 a.m. By 7:00 a.m., recognizing the futility of further resistance against overwhelming odds, the Americans surrendered.

Sources differ as to the number of casualties. The USMC Historical Division cites the following statistics:

- Of the 449 Marines, forty-six were killed, one died of wounds two were missing and thirty-two wounded.

- Of the sixty-eight Navy personnel, three were killed and five wounded

- None of the five Air Corps personnel were killed or wounded.

- Of the 1,146 civilians, seventy were killed and twelve wounded.

Beyond Belief: True Stories of Civilian Heroes

In total, of the 1,668 Americans on Wake Island, 122 were killed and 1,546 were taken as prisoners of war.

The prisoners were stripped to their underwear, bound, and marched to the edge of the airfield where they were seated in rows in front of machine guns. There, they remained with no food until Christmas day when they allowed to dress, bury their dead, and were fed. Informed that *"The Emperor has gracefully presented you with your lives."* An unidentified voice among the Americans called out *"Well, thank the son-of-a-bitch."*

The captured were marched to barracks at the north end of the island, where they were imprisoned until January 12, 1942, when all the military, with the exception of twenty-one severely wounded Marines and all but 360 civilians, were loaded aboard the Japanese liner *Nitta Maru* and transported to occupied China. Shank volunteered to remain behind with the wounded.

On May 11, 1943, the remaining military prisoners were taken aboard the *Asama Maru*, bound for China, and on September 30, all but ninety-eight U.S. civilian prisoners were evacuated to Japan aboard the *Tachibana Maru.* Shank again volunteered to remain behind to provide medical care to the remaining prisoners, many of them sick or wounded. Dentist James Cunha, and surgical nurse Henry Dreyer also remained behind to assist Shank.

As the fortunes of war shifted in the Pacific, Wake Island came under more and more frequent air attacks, beginning on February 24, 1942, by planes off the U.S.S. *Enterprise* (CV-6), and continuing with bombing raids and bombardment by naval gunfire. On October 6–7, a U.S. carrier task force launched a massive assault on the island.

Fearing that the island was going to be invaded, although post-war documents show the intent was to harass and isolate Wake Island with no intent to invade, Captain Shigimatsu Sakaibara, the Japanese commander, ordered the remaining ninety-seven prisoners executed. (One prisoner had earlier been beheaded for stealing food.)

On the evening of October 7, 1943, Lieutenant Commander Soichi Tachibana was ordered by Sakaibara to move the prisoners to an anti-tank ditch on the north end of Wake. Bound and blindfolded,

Dr. Lawton Shank

the prisoners were seated along the edge of the ditch, then mowed down by machine gun fire. They were buried in a mass grave. Sakaibara tried to cover-up the murders by radioing his superiors *"Riotous conduct among prisoners. Have executed them."*

On September 2, 1945, the Japanese officially surrendered aboard the U.S.S. *Missouri* in Tokyo Bay. Two days later on September 4, Brigadier General Lawson S. Anderson of the Fourth Marine Wing accepted the surrender of Wake Island from Admiral Shigematsu Sakaibara. Part of General Lawson's contingent, and the first man to go ashore on Wake Island since its fall four years earlier was Colonel Walter Bayler, the *"last man off Wake"* only days before its fall.

The American contingent quickly discovered that the Japanese had tried to cover the murders of the American POWs by disinterring the bodies and burying them in individual graves, marked with crosses, and claiming they had been killed in an air raid and subsequent uprising. An investigation was opened when every Japanese recounted the same story . . . word for word.

Lieutenant Commander Soichi Tachibaba, left, and Rear Admiral Shigematsu Sakaibara on trial before a military commission on Kwajalein.

Ultimately Sakaibara and Tachibana were tried and found guilty of war crimes by a military commission. They were sentenced to death, but Tachibana's sentence was later reduced to life in prison. Sakaibara was held on Guam where he was hung on June 18, 1947.

Beyond Belief: True Stories of Civilian Heroes

Dr. Shank's remains are in a mass grave along with 178 others from Wake Island in section G of the National Memorial Cemetery of the Pacific, Honolulu, Hawaii. The memorial is a large, flat, marble gravestone. At five by ten feet, it is the largest in the cemetery. On it are listed the names of the 178 men. Shank is also memorialized at the Circle Hill Cemetery in Angola, Indiana.

There was a lot of sentiment among the Marines who witnessed Dr. Shank's heroic actions on Wake Island, for him to be awarded the Medal of Honor. At first, since Shank was a first lieutenant in the Army Reserve, his Medal of Honor recommendation, drafted by Marines, was put through the U.S. Army's chain of command, but when the bureaucrats discovered he had *"performed under Navy jurisdiction and not under . . . MacArthur's command,"* the recommendation by Marine Captain John Hamas was returned with instructions to send it to the Navy Department.

Hamas and others made certain that the U.S. Navy was made aware of Shank's heroics and on November 6, 1946, and Hamas formally recommended Shank for the Medal of Honor. In addition to Hamas' recommendation, Marine Master Technical Sergeant Jesse L. Stewart, whose life was saved by Shank, wrote: *"due to his gallant actions above and beyond the call of duty, and to the circumstances surrounding his execution, he should be posthumously awarded the . . . [MoH]."*

Shank also received endorsements from Colonel James P. S. Devereux, senior Marine Officer, and Captain Winfield S. Cunningham, Senior Naval Officer at Wake Island. Although it appeared he met the requirements for a Medal of Honor, Rear Admiral Robert W. Hayler, head of the Navy Department for Awards

Dr. Lawton Shank

and Decorations, wrote, *"the Medal of Honor, as provided for by the act of August 7, 1942, is awarded only to any person who distinguishes himself 'while in the Naval service of the [U.S.]'. Since…Shank was a civilian, he is not eligible for this award."*

Although this statue was written nine months after Shank's demonstrated valor, this discrepancy was overlooked, despite the fact that Charles Lindbergh as a civilian had received the Medal of Honor a few years beforehand for his flight across the Atlantic.

The recommended Medal of Honor was thus disapproved by the Awards Board on March 6 1947, and confirmed by the Secretary of the Navy five days later.

Winfield Scott Cunningham did not forget the heroism exhibited by Dr. Shank and recommended him for the Navy Cross. The award was issued posthumously on May 6, 1947.

The Medal of Honor aside, Dr. Lawton Ely Shank remains the only American civilian to be awarded the Navy Cross.

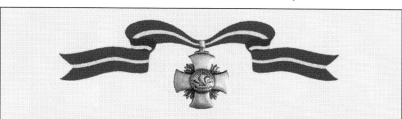

The President of the United States of America takes pride in presenting the Navy Cross (Posthumously) to Dr. Lawton E. Shank (U.S. Army Reserve), a United States Civilian, for extraordinary heroism in action against the enemy as Physician to American Contractors, Naval Air Station, Wake Island, while associated with the naval defenses on Wake Island on 9 December 1941. At about 1100,  while in the camp hospital, during an intensive bombing and strafing attack in the course of which the hospital was completely destroyed and several persons therein killed or wounded, Doctor Shank remained at his post and supervised the evacuation of the patients and equipment. With absolute disregard for his own safety, and displaying great presence of mind, he was thus enabled to save those

Beyond Belief: True Stories of Civilian Heroes

still living and to establish a new hospital in an empty magazine. Doctor Shank's display of outstanding courage and devotion to duty were in keeping with the highest traditions of the United States Naval Service.

Mr. René Malavergne

And A River Pilot Shall Lead Them:

By Dwight Jon Zimmerman

On August 7, 1942, U.S. Marines landed on the remote, and largely unknown to say nothing of at the time unpronounceable, Japanese-held Solomon island of Guadalcanal in the Southwest Pacific in Operation Watchtower. It was the first step in the campaign to defeat Japan in the Pacific.

Three months and one day later on November 8, and on the other side of the globe, a combined American and British invasion force landed on the coasts of Morocco and Algeria, then territories in French Northwest Africa, in Operation Torch, the first step in the American campaign to defeat Nazi Germany. Included in the invasion force was a

The U.S.S. *Dallas*, shown in this pre-World War II photograph, shows her superstructure and World War I-era four smokestacks which were removed for Operation Goalpost in order to reduce her profile and weight so she could better travel up the heavily defended, shallow Sebu River.
Naval History and Heritage Command

unit of Army Rangers aboard the converted destroyer *U.S.S.* Dallas.

127

Beyond Belief: True Stories of Civilian Heroes

Guiding the destroyer that would take those American troops to battle on distant shore was René Malaverge, a fifty-year-old French river pilot, who would become the first Frenchman, and civilian, to be decorated for heroism by the American military in World War II.

Operation Torch was a combined American and British amphibious assault at five locations, three in Morocco and two in Algeria, designed to oust the Axis from North Africa. The mission of the Army Rangers aboard the *Dallas* was to capture the modern airfield north of Port Lyautey in French Morocco, codenamed Operation Goalpost. Its seizure would provide a land base for P-40 Tomahawk fighters waiting on a nearby escort carrier that would provide air support for Western Task Force troops landing in Morocco. To reach the airfield the *Dallas* would have to run a twelve-mile gauntlet up the treacherous Sebu River. That Malavergne was on the warship's bridge and not in a Gestapo jail, or dead, was a testament to his extraordinary survival skills.

Malavergne was born on December 3, 1892, near Grenoble in the French Alps. He served in the French navy during World War I. Shortly after the war's end, he moved to the resort beach town of Mehdia, Morocco, where in 1920, he became Chief Pilot for the Société des Ports Marocain. That meant he was responsible for guiding ships in and out of the twelve-mile fishhook-shaped channel connecting the mouth of the Sebu River (Oued Sebu) to the ports of Mehdia and Lyautey. Sailors hated the Sebu River. It contained a nightmarish combination of high surf at the jetties, shallow depth, unpredictable currents, seasonal tidal variations, and shifting

128

sandbars. It took a skilled pilot to navigate such treacherous waters and Malavergne proved himself to be one of the best.

When war broke out in 1939, Malavergne was Chief Pilot of the Port of Mehdia/Port Lyautey. He rushed to volunteer for the French army, but he was turned away for, at age forty-seven, being too old. When Germany defeated France in 1940, it divided the country into occupied and unoccupied zones. A pro-German government was installed in the unoccupied section that became known as the Vichy government after the city it chose as its capital. The strongly patriotic Malavergne felt betrayed. When countryman Charles de Gaulle, a minor official in the previous government, escaped and made his appeal from London for Frenchmen to rally to his Free French banner to continue the fight against the Germans, he eagerly joined, becoming a Gaullist member of the guerilla Resistance.

A number of fellow Frenchmen in the North African territory shared his feelings and an active Resistance cell in Mehdia and Port Lyautey was organized that included the port captain, the chief customs inspector, and several other government officials. Malavergne's home in Mehdia, located on a riverbank near a heavily armed fortress not far from the mouth of the Sebu and later dubbed "the Kasbah" by the Americans, became a safe house and final stop for Allied aviators and refugees rescued by the Resistance. His job was to ferry them in his rowboat down the river and to a rendezvous location in the Atlantic where a blacked-out ship would pick up his charges and take them to Gibraltar.

But not long after they began their rescue work the cell was betrayed by an informant. On December 14, 1940, Malavergne and a number of others were captured. They were taken first to Rabat, the territorial capital, for interrogation, then to Casablanca, where they were further interrogated. In February 1941 the group was transported to Ceyrat in Vichy administered central France where Malavergne learned he was to be put on trial by court martial.

On June 4, 1941, Malavergne found himself before a military tribunal. He was charged with giving *"information of a military*

Beyond Belief: True Stories of Civilian Heroes

nature to a foreign power, to wit, Great Britain or its agents, with the intent of helping that power against France" and *"the clandestine embarkation of individuals joining the dissident elements"* (the Resistance). Had he been found guilty he very likely would have been executed, at the very least, jailed. Instead, he was acquitted of all charges.

Using himself as chief witness for the defense, he testified that the accusations against him, of repeatedly rowing a small craft down the Sebu, into the Atlantic and back—all at night—were impossible. He chaptered and versed the treacherous conditions of the river based on his years of experience as a pilot on the Sebu, even though he had done exactly what he said was impossible. His lie worked. The judges agreed and he was acquitted of all charges. But being set free was one thing. Being absolved of suspicion was quite another.

To return to Morocco he needed two visas from the Vichy government, one to leave France and one to enter Morocco. For months Vichy bureaucrats thwarted his attempts by approving the first and then allowing that visa to expire before "granting" the second, forcing him to start the process all over again.

Malavergne finally reached Morocco on December 14, 1941, a year to the day after his arrest. Denied his old job as chief pilot and denied permission to live with his common law wife in Port Lyautey, he found himself confined to Casablanca. There he accepted a job offer by the director of a large fishing business. Meanwhile the Office of Strategic Services (OSS), the forerunner of the CIA, had established intelligence operations in Morocco, covertly running them out of the American embassy. Upon learning of Malavergne's arrival in Casablanca and of his special knowledge and skills, contact was made and Malavergne was recruited. Using his day job as cover, OSS Captain Frank Holcomb later commented that Malavergne proved *"very useful in smuggling arms and communications equipment into Morocco for the OSS."*

In April 1942 he was instructed to begin gathering intelligence on water depth in ports, sandbar locations, defense

130

fortifications, and beach conditions, vital information needed for Operation Torch, then in the planning stages. In mid-September Malavergne was asked if he was willing to leave Morocco for an unspecified period of time and go to an undisclosed location, the reason for which would be explained upon his arrival. He agreed. He quit his job in Casablanca, telling his boss that he was "disgusted with sardines" and that he was going to join a colony in Tarodount, a remote town in southeast Morocco. He informed his common law wife, who regularly visited him in Casablanca because he could not afford an apartment there for them both, that he would not be seeing her for a long time.

On September 26 the OSS smuggled Malavergne in the back of a car to Tangier and then, by boat to Gibraltar. On October 2 an RAF bomber flew him to London. There he found himself briefly caught in the middle of a high command crossfire. Not everyone in the senior chain of command had been briefed of his extraction mission. The most important person left out of the loop happened to be the commander in chief of Operation *Torch* itself, Lieutenant General Dwight Eisenhower. Furious, he was worried that if Vichy French authorities got wind of Malavergne's disappearance it would alert them to landings on the Morocco coast scheduled to happen in little over a month.

But with no way to undo things without truly arousing suspicion, Malavergne was given the cover name of Victor Prechak and, on October 17, was flown to the United States. Five days later he was in Norfolk, Virginia. There he was briefed about his role as pilot of the *U.S.S. Dallas* in Operation Goalpost.

Of all the amphibious landings in Operation Torch, at Algiers, Oran, Mehdia/Port Lyauteym, Fedala, and Casablanca, the one at Mehdia/Port Lyautey, thought to be the easiest, proved to be one of the hardest fought. Instead of responding positively to American appeals, both broadcast from ships and delivered by American embassy and military personnel, to Vichy military commanders that they welcome American troops as comrades (in retrospect a naïve, even quixotic, effort), the commanders instead ordered their troops to fight. And fight they did.

American troops landing on the beaches north and south of the mouth of the Sebu Reiver on November 8 encountered such stiff resistance that Operation Goalpost, scheduled for that same day, had to be postponed.

On the night of November 9 a boatload of sailors led by Navy lieutenant Mark K. Starkweather entered the mouth of the Sebu and traveled up the channel to the boom that served as a ship barrier to sever it, thus allowing the *Dallas* free passage. There, with the guns of the Kasbah fortress ominously looming over them, the sailors managed to cut it. But during the effort to confirm their work and that no other obstacles existed to prevent passage, they were discovered. With a hail of gunfire raining down on them, Lieutenant Starkweather shouted, *"Let's get the hell out of here!"* Upon their return to the fleet Starkweather reported, *"Mission accomplished."*

Finally, at 5:30 a.m. on November 10, as dawn was breaking, *Dallas* skipper Lieutenant Commander Robert J. Brodie ordered Malavergne to take the *Dallas* up the Sebu, a river the pilot had not navigated in almost two years. As the destroyer began to enter the river, a violent storm broke out creating thirty-foot swells.

In his after-action report, Brodie wrote, *"As the seas were breaking astern the ship yawed violently, heading alternately for the south jetty and the patch of shoal water between the jetties. channel was narrow and immediately adjacent to the south jetty. [Malavergne] handled the ship masterfully, however, and kept to the channel. Shortly after entering between the jetties a shell splash was noted dead ahead of the ship and about thirty yards from us. It was estimated to be about 37-millimeter. Another was heard to pass by close aboard to starboard but the splash was not observed . . . . There was much small arms fire heard from the direction of*

Mr. René Malavergne

the Kasbah, both rifle and machine gun, and the occasional report of a larger caliber gun was also heard."

Malavergne successfully fought to keep the *Dallas* on course, aided by a sailor using an improvised hand lead made from a steel shackle who shouted out soundings. Suddenly the destroyer came to a halt, having run aground on a submerged sandbar. With French gunfire from the banks raking the *Dallas'* superstructure and cannons from the Kasbah bracketing the ship, Brodie ordered flank speed. Though the engine-

room dials showed twenty-five knots, the ship was barely crawling along at five knots in her struggle to break free of the sandbar. Finally the destroyer cleared the obstacle and shot forward. When the *Dallas* reached the boom Brodie and Malavergne discovered it had only been partially severed. It was still attached to three anchored buoys located at both banks and in the middle of the river. Brodie ordered full speed again and the *Dallas* rammed the section of the boom closest to where it had been severed and successfully cleared it.

This photograph shows the *Dallas*, still aground, located on the Sebu River near the Port Lyautey airfield. Note the absence of her smokestacks. Naval History and Heritage Command

Minutes later two scuttled steamers were seen, a third barrier attempt to block passage. But Malavergne cleanly threaded the passage between the two ships and rounded the river's oxbow bend. Now within sight of the airfield, the destroyer hit another submerged sandbar and this time ground to a halt. Though stranded, the ship was close enough for the Rangers to disembark and advance toward their objective. Twenty minutes later the airfield was in American hands. By 10:00 a.m., it was receiving P-40 fighters launched from the escort carrier *Chenango*.

For his role on the *Dallas*, on March 17, 1943, Major General Lucian Truscott, who commanded the force in Operation Goalpost, presented René Malavergne the Silver Star. Eight months later Malavergne and Truscott met again. On June 4, 1943, in an impressive awards ceremony at the American military cemetery erected near the Mehdia Kasbah Truscott pinned on Malavergne's chest the Navy Cross. René Malavergne was the first Frenchman, and civilian, to be decorated for valor by the United States military.

The President of the United States takes pleasure in presenting the Navy Cross to Monsieur Rene Malavergne, a French Civilian, for service as set forth in the following:

For extraordinary heroism as pilot of the U.S.S. DALLAS during the assault upon and occupation of the Port Lyautey Airfield in French Morocco on November 10, 1942. Taking the helm of the DALLAS and steering her across a dangerous bar while heavy seas were breaking, Monsieur Malavergne, with utter disregard for the possibility of death or capture, successfully piloted the vessel through a narrow entrance between the jetties of Oued Sebou and up that river to a point off the Port Lyautey Airfield. Although the channel was restricted at many points by wreckage of scuttled merchant ships and the entire passage was hampered by heavy fire from artillery, machine guns and snipers, he carried out his task with cool courage and competent skill, thereby enabling the DALLAS to accomplish a hazardous and extremely important mission. By his gallant conduct on this occasion, Monsieur Malavergne distinguished himself as a brave and patriotic Frenchman, loyally serving his country in the cause of right..

Mr. René Malavergne

After his service on the *Dallas*, Malavergne continued to work for the Americans, serving as a liaison with the provisional French government, and performing other duties. After the war he purchased a small bistro in Port Lyautey which he operated until his death on July 9, 1953, aged fifty-one.

Lt. General Mark Clark and an unidentified U.S. Navy captain lay a wreath during a ceremony at the temporary military cemetery near the Kasbah at Port Lyautey. At the end of the campaign in North Africa a permanent military cemetery was established at Tunis, Tunisia, where all the fallen in the North Africa campaign were buried. National Archives

The *Dallas* along with the destroyers *Bernadou* and *Cole* were awarded the Presidential Unit Citation for their roles in Operation Torch. Here Admiral Royal Ingersoll, Commander in Chief, Atlantic Fleet, presides over the award ceremony. Naval History and Heritage Command

The Over the Hill Gang

The Calcutta Light Horse and Operation Creek

BY DWIGHT JON ZIMMERMAN

"To drink to deeds of daring—and the men who'll have to do 'em."
—Alastair "Red Mac" MacFarlane, Calcutta Light Horse

The Calcutta Light Horse, a 186-year-old British auxiliary regiment, was in 1943 more a social club in India than a proud, active-duty territorial regiment. The unit's last military action had taken place in the Boer War almost fifty years earlier. Now its members, veterans who had separately seen service in World War I and though many were still fit, were resigned to watching from the sidelines as a new war was waged around them. Then Britain's Special Operations Executive (SOE), India, responsible for conducting unconventional warfare operations in the theater, gave these old warhorses an opportunity for some covert derring-do that seemed more in keeping with Hollywood.

On the night of March 9–10, 1943, volunteers from Calcutta Light Horse, assisted by some volunteers from Calcutta Scottish, another auxiliary regiment, conducted Operation Creek—arguably

Beyond Belief: True Stories of Civilian Heroes

the most improbable SOE mission of World War II. Their mission: capture or sink the German merchantman *Ehrenfels*.

The *Ehrenfels* was one of four Axis merchantmen (three German, one Italian) in the region when war broke out in 1939. All immediately sought refuge in the nearest neutral port, in this case Mormugao, Goa. Located on India's western coast about 300 miles south of Bombay (today, Mumbai), Goa was at the time a Portuguese territory.

British authorities were aware of the ships' presence in Goa, but as these were merchantmen, not warships, they were not seen as a threat. That perception began to change when forty-six Allied merchantmen were sunk by U-boats in the Indian Ocean over a six-week period in the fall of 1942. The toll continued to climb. Twelve ships were sunk in the first week of March. At this rate, the U-boats would be able to completely blockade India. Eventually SOE, India determined that the U-boats were getting detailed intelligence about merchant ship schedules, routes, even cargo, through a network of pro-Axis Indian agents providing information to the *Ehrenfels* which, in violation of neutrality laws, was passing the information to the region's U-boats via a secret radio transmitter.

Because Goa was neutral, an outright military operation was a non-starter. But a group of British civilians, using the cover story of a sea-going vacation-cum-drunken-dare boarding party gone awry (together with some well-placed bribes to Portuguese territorial government officials), could get away with an attack on the *Ehrenfels*.

Maybe.

That such a mad scheme was not only considered, but also approved, is a testament as to how desperate the maritime situation had become. Lieutenant Colonel Lewis Pugh was SOE, India's Director of Country Sections, part of Force 136 that conducted covert missions. In the latter half of February he contacted his friend Bill Grice, the colonel of the **Calcutta Light Horse**, and after swearing him to secrecy laid out the basic facts.

Pugh needed fifteen to twenty men. Their target was the *Ehrenfels* which they would either capture or sink. The mission would last about two weeks. The volunteers would be given some crash commando training. Because it was a top-secret mission, they'd get no credit, no pay, nor pensions should anything go wrong, and no medals. Grice wryly observed, *"How attractive you make the conditions sound, Lewis."* But Grice agreed to call a special meeting to ask for volunteers.

The following evening Grice addressed an assemblage of about thirty members, stating that he needed eighteen volunteers for a secret mission against the Germans. *"I can tell you nothing about it except that the operation should take about a fortnight and will involve a short sea voyage. There it is, gentlemen. I leave it to you. Is anyone willing to volunteer?"* To a man, everyone raised his hand.

The culling commenced. Those clearly too old or in poor health were dismissed. Among those accepted was the unit's corporal, Bill Manners, who asked, *"What about me? You know I've only got one eye."* He had lost an eye in a school accident.

"It was good enough for Nelson," replied Grice, referring to Admiral Horatio Nelson, the hero of Trafalgar. *"Why shouldn't it be all right for you?"* Insufficient men remained after the culling, and four members from Calcutta Scottish, another auxiliary, completed the roster.

Commando training was basic and brief. In addition the men studied blueprints of the *Ehrenfels* obtained by SOE and practiced boarding procedures. When the time came, to avoid arousing suspicion, they traveled separately in small groups by train to Cochin (Kochi) on the southwest tip of India where they rendezvoused with the ship that would take them to Goa.

The raiders expected to find in the harbor a destroyer, or a landing craft. At worst a trawler. Instead, to their astonishment, they found themselves boarding what was indisputably the most unlikely warship ever used in World War II.

Instead of an expected warship or trawler, Calcutta Light Horse Colonel Bill Grice and Operation Creek leader Lieutenant Colonel Lewis Pugh of SOE, India showed them the *Phoebe*, a hopper barge used to dredge rivers, the only available vessel, captained by Commander Bernard Davis of the Royal Navy.

Meanwhile, Light Horse member Jock Cartwright was in Mormugao using funds provided by SOE to secretly arrange the diversion. To reduce the number of crewmembers aboard *Ehrenfels* on the night of the attack, a ruse was devised involving a lavish festival and free prostitutes. Officially, the festival was for all the officers and sailors of ships in the harbor. Cartwright bribed key government officials and made the appropriate financial arrangements with the brothel owners. On the night of March 9, 1943, with the festival in full swing and the brothels bustling with sailors, everything was ready for the boarders.

At about 2:30 a.m. March 10, the *Phoebe's* hull ground against that of the *Ehrenfels*. Immediately the men of Operation Creek, led by Pugh, threw their grappling irons, clambered up makeshift boarding ladders, and began to fan out, Sten guns and explosive charges at the ready, to accomplish their assigned tasks.

Earlier the captains of the Axis ships had worked out individual defensive measures in the event of such an assault. An attacked ship would also blast a siren warning and upon hearing it the others would scuttle their ships to avoid capture.

Surprise was on the attackers' side, and response by the skeleton crew on the *Ehrenfels* was slow and uncoordinated, in part because her captain was among the first killed. Though the radio codebooks were destroyed, Pugh captured the transmitter. Twenty minutes into the raid, Davis on the *Phoebe* noticed the *Ehrenfels* beginning to list. Some members of the *Ehrenfels'* crew had opened sea valves, letting in tons of seawater. Immediately Davis ordered the lines to the *Ehrenfels* cast off, and pulled three times on the ship's horn, the signal for the attackers to return to the Phoebe.

Astonishingly, all the attackers returned to the *Phoebe* safely, with some suffering only minor injuries. Then they heard a series of explosions on the other Axis ships. Fearing an attack, the other captains pre-emptively scuttled their ships.

As Davis guided *Phoebe* out of the harbor before Portuguese authorities could intercept her, Pugh transmitted to headquarters the code word "Longshanks"—all Axis ships sunk. The "drunken-dare boarding party" action was a resounding success.

U-boat attacks plummeted. For the rest of March, U-boats sank only one ship. In April, only three merchantmen went down.

Meanwhile the volunteers of Light Horse and Scottish returned to their civilian careers. One such volunteer was Jack Breene, a partner in an insurance firm. As he settled in behind his desk to tackle business that had accumulated in his absence his partner entered, a worried look on his face. The partner handed Breene a newspaper, pointing to an article about the sinking of the Axis ships in Goa. Acting innocent, Breene looked at his partner, asking what that had to do with anything. His partner replied, *"Hell of a lot. Didn't you know I'd insured the damned things? They're worth over £4,500,000. There'll be a claim as long as your arm."* Breene laughed.

In 1947, with India achieving independence, Calcutta Light Horse and Calcutta Scottish stood down for the last time. Because theirs was a secret mission, the civilian volunteers of Operation Creek never received any honors, medals, or government message of gratitude. The members of Calcutta Light Horse designed their own memento for the mission—a sea horse, which subsequently appeared in the masthead of the organization's magazine and was fashioned into brooches for their wives.

The mission remained classified for decades. Then in 1978 a book about Operation Creek, Boarding Party by James

The cover of Boarding Party by James Leasor, the account of *Operation Creek*.

Beyond Belief: True Stories of Civilian Heroes

Lessor, was published. Two years later, "The Sea Wolves," a movie based on Lessor's book starring Gregory Peck, David Niven, Roger Moore, and Trevor Howard, was released. Though belated, and if not officially at least publicly, the volunteers of Calcutta Light Horse and Calcutta Scottish finally received their due.

The cast of the movie "The Sea Wolves" standing in front of the former headquarters of the Calcutta Light Horse: Gregory Peck, who played Lieutenant Colonel Lewis Pugh, Roger Moore who played Gavin Stewart, Trevor Howard who played Jack Cartwright, and David Niven who played Colonel W.H. Grice.

The Man Who Never Was

The Civilian Corpse Who Fooled the Nazis

BY DWIGHT JON ZIMMERMAN

On May 2, 1943, at precisely 12:30 p.m., in the oppressive mid-day heat of Andalusian Spain, the coffin containing the body of Major William Martin, Royal Marines, was lowered into its grave in the "English cemetery" section of the Nuestra Señora de la Soledad cemetery in Huelva, a fishing village about fifty miles northwest of Gibraltar. The funeral service and graveside ceremony had been conducted with full military honors, attended by military brass, government officials, and civilians from Britain and Spain. Some French attended as well. And, if one looked carefully, one would have spotted in the background a lone German. But, of all the mourners who began filing away to their cars, offices, homes, or shops after the graveside ceremony, only one man, the British consul Francis Hazelden, knew that the proceedings were all part of an elaborate sham.

The body in the grave that the gravediggers were now filling with dirt was not that of an English officer in the Royal Marines, had never been in the military for that matter, and, though his body had washed onto the nearby

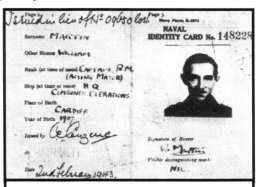

The forged Royal Navy identity card for Major William Martin contains the photograph of MI5 case officer Ronnie Reed, described as so closely resembling Glynwr Michael that he could have been mistaken for being his twin brother. Wikipedia

143

beach and was found by a local sardine fisherman, had not died in a plane crash in the Atlantic Ocean. In reality, the body inside that coffin buried in a Catholic cemetery was that of a Welsh Baptist, a derelict and probable suicide, who had died by eating rat poison, alone and unmourned, two months earlier in a London hospital.

He had been transported to Spain by submarine, and his real name would remain unknown for fifty-four years. In the meantime, his *nom de guerre* "Major William Martin" would become famous as the "Man Who Never Was," the pivotal player in Operation Mincemeat, the greatest deception operation conducted by British intelligence in World War II.

His real name was Glyndwr Michael. He was born on January 4, 1909, to Thomas Michael and Sara Ann Chadwick (they never married) in Aberbargoed, Wales. Aberbargoed was a grim, dirty village in the best of times and in the years leading up to World War I, whatever shred of prosperity this bleak coal town had possessed, vanished along with the coal from its mines.

At some point before he met Sarah, Thomas, a coal miner, contracted syphilis which he passed on to her. It's possible that Glyndwer suffered from congenital syphilis, which can cause damage to the bones, eyes, and brain. After the mines shut down, Thomas struggled from one job to another, increasingly seeking escape in drink. His health began to decline in 1919 and by 1924 it had reached a point where he could no longer work, and the family was reduced to surviving on government charity which insufficiently covered their living costs. In 1925 Thomas died of bronchial pneumonia. Glyn was sixteen years old. The widow Sarah and her three children from Tom (another son and a daughter, as well as Glyn the eldest) continued to barely survive on the government dole and whatever odd job Glyn was able to find.

When war broke out in 1939, the thirty-year-old Glyn was declared unfit for military service. Though the reason is not known, informed speculation suggests the most probable reason was for mental, not physical, disability. Sarah died in 1940 and was buried beside Thomas. After signing her death certificate, the same service he performed for his father, Glyn disappeared, slipping through the cracks of a society distracted by its need to focus on its own survival against the Nazi juggernaut.

At some point Glyndwr Michael went to London, perhaps lured by the opportunity to find work in the big city. Instead, he found death. On January 26, 1943, he was discovered in an abandoned warehouse in central London and taken to the nearby hospital of St. Pancras, suffering from acute chemical poisoning. Michael had ingested rat poison. While the probability that the act was deliberate cannot be dismissed—his father at one point had attempted suicide with a knife—it's also possible it was an accident. Regardless, on January 28, 1943, Glyndwr Michael died. Alone, unloved, unlamented—but, not unnoticed.

It was now that national wartime need intersected with individual tragedy to unite in an operation that would help save the former and make worthwhile in death the otherwise worthless life of the latter.

At **Symbol**, the January 1943 strategic conference in Casablanca between President Franklin Roosevelt and Prime Minister Winston Churchill, an overriding question was: After the Allies completed its victory against the Axis in North Africa, where to strike next? After much heated debate, the decision was made to conduct the next amphibious landing in the Mediterranean which meant, as Churchill cogently observed, *"Everyone but a bloody fool would know it was Sicily."*

So, the challenge then became how to convince the Germans that Operation Husky, the next Allied assault in the Mediterranean, was going to be anywhere else *but* Sicily? That's where the British Security Service, usually referred to as MI5, and its members of the XX System ("Twenty System" more famously referred to as the "Double Cross System") team responsible for counterespionage and deception against the Axis stepped in. It created a deceptive operation using the body of a dead military courier carrying false documents. But not only would the documents be false, so too would be the identity of the body.

Variations of this Trojan Horse-style deception were used by British officers in World War I and earlier in World War II and were known by MI5. But, as it turned out, in this particular case the genesis for creating a false identity for a corpse to trick the Axis came from a plot device in a detective novel published in 1937. In the otherwise forgettable *The Milliner's Hat Mystery*, its protagonist, Inspector Richardson, discovers that all the documents found on a dead body discovered in a barn are forged. The rest of the story is about how the inspector unravels the mystery and discovers the real identity of the corpse.

The plot device, like the poor-selling potboiler novel that utilized it, might otherwise have been forgotten but for the fact that one of its few readers was Ian Fleming, the future author of the James Bond spy adventures. In September 1939, Fleming was a lieutenant commander, the personal assistant to Rear Admiral John Godfrey, the chief of British naval intelligence, and tasked with writing what came to be known as the Trout Memo, to be disseminated to all intelligence chiefs, which contained a list of fantastical ideas whose purpose was to deceive the Axis.

Fleming remembered the plot device and number 28 on the list was the idea of a false flag identity of a corpse, mission for which TBD. For four years the idea lay dormant. Then, in 1943, with the need to deceive the Axis about the real location of Operation Husky, in the hands of MI5's Ewan Montague and Charles Christian Cholmondeley (pronounced "Chumly") the fictional plot device cum espionage high concept came to fruition and became the pivotal element in the deception plot indelicately named Operation Mincemeat.

Obviously, for the deception to work Operation Mincemeat needed a male body of military age. Though the war was producing a surfeit of bodies in England and London in particular, Operation Mincemeat's requirements drastically limited the inventory. Out were bombing victims as were victims of suicide by rope, gas, or easily detectable chemical means. Furthermore, not only did the body have to be that of a male of military age but also with next of kin who would have no objection to strangers taking the remains of their deceased loved one, whisking it away to some unknown location for purposes equally unknown.

Given the delicate nature of the request, discretion regarding inquiries for the obtaining of said corpse was paramount. Fortunately

The Man Who Never Was

Montague knew exactly the man who could help, the coroner of St. Pancras hospital, a man with a name that might have come out of a Charles Dickens novel: Bentley Purchase. A meeting was arranged, and Purchase agreed to contact Montague when a body fitting the requirements arrived at the hospital's mortuary. On January 28, 1943, Ewan Montague received a phone call from Purchase informing him that a candidate had arrived and would be "kept in suitable cold storage" until needed. After Montague confirmed that Glyndwr Michael's body and background fit the bill (Michael had had no contact with his siblings), Operation Mincemeat was activated.

To pull off the deception, the devil was definitely in the details. Not in the least of which was the fact that the central player in the hoax was already dead. As part of the forgery Montague and Cholmondeley needed a photograph of the subject's face for the military identity card. Unfortunately, the photo session to get one proved to be a disaster. No matter what they did in setting up the shot, the result was always the same. Glyn looked exactly like what he was: a dead man.

The Old Admiralty building where the plans for Operation Mincemeat originated.
Wikipedia

Felicitously, they found in MI5 case officer Ronnie Reed someone who so resembled Glyndwr Michael that it was observed he *"might have been the twin brother."* To round out "Martin's" history, Michael was dressed in a Royal Marine officer's uniform (a minor adventure in obtaining that), they created forged letters, both official (regarding the amphibious assault location) and personal (from a scolding father and love letters), as well as a photograph of a fiancée (in reality a female member of the XX team), pocket change, tickets to a London theater—no detail was too trivial.

In the end they created a well-rounded identity of Major William Martin that would have done any self-respecting mystery writer proud. And, to add to the deception, they made him a Catholic

Beyond Belief: True Stories of Civilian Heroes

and have him be found on the shore of Spain, a Catholic country, as Catholic nations had an aversion to conducting detailed autopsies—an important consideration because, despite all attempts to preserve his body, there was no getting around the fact that a thorough autopsy would reveal that "Major William Martin" had not recently died in a plane crash off the coast of Spain, but rather some time much earlier, and elsewhere.

Having completed the story of Major Martin—oh, and circumventing the legal nicety of deceptively accounting for the dead body, a process, though fascinating, is a digression, and your gentle author is already wrestling with enough of them—next came the logistical rub of getting the body from "Point A" (the hospital morgue) to "Point B" (a beach in Spain).

That involved placing the "major" in a coffin-like tube packed with dry ice, a high-speed trip by cargo van from London to a Royal Navy base in Scotland, and a submarine. The submarine in question, HMS *Seraph*, had a history of what is now known as Special Operations missions. Its captain, Lieutenant Norman "Bill" Jewell, was the epitome of a dashing and daring

The officers of the HMS *Seraph* stand on the deck of the submarine after the successful conclusion of Operation Mincemeat.

Wikipedia

British naval officer, who become a highly decorated officer in the war and who would retire in 1963 with the rank of captain.

After an uneventful voyage, the submarine arrived off the coast of Huelva on the morning of April 29, 1943. Just before dawn Jewell gave the order to dive. For the next few hours he conducted reconnaissance, viewing the beach and occasional fishing vessel through the submarine's periscope. At 1:00 a.m. on April 30, Jewell ordered the submarine toward shore, halting its progress when they were about a mile away. After waiting for the outgoing fishing fleet to

clear the area, the *Seraph* surfaced, the cannister brought out through the torpedo hatch and onto the deck, and two officers began unscrewing the bolts.

At 4:15 a.m. Major Martin was lifted out of the cannister. Jewell inspected the body. In his after-action report, he noted that there was "some little stink" to the body that had begun to decompose. Shortly before leaving Scotland, Jewell had been given an envelope containing the forged official documents (the personal letters and items were tucked into the uniform's pockets). He was instructed to put them in Major Martin's briefcase shortly before releasing him. This he now did.

He then inflated Major Martin's Mae West inflatable life vest, slipped the keys and military identity card into the corpse's pockets and, at 4:30 a.m. under the glow of the false dawn, gave an impromptu funeral service reciting what he could remember of Psalm 39: *"I will keep my mouth as if it were with a bridle: while the ungodly is in my sight. Held my tongue, and spake nothing: I kept silence, yea, even from good words; but it was pain and grief to me."*

Jewell and the other two officers on the deck then gently slipped the body into the sea. The *Seraph* turned around and headed toward Gibraltar at full speed, the wash of its screws helping push the bobbing corpse to shore. At 7:15 a.m., Jewell sent a wireless message to London: *"Mincemeat Completed."*

Now began the most nerve-wracking part of the operation: the waiting.

Later that afternoon Spanish authorities notified the British consulate that the body of a British officer had washed ashore and that it would arrive at Huelva dock the following morning.

Like Switzerland, neutral Spain during World War II contained a hotbed of spies from both sides. So long as things didn't get messy, Spanish authorities were content to turn a blind eye to the covert (and sometimes not so covert) goings on between the combatants' intelligence communities. Cooperation was further abetted by the fact that both sides freely, and generously, bribed everyone from high-ranking government officials and military

Beyond Belief: True Stories of Civilian Heroes

officers down to fishing boat captains, the latter who could provide valuable real-time information of warship traffic.

With Major Martin and his all-important briefcase in a Spanish morgue, the last thing that the British wanted was for the Spanish authorities to hand over the body of Major Martin and his briefcase untouched before the Germans had a chance to view its contents. To their horror, they discovered that such a scenario threatened to occur because the person responsible for Major Martin's body was an honest Spanish bureaucrat. Fortunately, the head of Germany's Abwehr intelligence agency in Spain was so anxious to copy the contents of Major Martin's briefcase that he finagled a way to obtain the briefcase long enough to do so.

Once copies were made, everything was returned in such a way as to give the impression that nothing had been disturbed. But the British had inserted clever traps that, after they received the body, briefcase, and personal effects, revealed that the Germans had succeeded in reading the forged documents. Full details of this, and other aspects of the caper are found in Ben Macintyre's excellent account, *Operation Mincemeat*.

The false intelligence rapidly went up the German intelligence ladder from Madrid to Berlin, eventually landing on the desk of Adolf Hitler himself. Long story short, Hitler bought the deception that the Allies were planning to invade Greece (in order to aid Russia) and Sardinia (in order to threaten Rome), and that proposed attacks on Sicily were a diversion. By deciphering German intelligence messages intercepted through ULTRA, those involved in Operation Mincemeat were satisfied that the Germans had swallowed Major Martin's bait, "hook, line, and sinker."

The operation's success continued even after Allied troops landed in Sicily on July 9, 1943. The night before the assault, the German high command in Berlin issued a *"Most Immediate"* intelligence analysis to commanders in the Mediterranean predicting a major Allied invasion of Greece, with joint attacks on Sardinia and Sicily. Field Marshal Erwin Rommel, the "Desert Fox" of North Africa fame, was dispatched to Greece to take command of forces there and repel an invasion that never came. And, hours after the Husky landings themselves, twenty-one ground-attack aircraft based in Sicily were dispatched to Sardinia, the reasoning being that the Sicily landings were a diversion.

The cruiser U.S.S. *Boise* (CL-47) firing on enemy tanks approaching the American troop landing beaches at Gela, Sicily, during Operation Husky. Note manned .50 caliber machine guns on several of the Army trucks on the LST's deck, a precaution against German air attack. Thanks to Operation Mincemeat, German high command had withdrawn most of the German troops stationed in Sicily. Naval History and Heritage Command.

As it must, life, and the war, moved on but, the story of the body laid to rest in grave number 1886 in Nuestra Señora de la Soledad cemetery did not end on that hot day in May 1943. Shortly after Major Martin was buried, the British government paid for a full-body gravestone to be placed over the grave. This was done for reasons less out of respect than for security—to reduce the likelihood that the Germans would exhume the body in order to conduct a complete autopsy. For decades it bore the following inscription:

William Martin
Born 29th March 1907
Died 24th April 1943
Beloved son of John
Glyndwyr Martin and the late Antonia Martin
of Cardiff, Wales

Dulce et Decorum est pro Patria Mort

Beyond Belief: True Stories of Civilian Heroes

In 1977, responsibility for the grave was taken over by the Commonwealth War Graves Commission and, in an ironic touch, maintained, on behalf of Britain, by the German consulate in Huelva. Every year, in April, an Englishwoman from the town lays flowers on the gravestone.

Then, in 1997, fifty-four years after Operation Mincemeat, the British government had a postscript carved on the base of the marble slab:

Glynwr Michael
served as
Major William Martin, RM

The grave of Glyndwr Michael/William Martin in the Nuestra Señora de la Soledad cemetery in Huelva, Spain. The post-script inscription at the gravestone's base revealing Major Martin's real identity as that of Glyndwr Michael was added in 1997. Benutzer:smashing/Wikipedia.

Miss Virginia Hall

An Extraordinary Woman and an Exceptional Spy

BY: JAMES G. FAUSONE

The State Department stuck Virginia Hall in a series of dead-end jobs as a clerk and secretary, and then denied employment, let alone a promotion, because of a disability even though she was college educated, was fluent in six languages, and had years of multicultural experience. But the State Department's short-sighted loss was first the British Special Operations Executive (SOE) and later the American Operation for Strategic Services' (OSS) long-term gain. But as *la Dame Qui Boite, "the Limping Lady,"* Virginia Hall became a formidable agent for both special operations services. She was so effective in Occupied France during World War II that she became the Gestapo's Enemy No. 1. But no matter what the Nazis did, she was never caught. Gestapo leader Klaus Barbie, the notorious *"Butcher of Lyon,"* mistaking her nationality, cursed, *"I would give anything to get my hands on that limping Canadian bitch."* After the war, she became the only civilian woman to be awarded the U.S. Army Distinguished Service Cross.

AMERICAN UPBRINGING

Virginia Hall was born in Baltimore, Maryland, on April 6, 1906, to Barbara Virginia Hammel and Edwin Lee Hall. She had a privileged upper-class upbringing. She attended Roland Park Country

Beyond Belief: True Stories of Civilian Heroes

School, Radcliffe College, one of the historic "Seven Sisters" that offered college degrees to women, and then Barnard College (Columbia University), where she studied French, Italian, and German. She also attended George Washington University where she studied French and Economics.

Pre-World War II and Tragedy

Hall's goal was to be a member of the diplomatic corps. This was not a goal that was easy to achieve in the 1920s – there were very few women in the diplomatic corps at that time. Virginia did find work as a State Department, but as a lowly clerk in the Warsaw Embassy in 1931. Though overqualified for the job, she took it, believing that the most important thing was to get in. From there, find a way to get promoted.

Virginia Hall - (photo courtesy of Central Intelligence Agency)

She transferred to Smyrna, Turkey. At the time she arrived, the economy was driven by cotton dying, mills spinning thread, iron works, and soap works owned by British and French companies. Much of the area was still undeveloped and outdoor shooting sports were regular activities of the educated class. Virginia was a regular participant in the hunts for Gallinago—a marsh snipe found on the shore of the Gediz Peninsula in Turkey.

Virginia was competitive even in hunting outings. In 1933, she was out early and hoping to bag the first snipe of the day. While going over a fence she tripped, and her shotgun went off, accidentally shooting herself in the left foot. Though doctors were able to save her life, they could not save her limb. Virginia lost a portion of her left leg just below the knee.

She was given a leave from the State Department and returned to the United States for care and recovery. Back at the family farm in Parkton, Maryland, Virginia learned to walk with a prosthetic limb that she called "Cuthbert." Cuthbert was an Angelo-

Saxon monk, mystic, miracle worker and saint in England in the seventh century AD. It is unclear if Virginia knew of the saint from her studies or travels.

Virginia Hall's driver license, 1930s. - (Lorna Catling Collection)

After her leg injury, she worked again as a consular clerk in Venice, Italy, and in Tallinn, Estonia. Despite several attempts to become a U.S. diplomat, she was turned down because of an obscure rule against hiring people with disabilities as diplomats. Secretary of State Cordell Hull dismissed her request writing, *"Hall could become a fine career girl in the Consular Service."*

She was not going to be *"a fine career girl."* However, even her appeal to disabled President Franklin D. Roosevelt was unsuccessful. Six years after her accident, Hall resigned from the Department of State in March 1939, still working as a consular clerk.

When war broke out in Europe in September 1939, Virginia Hall was not one to cautiously wait or sit out the next great adventure. Looking to help in France, Hall became an ambulance driver for the French army's Services Sanitaires de L'Armee. As a private, she received training in first aid and ambulance driving. When the German army invaded France in May 1940, the work was around the clock. After the France's defeat in June 1940, it became obvious it was time to leave France and contemplate her options.

When she arrived in London, the U.S. Embassy wanted her firsthand information on the status of France. And she was again hired by the U.S. Defense Attaché Office but knew this was a dead end with no career opportunities. She endured the Luftwaffe's bombings of London in the Battle of Britain. After a chance meeting with a British undercover agent on a train who, at one point during their conversation, gave her a business card with a phone number on it. Virginia called the number. Virginia left her position as a clerk in the in February 1941, having been recruited by the SOE.

Beyond Belief: True Stories of Civilian Heroes

AN AMERICAN IN BRITISH SERVICE

The SOE was a secret World War II organization created to conduct espionage, sabotage, and intelligence gathering, and other clandestine activities in Axis occupied territories for the British. It began in July 1940 and was known as "Baker Street Irregulars" or "Churchill's Secret Army," or "Ministry of Ungentlemanly Warfare."

The importance of this clandestine work could not be underestimated. Neither could the danger of such work. Virginia Hall was uniquely qualified to participate in behind-enemy-lines spy activity. Importantly, the British saw a role for women to play in this work. The SOE directly employed or controlled more than 13,000 people, about 25 percent of whom were women.

Hall received training in such things as armed and unarmed combat, parachute jumping, radio operations, demolition techniques, trade craft, etc.

Because Hall was an American citizen at a time when the United States was neutral, she was a particularly valuable asset for SOE. She was sent to Vichy France in August 1941. Her cover was that of a *New York Post* reporter, which gave her an ability to interview people and populate stories with facts of importance to British military planners.

From August 1941 until November 1942, her headquarters were in the Haute Loire Department between the cities of Toulouse and Lyon. Her code-name was *Geologist-5*, with a mission to provide SOE with information on Vichy France, including reports on political developments, economic conditions, and the pulse of the resistance. Lyon, in southern France, is closer to Geneva Switzerland than it is to Paris.

She created the Heckler Network in Lyon. Over the next fifteen months she focused on support operations—organizing resistance movements' supplying agents with money, weapons, and supplies; helping downed airmen to escape; and offering safe houses and medical assistance to wounded agents and pilots.

A network would be made up of numerous spies that in turn, had a chain of agents that helped the network by providing information, safe houses, food, and logistical support. But Virginia went beyond her charter and proved adept at recruiting spies. The Heckler Network she established had a reported 90 agents in southern France. The group provided intelligence on ammunition and fuel depots, German troop movements, and industrial production. Virginia's encoded communications were sent via Western Union telegram to her cutout at the *New York Post*, who forwarded the information to SOE London.

When the United States entered the war in December 1941, Hall's neutral status vanished and, even though she was operating in nominally free Vichy France, her situation became increasingly dangerous.

In September 1942, she sent a message to SOE in London that *"my time is about up."* Virginia stayed another two months after her message, changing names and safe houses frequently to avoid capture. Hall knew the border with Spain would be sealed and more men would be hunting her.

When the Allies landed in French Northwest Africa in Operation Torch, German response in France was to seize control of the rest of the country. As a result, Hall's already fraught situation became untenable. She knew if she stayed, she'd be caught. After a car ride south with two companions, Hall was deposited at the start of a trail that led through the Pyrenees Mountains into Spain. The trail took days to navigate. This was not a walk in the park for anyone, especially a woman with a prosthetic leg. The mountainous trail rose 7,500 feet before coming down in Spain. It was a forty-four-mile trail that normally took three to four days to traverse. The exact time for travel, and the pain she endured, was never discussed by Hall.

Unfortunately, getting to Spain was not the end of Hall's problems. She arrived at the train station at San Juan de las Abadesas hours before the Barcelona-bound train. She was spotted and jailed by Spanish authorities for illegally crossing the border. Eventually, the U.S. Embassy secured her release and she returned to the United States.

Britain's King George secretly awarded her the honor of Member of the British Empire in 1943, the third highest ranking Order of the British Empire award, behind Commander of the Order

Beyond Belief: True Stories of Civilian Heroes

of the British Empire (COB), and Officer of the Order of the British Empire (OBE).

IN SERVICE TO AMERICAN

Hall wanted to return to France but SOE knew it was too dangerous. The Nazis were looking for her and her network had been rolled up. Undeterred, she sought another way to serve. She found it with the Office of Strategic Services. She was commissioned a second lieutenant and, after completing training, she was given the false identity of Marcelle Montagne, codename Diane. She had another codename as well, Artemis. She was then sent to France to help organize, supply, and lead Resistance networks in support of Operation Overlord, the Allied landings in Normandy scheduled for the spring. Standard operating procedure was for operators to be parachuted into occupied territory. But, because of her prothesis, on March 21, 1944, she was taken to France by motor gunboat, landing at Beg-an-Fry near the Breton port of Brest.

A painting of Hall as a wireless operator during her second mission to France. (Jeffrey W. Bass, Public domain, via Wikimedia Commons)

Landing with her was sixty-two-year-old Henri Lassot, who was to be the organizer and leader of the new Saint network, it being too radical a thought that a woman could lead an OSS network of agents. She was assigned as Lassot's wireless operator. Lassot carried with him one million francs, equivalent to 5,000 British pounds; and Hall had 500,000 francs with her. Hall quickly separated herself from

Lassot, whom she characterized as too talkative and a security risk, instructing her contacts not to tell him where she was. Aware that her accent would reveal that she was not French, she engaged a French woman, Madame Rabut, to accompany and speak for her.

Hall was disguised as an older woman, with gray hair, her teeth filed down to resemble that of a peasant woman. She disguised her limp with the long skirt and shuffle of an old woman.

Hall roamed around France south of Paris, from March to July 1944, posing sometimes as an elderly milkmaid. She found and organized drop zones, established several safe

The OSS of World War II forged a French identification certificate for "Marcelle Montagne," an alias of spy Virginia Hall - (Photo by Rudi Williams, Public domain, via Wikimedia Commons)

houses, and organized and supplied with arms several resistance groups of a hundred men each in the Cher and Cosne departments along the Loir Valley.

Following the D-day landings in Normandy on June 6, 1944, from July to September 1944 Hall operated in Haute-Loire Department. She was next given the job of assisting the Maquis in southern France harass the Germans in support of the Allied invasion on France's Mediterranean coast in, Operation Dragoon, scheduled for August 15, 1944. As a civilian woman but with the rank of second lieutenant, she had problems asserting her authority over the Maquis groups and the self-proclaimed colonels heading them. She complained to OSS headquarters, *"you send people out ostensibly to work with me and for me, but you do not give me the necessary authority.'*

She told the Maquis leaders that she would finance them and give them arms on condition that they would be advised by her, but the prickly Maquis leaders, reluctant to take orders from a woman junior officer, at first balked and continued to be a problem. But the three planeloads of supplies she received in late July, and the money she distributed for expenses, gained their grudging acquiescence.

The three battalions of Maquis (about 1,500 men) in her area undertook a number of successful sabotage operations. Now part of the French Forces of the Interior (FFI), they forced the German occupiers to withdraw from Le Puy-en-Velay, in the Auvergne region of south-central France, and head north with the rest of the retreating German forces.

In August 1944, Paris was liberated amid celebration in the streets, and American troops rumbled through the avenues on August 26th. The following year in April 1945, she returned to Paris where she wrote reports and identified people who had helped her and were deserving of commendations. Her work complete, she then resigned from OSS. But her efforts were not forgotten.

In May 1945, Gen. William Donovan, the legendary head of the OSS, presented her with the Distinguished Service Cross. President Truman wanted to give Hall the award himself in a public ceremony, but she declined such a public event worried the fanfare would make her non-operational in the future and reveal too much to the enemy.

It was the only DSC awarded to a civilian woman in WWII.

Branch receiving the Distinguished Service Cross from General Donovan, September 1945. CIA People, Public domain, via Wikimedia Commons

The Distinguished Service Cross (DSC) is the United States Army's highest military decoration for soldiers who display extraordinary heroism in combat with an armed enemy force. Ranking after the Medal of Honor, the nation's highest decoration for military valor, it is the highest award that can be given to civilians and foreign allies.

The French government awarded Hall the Croix de Guerre avec Palme in 1988 as part of the inaugural class of the Military Intelligence Corps Hall of Fame.

In 2006, the French and British ambassadors honored Hall, who died in 1982, in a ceremony at the home of the French ambassador in Washington. The British ambassador to the United States presented a certificate signed by King George VI to Ms. Hall's niece. Hall should have received the document in 1943, when she was made a member of the Order of the British Empire. However, it had remained in a British government vault for over fifty years.

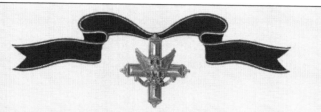

The President of the United States of America, authorized by Act of Congress, July 9, 1918, takes pleasure in presenting the Distinguished Service Cross to Miss Virginia Hall, a United States Civilian, for extraordinary heroism in connection with military operations against an armed enemy while serving as an American Civilian Intelligence Officer in the employ of the Special Operations Branch, Office of Strategic Services, who entered voluntarily and served in enemy-occupied France from March to September 1944. Despite the fact that she was well known to the Gestapo because of previous activities, Miss Hall established and maintained radio communications with London headquarters, supplying valuable operational and intelligence information. With the help of a Jedburgh team, she organized, armed, and trained three battalions of French resistance forces in the Department of the Haute Loire. Working in a region infested with enemy troops and continually at the risk of capture, torture, and death, she directed the resistance forces with extraordinary success in acts of sabotage and guerrilla warfare against enemy troops, installations, and communications. Miss Hall displayed rare courage, perseverance, and ingenuity. Her efforts contributed materially to the successful operations of the resistance forces in support of the Allied Expeditionary Forces in the liberation of France.

Beyond Belief: True Stories of Civilian Heroes

<u>Life After WWII</u>

Life back in the United States had to be slow paced and dull for Hall. She did not have a "normal "life to return to having left and explored the world. But adjust she must. She did return to Lyon to see how her friends and comrades had fared after the war. Heartbreak and happiness would be in store for her.

Her closest associates, brothel-owner Germaine Guérin and Dr. Jean Rousset, had both been captured by the Germans and sent to concentration camps, but they survived. She arranged 80,000 francs (400 British pounds) compensation from the United Kingdom for Guérin, but most of her network received nothing other than freedom. Unfortunately all too many of her network did not survive – some were executed at Buchenwald concentration camp. The German agent, Robert Alesch, who had betrayed her network in Lyon, was captured after the war and executed in Paris.

Hall joined the Central Intelligence Agency, the successor to the OSS, in 1947, one of the first women hired by the new agency. Her desk-bound job as an intelligence analyst was to gather information about Soviet penetration of European countries. She resigned in 1948 and then was rehired in 1950 for another desk job.

In 1951, she worked alongside fellow former spy Paul Golliot, supporting undercover activities to prevent the spread of communism in Europe. She simply was not cut out to sit at a desk and be subservient to men that had less knowledge and experience. In 1966, she retired, at the mandatory retirement age of 60. Those who did not know her background would have viewed her as just another federal bureaucrat buying time to retire.

Virginia Hall and Paul Golliott

Her personal life took a positive turn in 1957 when she married Golliot after living together off-and-on for years. They retired to a farm in Barnesville, Maryland, where she lived until her death on July 8, 1982. She packed a lot of living into her seventy-six years. Her husband survived her by five years. She is buried in the Druid Ridge Cemetery, Pikesville, Maryland.

Virginia Hall left no memoir, granted no interviews, and spoke little about her overseas life—even with relatives. She left behind no daughters, but she changed perceptions about what everyone's daughters could accomplish. Her life is a road map of how to raise a strong and independent woman.

Mr. Morris (Moe) Berg

The Catcher is . . . an Assassin?

BY JIM FURLONG

Among the colorful characters who became spies during World War II, no one was more unusual than Morris "Moe" Berg. Tall, handsome, charismatic, erudite, a professional baseball player, lawyer, scholar, linguist, and spy, Berg was a modern-day Renaissance man who embodied the adage that truth is stranger than fiction.

Depending on your source, Moe spoke seven languages fluently and could converse in twelve or more. A graduate of Princeton, he also played second base on the baseball team. He went on to play baseball, originally signed by the Brooklyn Robins, he also played for the Chicago White Sox and ended his career with the Boston Red Sox which he coached for a couple of years after his playing days were over. He would sometimes report to his baseball team after the season started so he could continue his studies for a Law Degree from Columbia University in New York. Moe began his career as a catcher because, reporting to the team late, his replacement at his original position of second base was batting over .300. However, the team's starting catcher had just gotten injured, so he grabbed a catcher's mask and became a catcher. He was a voracious reader consuming about ten newspapers every day.

There was a joke around the baseball that went something like this: *"Berg can speak twelve languages but can't hit in any one of them."* He was a lifetime .243 hitter. In 1934 when baseball went on a barnstorming tour of Japan, Berg addressed the Japanese legislature (The Diet) in Japanese. His reputation as an intellectual was supported by several appearances as a contestant on the radio quiz show "Information Please," answering questions about the etymology of words and names from Latin and Greek, historical events in Europe and the Far East, and going to international conferences.

But it was his work after his baseball career ended that earned Moe Berg a spot in this book. You see, during World War II he was a spy for the Office of Strategic Services (OSS).

BIRTH AND EARLY LIFE

Berg was the third and last child born to Bernard and Rose (Tashker) Berg. Both parents were Jewish immigrants. Bernard, a pharmacist, emigrated from the Ukraine. Rose was a homemaker. Early on the family lived the Harlem section of New York City, practically in the shadows of New York's Polo Grounds baseball stadium.

Bernard Berg bought a pharmacy in West Newark in 1906 and resided in the back of the store until 1910, when the family moved to the Roseville section of Newark.

Berg began playing baseball at the age of seven for the Rosewood Methodist Episcopal Church baseball team under the pseudonym "Runt Wolfe," Apparently those with a Berg surname were not welcomed on a Christian church league.

In 1918, at the age of sixteen, Berg graduated from Barringer High School. During his senior season, the Newark *Star-Eagle* selected a nine-man all-star team from the city's best prep and high school baseball players, and Berg was named the team's third baseman. Barringer was the first in a series of institutions where Berg's religion made him unusual at the time. Most other students were East Side Italian Catholics or Protestants from the Forest Hill neighborhood. Berg's father had wanted him to experience an environment with few Jews.[1]

After graduating from Barringer, Berg enrolled in New York University. He spent two semesters playing baseball and basketball on the school teams. In 1919 he transferred to Princeton University

---

[1] Dawidoff, Nicholas, *The Catcher Was a Spy, The Mysterious Life of Moe Berg.* Vintage, (1995).

and never again referred to attending NYU, presenting himself exclusively as a Princeton man. Berg received his BA, magna cum laude in modern languages. He had studied seven languages, Latin, Greek, French, Spanish, Italian, German and Sanskrit, studying with the philologist Harold H. Bender. His Jewish heritage and modest finances kept him on the fringes of Princeton's Ivy League social life.[2]

During his freshman year, Berg played first base on an undefeated team. Beginning in his sophomore year he was the starting shortstop. He was not a great hitter and was a slow baserunner, but he had a strong, accurate throwing arm and sound baseball instincts. In his senior season he captained the baseball team and had a .337 batting average, highlighted by batting .611 against Princeton's arch-rivals, Harvard and Yale. Shortstop Berg and Princeton's second baseman Crossan Cooper, communicated plays in Latin when there was an opposing player on second base.

On June 26, 1923, Yale defeated Princeton 5–1 at newly built Yankee Stadium to win the Big Three title, despite Berg's having had an outstanding day going 2–4 batting with a single and a double as well as putting in his usual defense at shortstop. Both the New York Giants and the Brooklyn Robins (later becoming known as the Brooklyn Dodgers in 1932) desired "Jewish blood" on their teams, to appeal to the large Jewish Community in and around New York. Both teams expressed an interest in Berg, but the Giants had future Hall of Famer shortstops in Dave Bancroft and Travis Jackson. The Robins were a mediocre team, on which Berg would have a better chance to play. On June 27, 1923, Berg signed his first big league contract for $5,000 (the equivalent of $84,000 in 2022) with the Robins.[3]

PROFESSIONAL BASEBALL CAREER

So, Berg played his first and only season in the "Senior Circuit," National League, with the Brooklyn Robins. It is doubtful that Moe received any votes for Rookie of the Year, batting a paltry .186 in forty-nine games and 129 at bats. At the time, Berg was an infielder, mostly at shortstop or third base. Spring training for

---

[2] Ibid.
[3] Ibid.

Beyond Belief: True Stories of Civilian Heroes

Brooklyn in 1924 was in Clearwater, Florida. Because of his less than stellar batting average in "the Bigs" Berg was sent to the Minneapolis Millers of the American Association, a minor league team. It was this demotion which reportedly triggered an immortal baseball phrase. Mike Kelley, the Millers Manager, knew Mike Gonzales who was playing for Brooklyn and queried Gonzales as to Berg's potential. In a telegram to Kelley, Gonzales uttered a phrase that to this day are four dreaded words no prospective ballplayer wants to hear: *"Good field, No hit."*

To say Moe Berg, in addition to being highly intelligent, was also very eccentric might be an understatement. Daily, he read upwards of a dozen newspapers or more. He considered an unread newspaper "alive" and wouldn't let anyone else read them until he finished reading them at which time, he considered a paper "dead." If someone had touched an *"alive"* paper before he read it, it became "dead," and he would go out and buy another one.

Casey Stengel, no stranger to eccentricities himself, once called Moe Berg *"the strangest man ever to play baseball."*[4] He often would disappear for days—even weeks on end—and return without explanation. This continued even into his days as a spy for the OSS.

Berg tags out a Cleveland player at the plate.

Berg would go on to play fourteen more seasons, all in the American League, with the Chicago White Sox, Washington Senators, and Boston Red Sox, playing mostly as a back-up catcher and substitute short stop. During that time his playing time was interrupted when he enrolled in Columbia Law School, passing his bar exam in 1929 and getting his law degree in 1930. Only once did he crack .300, and that was in 1938 when, for the Red Sox, he batted .333—in twelve at bats. Hitting only six home runs during his career, his biggest accomplishment as a hitter was sixteen doubles for the

---

[4] Berger, Ralph *Moe Berg,* Society for American Baseball Research

Mr. Morris (Moe) Berg

White Sox in 1928. When his career ended in 1939, he possessed an unremarkable slash line of .243/.278/.299

But, toward the end of his career, a new, mysterious chapter opened in his life—one that continues to mystify historians to this day.

MAJOR LEAGUE BASEBALL BARNSTORMS THROUGH JAPAN

Doing research for this book it intrigued me that a career .243 hitter and backup catcher who bounced from team to team in baseball—this non-All Star—would be invited to All-Star Barnstorming Tours in 1932 and 1934. These tours included future Hall of Famers Babe Ruth, Jimmy Foxx, Ted Lyons, Lefty O'Doul, Lou Gerhig, Earl Averill, Charlie Gehringer, Lefty Gomez, Connie Mack and . . . Moe Berg? One possible explanation is that Berg could speak and write in Japanese. Certainly, the squad could have hired any interpreter, but for some unknown reason they chose Moe Berg.

One possible explanation points to William J Donovan, who would eventually form the Office of Strategic Services (OSS), harbored a belief even during the mid-1930's that war with Japan was inevitable. So, Donovan and some of his associates with the same beliefs began clandestinely assembling intelligence on Japan. Despite Donovan being several years older than Berg, both were Columbia Law School graduates practicing in New York City (Berg when he wasn't playing baseball). Both Donovan and Berg knew Nelson Rockefeller who, during the war, offered Berg his first job working for Rockefeller's Office of Inter-American Affairs (OIAA).

Regardless of who and how the strings were pulled, Berg was on the roster and traveled with the team to Japan where he gave a speech to the welcoming committee and later addressed The Diet (legislature) in Japanese. He was little used during games in Japan and was known to walk the streets in a long black kimono while his teammates were giving exhibition games at the various universities. On November 29, 1934, with his team playing elsewhere, Berg went to St. Luke's Hospital in the Tsukiji section of Tokyo armed with a bouquet of flowers and a hidden 16-mm. movie camera hidden beneath his kimono. Supposedly he was there to visit the daughter of the American ambassador, Mrs. Cecil Burton, who had just given birth to a daughter. But instead of visiting the ambassador's daughter, he went straight to the roof of the hospital which at that time was the tallest building in Tokyo, to take photographs

During the daring Doolittle Raid a little over seven years later, the purpose of the raid, besides striking fear into the hearts of the citizenry that the U.S. could bomb Japan's capital, was also to cripple as much as possible the Japanese war machine. There is scholarly dispute as to whether the Berg's film was used in the planning of the Doolittle Raid. His biographer, Nicholas Dawidoff, states that Berg didn't show the film to Intelligence Analysts until the summer of 1942, months after the Doolittle Raid on April 18, 1942. Nick Accoella, writing for ESPN Classic *Sports Century* Biography, declares that the film was viewed by Doolittle and his Raider pilots for orientation during the raid. Ralph Berger writing an article on Berg for the Society of American Baseball Research (SABR) asserts the pilots did use the film, but it was not useful because the film was *"too old to be useful to the pilots."*

BASEBALL IN BERG'S LATER CAREER

Having been released by the Indians while on the 1932 tour, Berg stayed behind and continued a personal tour of the Far East, even visiting Moscow in the Soviet Union. He was then given a contract by the Boston Red Sox for whom he played for five more years as a backup catcher, never averaging over thirty games in a season. After his playing days ended following the 1939 season, Berg coached with the Red Sox until the outbreak of war.

ESPIONAGE*

Berg was still working for Nelson Rockefeller's Office of Inter-American Affairs and had attracted the attention of the Office of Strategic Services (OSS), perhaps at the behest of Rockefeller himself. What impressed OSS the most was: Berg's work at OIAA,

---

* Author's note. I'd to thank Dr. John Arnold of NICOM (www.nicom.com) who provided me invaluable material to do research into Moe Berg's life as an OSS spy during World War II. This research was done at the National Archives and include previously classified materials. Thanks John.

his high level of intelligence, his ability to speak several languages including German, French and Italian, and his affable manner

Berg was interviewed for an OSS Special Operations position in early in July 1943 and on July 17, 1943, Lieutenant Commander Davis Halliwell, Chief of the OSS Special Operations Section wrote the OSS Security Chief William Mudge asking him to "expedite" the security clearance for Berg. As justification Halliwell said it was his *"belief that we should get our hands on him as fast as possible, and will you please suggest to Mr. Howland that I believe he can arrange for provisional security."*

Berg's OSS credentials

This provisional security clearance was granted on July 22, 1943. It had already been determined that Berg would first be sent to North Africa to "solve the North Africa problem." Although the North African Campaign had been declared over on May 13, 1943, the aftermath had left terrible food shortages. This, in turn, was fueling increasing nationalist flames in Tunisia and Algeria, both at the time being French territories. It was believed Berg, with his fluency in French would be able to root out pockets of nationalist desires and identify where food assistance would be most needed.

After training, Berg was sent to North Africa with his travel orders cut on April 13, 1944. He was authorized to wear civilian clothing, and to have a .45 cal. pistol and "Special OSS Equipment" (the cyanide capsule).

After completing that assignment, he was selected for a special mission codenamed Project Larson, as part of the ongoing Alsos Mission. The purpose of Project Larson was to interview top Italian physicists to see if they knew anything about a German bomb program.

In 1944, Berg traveled to Italy and met with physicists Edoardo Amaldi and Gian Carlo Wick, who admitted that they had not done any atomic research for the Germans and suspected that even if the Germans were working on an atomic bomb, it would have taken them at least a decade to complete it. Berg continued to visit with other Italian scientists throughout the summer, though little was learned about a German nuclear program.

THE HEISENBERG AFFAIR

Germany, already at war, began its secret project, called *Uranverein*, or "uranium club" in April 1939, just months after German scientists Otto Hahn and Fritz Strassmann had inadvertently discovered fission. Germany had a significant head start over the Allies as well as some of the best scientists, a strong industrial base, sufficient materials, and the interest of certain military officers, though not Adolf Hitler.

President Roosevelt became aware of the German nuclear program four months later when, in August 1939, he received the now-famous letter from Albert Einstein in which Einstein warned the president that it *"may become possible to set up a nuclear chain reaction . . . by which vast amounts of power would be generated."*

Robert Furman, Chief of Foreign Intelligence for the Manhattan Project, the top secret American atomic bomb program, described how *"the Manhattan Project was built on fear. Fear that the enemy had the bomb or would have it before the Allies."*

The United States government remained equally afraid. Major General Leslie Groves remembered, *"Unless and until we had positive knowledge to the contrary, we had to assume that the most competent German scientists and engineers were working on an atomic program with the full support of their government and with the full capacity of German industry at their disposal. Any other assumption would have been unsound and dangerous."* There was even consideration of kidnapping Werner Heisenberg in Switzerland in 1942, although this plan never came to fruition. In 1943, the United States launched the Alsos Mission, a foreign intelligence project focused on learning the extent of Germany's nuclear program.

Mr. Morris (Moe) Berg

In December 1944, the OSS learned that renowned German physicist Werner Heisenberg was leaving Germany to give a lecture in Zurich. Berg was ordered to attend the conference and to make contact with Heisenberg.

When Heisenberg entered that lecture hall in Zurich, sitting only a few feet away was Moe Berg. Under cover as a German businessman, Berg had his .45 caliber pistol and a cyanide capsule in his pocket. If, during the course of the lecture, Berg believed that Germany was close to developing the atomic

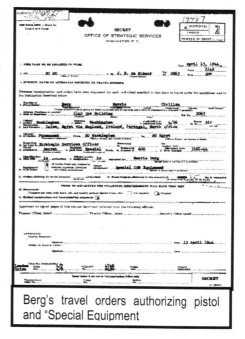

Berg's travel orders authorizing pistol and "Special Equipment

bomb, he was ordered to kill Heisenberg and if captured, swallow the cyanide capsule and commit suicide.

As it was, Heisenberg's lecture was simply about S-Matrix Theory: atomic particles and the possibility that they could change their state. And while this does occur during nuclear fission, the lecture was not otherwise sufficient to determine whether Germany had other means to produce a bomb, such as sufficient uranium and the industry necessary to produce a bomb. Berg did not get a degree in physics at Princeton University, only in Modern Languages. So, he contrived to get an invitation to a dinner being hosted that evening a Swiss physicist Paul Scheerer, an OSS source who was feeding information about Germany to Bern Station Chief Allen Dulles who would later become the Director of the CIA. That dinner party did nothing to cause Berg to determine that Germany was very close in development of their bomb. So, Berg walked Heisenberg to his hotel still carrying his pistol and cyanide capsule. During the walk Berg concluded that Germany was not close to having the bomb and decided not to assassinate Heisenberg.

Beyond Belief: True Stories of Civilian Heroes

BERG IN THE IMMEDIATE POSTWAR

With the death of President Franklin Roosevelt on April 12, 1945, support for the OSS dramatically declined in the new Truman Administration. In fact Donovan and the OSS had many enemies who seemed to have the ear of the new Administration, not the least of whom was J. Edgar Hoover of the FBI who despised and was jealous of the OSS and wanted foreign intelligence gathering brought under the FBI umbrella. So, it was decided by Truman, that the OSS would be shut down after the war—it was just a matter of when.

But the OSS would not come in from the cold without a fight.

Brigadier General John Magruder of the OSS sat down with an old friend of Donovan's, the Assistant Secretary of War, John McCloy, one of the great movers and shakers of Washington. Together, they countermanded the president. Magruder left the Pentagon that day with an order from McCloy that said, *"the continuing operations of OSS must be performed in order to preserve them."* That piece of paper kept the hope for a Central Intelligence Agency alive.

The spies would stay on duty, under a new name, the Strategic Services Unit—the SSU. McCloy then asked his good friend Robert A. Lovett, the Assistant Secretary for Air War and a future Secretary of Defense to set up a secret commission to plot the course for American intelligence-and to tell President Truman what had to be done. Magruder confidently informed his men that *"the holy cause of central intelligence"* would prevail.

General Magruder would eventually receive the Army Distinguished Service Medal for his OSS/SSU efforts.

WHERE'S MOE?

Several research articles I read indicated Moe Berg returned to the United States in April 1945 and resigned from the Strategic Services Unit (SSU). But, confusingly, the SSU hadn't even been formed yet and the OSS was still operational. The SSU was established on October 1, 1945, through Executive Order 9621, which simultaneously abolished the OSS. The SSU was headed by General John Magruder.

It seems that as the war was ending and the immediate aftermath, Berg, along with a foreign intelligence specialist from the Manhattan Project, Lieutenant Colonel Calvert, were crossing Europe looking for Axis scientists. Because the intelligence specialist did not speak the languages, Berg, who did, was invaluable in using his contacts to find those scientists before the Soviets did. Berg then safely returned them to either the British or to American soil. He would later be awarded the Presidential Medal of Freedom for his service both during the war and its immediate aftermath. The citation reads as follows:

> Mr. Morris Berg, United States Civilian, rendered exceptionally meritorious service of high value to the war effort from April 1944 to January 1946. In a position of responsibility in the European Theater, he exhibited analytical abilities and a keen planning mind. He inspired both respect and constant high level of endeavor on the part of his subordinates which enabled his section to produce studies and analysis vital to the mounting of American operations.

When this citation was written it was noted in Moe Berg's supporting documentation that the testimony would need to remain Top Secret forever. But the documentation has been declassified. It is over ten pages long and I will try to summarize it as best I can.

First, one has to remember that Berg was a civilian when he worked as a spy. As such he was without the protection of the Geneva Convention. If captured, he would have been executed.

- There were many times, especially when Rome was falling, that Berg inserted himself into the action in an attempt to find Italian scientists by being between Italian guerilas and retreating Germans. Without credentials, he would have probably been shot by either side. These scientists' engineering specialties saved the United States at least two years in fighter jet design.

- I already detailed the Heisenberg Affair. I would also add there were many pro-Nazi scientists in that room.

- General Leslie Groves of the Manhattan Project used the information received from Berg about the lagging German bomb effort to ease the work schedules of some of his scientists. He had become concerned about their health because they were driven to overwork by the race between the United States and Germany to develop the bomb.

- During the war and afterward, Berg was able to pinpoint exact locations of vital stockpiled bomb materials and vital bomb making equipment such as cyclotrons used to develop uranium. He even took photos of the barrels of 700 tons of Belgium Congo uranium. The knowledge of these locations allowed the Allies to secure these materials and prevented them from falling into Soviet hands.

- While in Zurich he helped uncover a British spy.

- In January 1946 a Soviet visited top bomb scientists in Copenhagen. Berg learned of this within forty-eight hours knew who the Soviet was, who he visited, and what he wanted. Berg secured the cooperation of the scientists

- In the aftermath of the war Berg was constantly crisscrossing Europe securing the cooperation of many scientists and convincing them to immigrate to America and work for us.

Moe Berg finally did leave Europe and return to the United States in July 1946, about fourteen months after the war's conclusion.

POST SERVICE

Upon Moe's return the pencil pushers in Washington immediately demanded an accounting of the use of Berg's advances right down to the number of bullets used in his .45. At least six letters were sent to Berg demanding the accounting. Berg offered to repay the full amount that had been advanced, but for some reason the bureaucrats declined his offer. Yet, the letters demanding an accounting continued. When asked to come to the White House to receive the Medal of Freedom, he turned down the medal.

Berg spent the rest of his life living between his brother, Dr. Samuel Berg, and his sister Ethel. He turned down offers to coach baseball. In 1952 he briefly returned to the spy craft to work for the

CIA to find out the status of the Soviet bomb program. He was not successful.

Berg died on Memorial Day, May 29, 1972, in Belleville, New Jersey, being hospitalized after a fall in Ethel's home. Reportedly, his last words were, *"Did the Mets win today"?*

After his death Ethel accepted the Medal of Freedom on his behalf. She donated the medal to the Baseball Hall of Fame where it is on permanent display in Cooperstown, New York. In 1996 he was inducted into the Jewish Sports Hall of Fame. In 2000 he was inducted into the Baseball Reliquary Shrine of the Eternals. Berg's is the only baseball card on display in the lobby of the Central Intelligence Agency in Langley, Virginia.

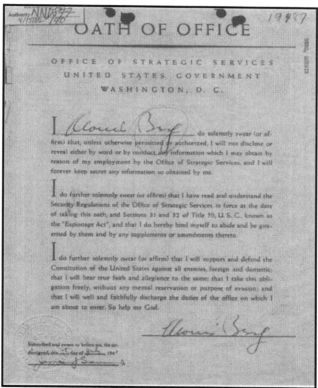

Morris Berg's OSS Oath of Office July 25, 1943.

Mr. Justus Rosenberg

A Profile in Survival: The Holocaust, French Resistance, and U.S. Army

BY DWIGHT JON ZIMMERMAN

Miriam Davenport knocked on the hotel room door of Justus Rosenberg and when he opened it, she excitedly said, *"Gussie, I think I may have found a real job for you."* And with that one sentence, Rosenberg, a Polish Jew and former undergraduate student at the Sorbonne in Paris, would find himself embarking on an epic adventure, first as a courier for an organization helping refugee artists, writers, and intellectuals escape France following its defeat by Germany in 1940, later joining the French Resistance, narrowly escape from being shipped to a concentration camp, service as an aide to a U.S. Army battalion, and finally as an officer in the United Nations Relief and Rehabilitation Administration (UNRAA) —all before the age of twenty-five.

The cover to Justus Rosenberg's memoir in which he recounts his extraordinary experiences as a courier, French Resistance soldier, U.S. Army aide, and United Nations Relief and Rehabilitation Administration officer.

Justus Rosenberg was born on January 23, 1921, to Jacob and Bluma Rosenberg in the Free City of Danzig (now Gdansk), a semi-autonomous city-state in Poland.

Beyond Belief: True Stories of Civilian Heroes

Rosenberg's father was a successful international wholesale businessman and young Rosenberg was expected to enter the company when he came of age. That began to change after the Nazis came to power in 1933. Because it had once been a part of Germany, Danzig had a large German population. A local Nazi party, taking its cue from what was happening in Germany, began a campaign of harassment and attacks against Jews and their businesses. In 1937 the family decided that the sixteen-year-old Rosenberg should go to France and continue his studies at the Sorbonne in Paris. Justus left Danzig that summer, not suspecting that he would not see his parents and younger sister again for fifteen years.

Paris was the center of the world during the interwar years and when he wasn't studying, Rosenberg took full advantage of all that the City of Light had to offer. All that came to a dramatic end when the German army invaded France on May 10, 1940. At first, everyone thought that the powerful French army, together with its British army ally, would successfully repel the Germans. But as the days passed, confidence turned into consternation, and finally, panic, as increasing numbers of Dutch, Belgian, and French refugees fleeing ahead of the advancing Germans flooded Paris. On June 10, the French government declared Paris an open city, with the German army occupying it four days later. Finally, on June 25, the new government formed under Marshal Philippe Pétain signed an armistice dividing France into two zones, one occupied by German forces in the north and along the Atlantic coast, and an unoccupied zone ruled by the new government based in the spa city of Vichy.

But long before then Justus had joined the chaotic refugee flight south. It was at Toulouse, part of the unoccupied zone, that he met Miriam, an American who he learned had been studying for her master's degree in art at the Sorbonne. As so often happens in time of war, they formed a quick friendship with her giving him the nickname "Gussie." Her fiancé was in Yugoslavia and she planned to get the visas she needed at the American consulate in Marseille, pick up her fiancé, and eventually take him with her to the United States. Rosenberg's goal was more straightforward: find a way to leave France. She suggested he'd have better success escaping through Marseille, gave him the name of her hotel, and suggested he see her should he need help.

Mr. Justus Rosenberg

Two weeks later and in the middle of the night he was at her hotel room doorstep, a refugee seeking refuge. Earlier, while waiting for her visa application to be processed, Miriam had taken a job as a typist at the Emergency Rescue Committee (ERC), a privately funded American organization set up immediately after France's defeat to help artists, writers, and intellectuals, most of them Jews, escape Vichy France. In August, journalist and co-founder Varian Fry arrived at Marseille carrying $3,000 and a list of 200 names. Before the French government shut down the operation in September 1941, the organization would help as many as 4,000 people escape Nazi persecution, among them Hannah Arendt, Marcel Duchamp, Marc Chagall, Max Ernst, and André Breton.

Shortly after he had arrived at her hotel room, Miriam told Justus that she had given Fry his name and told him that Justus was fluent in German and French, knew some English, and that, though Jewish, he could pass as a gentile with his blue eyes and blond hair. He was also familiar with the contemporary political situation; and most importantly, could be trusted. Justus agreed to meet Fry. He arrived at Fry's office first thing the following morning and was promptly hired.

During his first week of work, Justus was kept busy sending coded telegrams from the Marseille central post office to the organization's home office in New York City and dropping off blank identity cards to a forger who used them to create false identities for the people on Fry's list.

Rosenberg's work for the ERC came to an abrupt end in September 1941 when the Vichy government ordered Fry expelled from France. Rosenberg subsequently attempted to smuggle himself into Spain by way of Andorra, a postage stamp-sized country lodged between France and Spain in the Pyrenees Mountains. But as he neared the border, French gendarmes found and arrested him, charging him with unauthorized trespass. Instead of prison, Rosenberg was let off with a small fine and parole by a sympathetic judge.

Upon his return to Marseille, Rosenberg reconnected with Jean Gemähling, a former co-worker at the ERC who was also a member of the nascent French Resistance. Gemähling had attempted to recruit Rosenberg for the Resistance after the ERC closed, but Rosenberg told him he wanted to leave France. Now, Rosenberg told Gemähling, he wanted in.

Following Gemähling's advice, Rosenberg moved to Grenoble in the French Alps and enrolled under his real name as a student at the local university. There he served as a "talent scout," identifying potential candidates for the Resistance.

For seven months his dual life proceeded without incident. Then, on August 27, 1942, two gendarmes arrived at the house where he was staying and ordered him to pack and follow them. He was loaded on a bus containing three men. By the time the bus stopped later that day at a former military camp in a suburb outside of Lyon, the bus was filled, having stopped at numerous villages along the way to pick up others similarly rounded up by the gendarmes. That night Rosenberg discovered that the complex was serving as a detention camp and that once it was filled with foreign refugees, everyone would be shipped to labor camps in Poland. Justus knew he had to escape. The question was, how?

During one of their many conversations, Justus recalled Gemähling mentioning that if captured, the best way to escape was to find an excuse, faking either insanity or a serious illness, in order to be sent to the hospital, the reason being that it was easier to escape from a hospital than it was from jail or a prison. While walking in the parade ground, Justus mulled his options. He dismissed insanity as not being viable. But what sort of illness to fake?

He spotted an acquaintance from the Sorbonne whom he knew to be a medical student. After telling her of his plan, she suggested peritonitis and described its symptoms. A short time later he collapsed onto the ground, groaning and writhing in extreme pain. He was taken to the infirmary for examination. To fake a fever he used a trick he had learned years ago to fool the school nurse when students wanted to get out of going to class. After the nurse left him to go about her rounds, Justus took the thermometer out of his mouth and furiously rubbed it until it registered 104 degrees. That temperature, and his howls of pain when the doctor poked his abdomen, caused Justus to be put in an ambulance and taken to the hospital where doctors removed his healthy appendix.

Mr. Justus Rosenberg

In his memoir, The Art of Resistance, Justus wrote, *"I never found out what went through the minds of those physicians once they saw that I didn't have anything wrong in my gut. Were they sympathetic people, willing to ignore my fakery and perhaps even help me get away? In any case they actually did take my appendix out!"*

During recovery he persuaded a nurse to mail a letter for him, instructing her to put it in a specific mailbox that he knew was nearby, part of a network of mailboxes used by the Resistance for communication amongst its members. His message simply stated his name and which hospital he was at.

Four days later a priest working for the Resistance arrived at his bedside. The priest quietly told Justus that his escape was planned for Sunday—visitors' day—where there would be a high volume of traffic in and out of the hospital that he could blend in with. The priest told him which toilet stall on the floor would contain a bundle of street clothes for him, and the location of a bicycle outside the hospital for his escape. At the appointed time on Sunday afternoon, Justus left his bed to "go to the bathroom." He entered the toilet, changed clothes, bundled up his hospital garb for the priest to gather after he left, and walked out of the hospital without arousing suspicion. He quickly found the bicycle and, with one hand pressed against his stitched-up incision, pedaled to a safe house whose address the priest had him memorize.

Two days later he was taken by a member of the Resistance about seventy-five miles south to a farm near Montmeyran in southeast France, not far from the French Alps. There he would remain for the next two years, a member of the Maquis—a full-fledged soldier in the Resistance.

After he had fully recovered from surgery, he was given a false identity and underwent two months of vigorous training in guerilla operations. After that his missions ran the gamut, including work as a spy, gathering intelligence of German troop strength and movement, collecting weapons and supply bundles dropped by British aircraft, and ambushing German convoys. On one such ambush mission, he was wounded in the foot.

The long-awaited Allied return to France finally came to pass at Normandy on June 6, 1944. Operation **Overlord** was a watershed moment in the Allied campaign. But it was Operation **Dragoon,** the Allied amphibious assault on the Mediterranean coast near Marseille and Toulon on August 15, that had a more immediate impact in the area where Justus' Resistance cell operated because it was much closer, only about two hundred miles away.

Three days after the Dragoon landings, twenty-three-year-old Justus was the leader of a heavily armed squad assigned to ambush an expected German convoy retreating from a nearby airfield. Shortly after dawn the next day they saw three soldiers on the road approaching their position. But the soldiers were coming from an unexpected direction. With the sun at their back, Justus couldn't clearly identify them. The *maquis* soldier manning the machine gun wanted to open fire, but Justus countermanded him. He wanted to be absolutely certain of their identities. Also, the trio was undoubtedly an advance patrol of a larger force, which he didn't want to prematurely alert.

As the soldiers closed, Justus saw that they weren't German. Were they, perhaps, American? Taking a chance that they were, he emerged from his hiding spot and met Lieutenant Peter Rogers, leader of a reconnaissance squad in the 636th Tank Destroyer Battalion of the Seventh U.S. Army. Rogers took Justus to battalion headquarters that had been set up in nearby Montmeyran. There Justus pointed out on the commanding officer's map the location of all the German units in the area. After learning that Justus was fluent in French, German, English, Polish, and some Russian, the commanding officer phoned a French army liaison officer at division headquarters and got Justus assigned to the battalion as an aide to Lieutenant Rogers.

Justus served as an interpreter, interrogator, and guide. On October 11, he was wounded when the jeep he was riding in ran over a Teller mine, severely wounding the driver and killing the soldier in the front passenger seat normally occupied by Justus.

Mr. Justus Rosenberg

In early December 1944, shortly before the German army launched the Ardennes offensive that came to be known as the Battle of the Bulge, Justus and Lieutenant Rogers were on leave in Paris. Justus took the opportunity to visit his pre-war haunts, including the Sorbonne campus. There he met one of his professors, Albert Bayet, who remembered that Justus had been one of his students. Bayet told him about the plight of the more than twelve million refugees and people displaced by the war and that the new United Nations organization had created an agency, the **United Nations Relief and Rehabilitation Administration**, to help them. Because of the immense scope of the problem, UNRAA was in desperate need of qualified people. Bayet said that Justus' language skills and recent background made him an ideal candidate and urged Justus to visit UNRAA's Paris office.

Justus told Lt. Rogers about UNRAA and, after receiving assurance from him that Justus would have no problem being released from the Army, Justus went to the UNRAA office where he was offered the position of supply officer.

He became a member of UNRAA Team 9, eventually stationed in Darmstadt, Germany, responsible for seventeen thousand displaced Poles, Latvians, Lithuanians, Estonians, Yugoslavs, Jews, Russians, and Ukrainians. He also served as liaison with the American Office of Military Government (AOMG) in Darmstadt, becoming deeply involved in German reconstruction. When he resigned from UNRAA on October 25, 1945, to pursue his interrupted studies at the Sorbonne he had received numerous letters of commendation for his work as supply officer which Major Leon P. Ervin, commanding officer of the Darmstadt AOMG, described as *"the most difficult in DP* [Displaced Person] *work."*

After graduating with the equivalent of a master's degree, in 1946, thanks to his service with the 636th, he was able to immediately get a visa to the United States where he had been offered a job as a college professor in Ohio. Once in the United States, he began a search for his family. He learned that though an uncle, his father's brother, had perished in the Holocaust, but his parents and sister were living in Israel, having escaped to Palestine shortly after he had gone to France. Fifteen years after leaving Danzig, Justus stepped off the boat at Haifa and was reunited with his family.

Beyond Belief: True Stories of Civilian Heroes

Justus chose to continue to live in the United States. Eventually he became a professor of literature at Bard College in upstate New York. For decades he never talked about his experience in the war. Finally he decided to write about it. In 2020, at age ninety-nine, *The Art of Resistance*, was published to critical acclaim. When Justus Rosenberg died on October 30, 2021, at age 100, among his honors were the Bronze Star and Purple Heart from the U.S. Army and, from France, that nation's highest decoration, the Légion d'honneur, rank of Commandeur.

Justus Rosenberg receives the French Legion of Honor medal from Ambassador Gérard Araud at a 2017 ceremony in New York

Mr. John Randolph
and Mr. Bernard Ullmann
Into the Maelstrom Armed with a Pen

BY SCOTT BARON AND C. DOUGLAS STERNER

The battlefield has never been the exclusive domain of warriors. Its bloody fields have always been the workplace of numerous other professions, from doctors and nurses to priests and ministers, and photographers and journalists who risked death and serious injury to carry out their duties. In some cases, they have gone far beyond and outside their responsibilities.

Ironically, it was not a war—but a cow—that thrust Associated Press reporter John Robert Randolph into the spotlight in 1949, a year before the start of the Korean War. A native of Detroit, Michigan, Randolph began reporting for the *Seattle Star* in 1936. During World War II, like millions of other American men and women, Randolph entered military service, choosing to serve in the U.S. Army Air Forces. He was assigned to posts in the United States during the war, and saw no combat action.

Discharged after the war ended, he joined the Associated Press as a reporter in the syndicate's headquarters in New York. How he came to cover the most riveting story of 1949 is unknown—it was breaking news out in the middle of nowhere—the small town of Yukon, Oklahoma. It was the kind of story often assigned to a cub reporter, the kind of story most reporters would never have wanted—a *fluff piece* in a far distant rural location about a cow stuck in a silo. Within days, however, Grady the Cow would become a household name across the nation and around the world, and the AP reporter covering it would become an instant celebrity with a quickly recognizable byline: John Randolph.

Grady was a six-year-old, 1,200-pound Hereford cow that belonged to Yukon famers Bill and Aylene Mach. On February 22, 1949, the pregnant cow was preparing to give birth to a still-born calf, and Mach had moved her to a small shed next to a silo. As Grady was having complications with delivery, and becoming quite anxious, Mach called local veterinarian D. L. Crump to help. Crump tied Grady to a post so she would hold still during delivery, and when he had finished his unenviable chore and Mach untied her, Grady whirled and began chasing Dr. Crump, who ran and jumped on a pile of cottonseed to escape.

Grady made a dive for the only light in the shed, which was coming from a small seventeen-inch by twenty-five-and-a-half-inch opening to the silo. How the massive Hereford got through the opening was difficult to understand—it was a desperate escape attempt by a very unhappy cow. The opening itself was framed with heavy steel, and there appeared no way to get Grady back out of the silo. The poor cow was trapped. The only possible solution was to tear down the expensive silo, which was really not an option.

Mach appealed to the local newspaper for help and the response was immediate and overwhelming. Over the next four days he received 5,400 letters and 700 telegrams from forty-five states and from Canada. It also drew the attention of local newspapers around the country as well as the Associated Press and other major news agencies.

Yukon farmer Bill Mach with Grady the Cow when she was in his silo in February 1949

Randolph would later report: 'The **Bangor (Maine) Daily Commercial** *started a contest to find the best method to help Grady.* – The Toledo (Ohio) Times *appointed a cow editor and started firing ideas to Mach.—Another newspaper, in Toronto, Canada, opened its editorial columns suggestions.—*The Atlanta

Mr. John Randolph and Mr. Bernrd Ullmann

(Georgia) Constitution *suggested a drug to relax Grady so she could be folded up and eased back through the door. This last idea also came from Oklahoma's Gov. Roy J. Turner, once a farm boy but now an oil millionaire who raises prize Herefords."*

Hundreds of interested people drove to Yukon to monitor the rescue effort, as well as add their own suggestions to the thousands pouring in daily by mail and telegram. They ranged from tunneling under the silo to free her or rigging a pole to swing her out of the open top, to even bringing in an attractive bull to lure her out. An Air Force officer even informed Mach he knew of a helicopter that could lift the 1,200 pound cow out, but it was in San Marcos, Texas.

It was Ralph Partridge, the farming editor of *The Denver Post* however, who finally came through. He flew to Oklahoma while a ramp was being built from the floor of the silo to the small opening. He coated the ramp and Grady herself with axle grease and put her into two heavy halters.

Dr. Crump suggested that they milk Grady before the planned rescue effort commenced on the morning of February 26. Mr. Jo. O. Dickey, Jr., a local school's vocational agriculture teacher, entered the silo to milk her. Then Dr. Grady climbed into the silo to administer tranquilizers. He and Dickey then got behind Grady to push, while Partridge, Mach, and others began to pull on ropes attached to Grady's harnesses. Randolph reported, *"More than 40 early risers gathered in the raw, gray dawn to watch the solution of a problem that stirred North America . . . Knock-out drops, cup grease and a strong push-pull freed Grady the cow from her silo prison at 8:09 a.m. Saturday . . . It was a triumph for the* Denver Post*, which invaded Oklahoma to rescue this damsel in distress."*

The days of entrapment and desperate efforts to free Grady the Cow made her an instant celebrity. *Life* magazine published a photo of her stuck in the silo, taken from above, in the March 7, 1949 issue. Grady marched in the Capitol Hill '89ers Parade in Oklahoma City on April 21, and she went on exhibit that year at the

Beyond Belief: True Stories of Civilian Heroes

Oklahoma State Fair. The book *The Cow in the Silo* was published in 1950, and as proof that her story is timeless, the 2005 book *Grady's in the Silo* won the Oklahoma Book Award for Children's Literature. Grady went on to successfully give birth to four heifers and two bulls, and she was so popular with tourist who wanted to visit her at her special pen on the farm that Mach even had a special sign installed on Route 66. Grady the Cow died on July 24, 1961.

In addition to his coverage of Grady's rescue, Randolph followed up on March 3 with a report of Grady's post-rescue condition. Grady's story had captivated the world, and Randolph's reporting had given him a high profile.

The following year Randolph was sent to the Associated Press' headquarters in Japan, and then to South Korea when war broke out in 1950. Thereafter, the now thirty-one-year-old AP reporter who had captivated the world with his stories about a hapless cow little more than a year earlier, began reporting from the front lines, his stories bringing the reality of war home to the United States.

Wanting to report on what he saw, Randolph requested permission to accompany the troops in battle. On April 23, 1952, he was joining the 3rd Infantry Division's 7th Infantry Regiment into one of the deadliest battles of the war. The Regiment's 1st Battalion was commanded by Lieutenant Colonel Frederick Carlton Weyand, who would later earn a Distinguished Service Cross in the Vietnam War, and would one day achieve the rank of a four-star general and serve as the fourteenth Army Vice Chief of Staff and twenty-seventh Army Chief of Staff.

In the spring of 1952, the communist Chinese People's Volunteer Army had a battalion of Belgian troops enveloped along the Imjin River, near the 38th Parallel in northeast South Korea, and his battalion's mission was to break through and relieve the beleaguered United Nations force. Lieutenant Colonel Weyand was preparing to depart when he was approached by what he later described as a *"lanky eager war correspondent."* Randolph was determined to once again, report from the front, and Weyand assigned him to accompany Master Sergeant Joseph Dix with 3rd Platoon of Company B. The 150 men of Baker Company were tasked

Mr. John Randolph and Mr. Bernrd Ullmann

with seizing the hills south of the river to provide covering fire for the withdrawal of the trapped Belgian unit.

But Randolph was not the only "eager war correspondent." Bernard Ullmann, a French civilian and correspondent for the Agence France Presse had also come along in what Randolph later reported was a "spur of the moment" decision. Weyand had explained to both men that his battalion was expecting to confront a large enemy force and tried to dissuade them, but eventually relented and reluctantly granted permission for both men to accompany his soldiers.

Ullmann was a veteran reporter who had already seen war first-hand. The son of Jewish bourgeoise, he was born in Paris, France, on January 13, 1922. His mother later divorced, and then remarried journalist Ferdinand de Brinon. His mother's second marriage gave Ullmann opportunity to meet some of the most prominent and famous people in Paris. Brinon was later destined to play an important role in  the pro-Axis Vichy government, and, after World War II concluded, was convicted of treason, sentenced to death, and shot in 1947. When France fell to the Germans in 1940 and Brinon went onto the side of the Axis, the rebellious young Ullman joined the Allies. As a twenty-year-old correspondent, he had even been given permission at one point to fly aboard a U.S. Army Air Forces Marauder bomber assigned to strafe German ground troops.

Now Ullman was in Korea with fellow correspondent John Randolph, and both were observers as the Battle of the Imjin River was about to unfold. As night fell on the night of Monday, April 23, 1951, and temperatures were dropping into the mid-thirties, troopers of the 1st Battalion, 7th Infantry Regiment, were preparing to advance on the enemy in the vicinity of Onglon-dong, South Korea.

Weyand later described the action: *"Company B was stalled by the heavy Chinese resistance it encountered. Company A, on its left took its objective. The Chinese had to commit a reserve battalion against it, and thereby took pressure off a trapped*

Beyond Belief: True Stories of Civilian Heroes

Belgian battalion. Company B was ordered to withdraw. It was pitch black and the company was virtually surrounded."

Advancing over rugged, mountainous terrain to the crest of the hill objective, Company B came under heavy and sustained machine gun, mortar, and artillery fire, and suffered numerous casualties. Several men in the lead platoon fell in the open.

As Weyand recalled: *"With complete disregard for his safety, Mr. Randolph moved forward to carry these wounded men to less exposed positions where they could receive medical attention. All in all, I believe he made four trips. Several men in this battalion undoubtedly owe their lives to his efforts to get them immediate medical attention. When the company moved to the rear, out of the assembly area, Mr. Randolph, helping the wounded, was one of the last out."*

Randolph remained behind with the covering force as the Chinese infiltrated into the immediate area and began firing and throwing grenades from a distance of less than 100 yards. During this action, Platoon Sergeant Jay T. Bare was mortally wounded.

Again, disregarding his own safety, Randolph lifted the sergeant into his own jeep and drove through a hail of enemy fire. As Randolph reported in the story, he cabled the following day, *"The worst part was when we got down from the hill and had to run Chinese crossfire with the Chinese starting to attack from one side. I got a slug through my jeep hood and a moment later, a platoon sergeant was shot down by my right fender. We hauled him into the jeep and got him to the aid station. All in all, it was a bit of a mess."*

Although Platoon Sergeant Bare did not survive his wounds, John Randolph's efforts to help him won the admiration and respect of the entire battalion. Randolph's report of the battle modestly made no mention of his role, stating only that he *"helped carry some wounded."* It was only after Weyand read Randolph's account of that night that he decided to take action.

Writing a letter to the management of the AP, Weyand stated: *"Although his account was completely factual, his modesty obviously forbade mention of his own contributions. I am taking*

Mr. John Randolph and Mr. Bernrd Ullmann

action through Army channels to secure official recognition of his courageous actions under fire on behalf of my men. I thought however you would be personally interested in knowing the type of man you have working for you. . . . He has won himself a place in our hearts and he will always be welcome in our mess as a guest or in the line as our comrade.

"Later, when Company B returned under orders to the assembly area, another soldier was severely wounded by automatic weapons fire sweeping the terrain occupied by the unit. Again, Mr. Randolph braved intense hostile fire, rushed to the aid of the wounded man, picked up and carried him to his jeep, then drove through a hail of enemy fire to the aid station. During this heroic drive, his jeep was spattered by bullets from enemy weapons, but he reached the aid station safely. The courageous and aggressive action taken by Mr. Randolph reflects great credit on himself and the United States Army."

Baker Company lost two men killed, seven wounded, with the battalion suffering a total of thirty casualties. The next night, Randolph reported that *"the same battalion was attacked in a dug-in position by an extraordinary number of Chinese. The company I was with the night before counted 300 Chinese bodies in front of it the next morning. The next night they were fighting again. at the moment, two and a half weeks later, they are at the front again, patrolling every day into Chinese territory."*

For his own gallant leadership in the battle, Lieutenant Colonel Weyand was awarded the Silver Star. Further, he submitted eleven soldiers of his battalion for the Silver Star as well:

- Sergeant William A. Bonacci - Company B (2nd award)
- Private Lee Roy Calhoun – Company B
- Master Sergeant Jacob Frick – Company B
- Private First Class Tautomo Hironaga – HQ Company
- Master Sergeant Adam J. Michalski – Company A
- Captain (Infantry), [then 1Lt] Harley F. Mooney – Company A
- Private First Class Russel Merlin Odberg – Company C (Posthumous)
- Private William W. Pearson – Company C
- Corporal Milos S. Polovina – Company A

Beyond Belief: True Stories of Civilian Heroes

- First Lieutenant (Infantry) George O. Rabideau – Company C
- First Lieutenant (Infantry) Robert K. Williams – Company A

Weyand had not, however, forgotten the two war correspondents who had been with him and his men on that horrible night. On September 19, 1951, Gen. James A. Van Fleet presented Randolph with the Silver Star medal.

The President of the United States of America, authorized by Act of Congress July 9, 1918, takes pleasure in presenting the Silver Star to Mr. John Randolph, a United States Civilian, for gallantry in action as a Correspondent, Associated Press, in action at Ongion-dang, Korea, on 23 April 1951. Voluntarily attaching himself to Company B, 7th Infantry Regiment, during an attack against an estimated regiment of Chinese Communists, heedless of the risk involved, he proceeded four times through heavy enemy fire to pick up and carry wounded riflemen to places of safety. Later, when Company B returned under orders to the assembly area, another soldier was severely wounded by automatic weapons fire sweeping the terrain occupied by the unit. Again, Mr. Randolph braved intense hostile fire, rushed to the aid of the wounded man, picked up and carried him to his jeep, then drove through a hail of enemy fire to the aid station. During this heroic drive, his jeep was spattered by bullets from enemy weapons, but he reached the aid station safely. The courageous and aggressive action taken by Mr. Randolph reflects great credit on himself and the United States Army.

Randolph would remain in the front lines for the remainder of the Korean War, as did French journalist Bernard Ullmann. He, too, had not been forgotten by Lieutenant Colonel Weyand, for Randolph had not been the only heroic civilian on the field of battle that day. In 1953, Ullmann was also awarded the Silver Star.

During the Korean War, 457 newspapermen and women covered war. with six of them winning Pulitzer Prizes. Eighteen

Mr. John Randolph and Mr. Bernrd Ullmann

newsmen (seventeen UN, one South Korean) were killed in action and three (Maurice Charrieloup, Frank "Pappy" Noel and Phillip Deanne) were Prisoners of War, held in captivity by the Communists for three years. But Randolph and Ullmann are the only two civilian journalists to be awarded a Silver Star in the Korean War.

The President of the United States of America, authorized by Act of Congress July 9, 1918, takes pleasure in presenting the Silver Star to Mr. Bernard Ullmann, a French Civilian, for gallantry in action as a French Correspondent, Agence France Presse, attached to Company B, 7th Infantry Regiment, in action against an armed enemy of the United Nations near Onglon-dong, Korea, on 23 April 1951. Advancing over rugged, mountainous terrain to the crest of the hill objective, Company B came under vicious machine gun and rifle fire at approximately 2000 hours and suffered numerous casualties. Fully aware of the danger involved, Mr. Ullmann left his place of comparative safety and repeatedly crossed open, fire-swept terrain to aid and evacuate the wounded from the path of the rapidly advancing enemy. After darkness had descended and upon orders to withdraw, Mr. Ullman continued to pursue his heroic, self-imposed task until all the wounded had been removed from the area. Mr. Ullman's intrepid actions saved the lives of many wounded, and his unflinching courage and consummate concern for his fellow men reflect the highest credit on himself and the members of his profession.

After war, John Randolph was assigned as Associated Press News Editor in Tokyo, becoming Bureau Chief in 1956. He was a member of the Foreign Correspondents Club of Japan, serving as President from 1961–62. He became a general executive for the Associated Press before resigning in 1963 to work as a freelance journalist. He served as a member of the *New York Times* bureau early in the Vietnam War, again often reporting from the front.

Returning to Japan, he joined the editorial department of *Pacific Stars and Stripes* in Tokyo and was working there at the time of his death. On January 5, 1977, Randolph died of a heart attack while at home in his Tokyo apartment. He was fifty-seven years old.

Bernard Ullmann continued his adventurous, globe-trotting lifestyle as a journalist for Agence France-Presse for decades. He headed its offices in Beijing China, from 1959–1960); Moscow, Russia, from 1962–1977; and Washington, D.C. (1977–1987). He was an editorial advisor for *L'Express* magazine, and covered not only the war in Korea, but also the Bangladesh Liberation War. He was a member of the Albert-Londres Prize jury and authored several books. In addition to the U.S. Army Silver Star, he was awarded the Croix de guerre and Chevalier of the Légion d'honneur. He died December 31, 2008 at the age of eighty-six.

John Randolph understood, and had empathy for, the role of infantrymen in America's "Forgotten War," as the Korean War came to be called In one of his articles he wrote: *"The real tragedy is that our infantry have to go on doing that sort of thing day after day after day, and since we are so short of ground troops it amounts to a death sentence if a man has been at it long enough. The most shocking thing about the Korean War is that with a nation of 150,000,000, we have put the whole burden on less than 100,000 infantrymen."*

Mr. John Paul Vann

The Rise of the Phoenix

BY JIM FURLONG

If one were to call John Paul Vann an enigma it would probably be an understatement. He was born out of wedlock to a mother who was a prostitute, raised in hardscrabble living conditions, sent to an elite boarding school by a church minister later convicted as a pedophile, enlisted in World War II but the war ended before he saw combat. He was a logistics expert who shined during the Korean War. As a garrison soldier between the wars in Korea and Vietnam, he was investigated for moral shortcomings, and eventually resigned from the Army under this cloud. He went to Vietnam as a civilian for the U.S. Agency for International Development (USAID). He was a primary architect of the U.S. policy of Vietnamization, and he was the only known civilian who would lead U.S. military troops into battle in Vietnam. He was killed in action in 1972 and was posthumously awarded the Presidential Medal of Freedom and the Distinguished Service Cross for extraordinary heroism. He was the only civilian to receive the Distinguished Service Cross since World War II. Many accounts were written about Vann—probably the most widely read was the Pulitzer Prize winning *A Bright Shining Lie* by Neil Sheehan. When you consider the circumstances of his life, it is almost . . . well . . . *Beyond Belief.*

Vann was born in Norfolk, Virginia to Myrtle Lee Tripp and Johnny Spry on July 2, 1924, and was originally named John Paul

Beyond Belief: True Stories of Civilian Heroes

Tripp. He and his siblings grew up in impoverished circumstances in nearby Roanoke, Virginia. In 1929, when Vann was only five years old, Myrtle Lee married Aaron Frank Vann and young John Paul took his stepfather's surname. But it wasn't until 1942, thirteen years later, that Aaron Vann officially adopted John Paul. Initially attending public schools, Vann was able to enroll in a boarding school at Ferrum College sponsored by Garland Hopkins, a prominent Methodist minister at a church in Arlington, Virginia. Hopkins, however, was a troubled man in his own right. He was a pedophile who tended to seek out troubled boys much like Vann and committed suicide in 1962 while the adult John Vann was a guest in his home.

Vann graduated from Ferrum secondary school in 1941 and immediately began attending Ferrum Junior College, graduating in 1943. With World War II raging in Europe and the Pacific, Vann decided to seek out military life rather then return to his poverty-stricken roots.

Like many young boys during the 1920s and 1930s, Vann had seen barnstormers visit his communities and developed a passion for flying. So, when it came time to join the military in March 1943, Vann enlisted in the U.S. Army Air Forces, hoping to become a pilot. Unable to complete pilot training, he was shifted to Navigation School. He completed Navigation School and was commissioned a second lieutenant in February 1945. By this time World War II was nearly over and Vann never saw combat. He chose to remain in the military but when the U.S. Air Force was created as a separate branch of service in 1947, he opted to remain in the Army as an infantryman and specialized in logistics.

After segueing into the Army and receiving requisite infantry training, Vann went to Fort Benning to attended jump school and became a paratrooper. He eventually was assigned to the 25th Infantry Division, then part of the Allied Occupation Forces in Japan on the Island of Honshu.

KOREAN WAR

On June 25, 1950, the Korean War began when close to 100,000 well-equipped and well-trained North Korean troops stormed across the border into the Republic of South Korea. The 25th Infantry Division was alerted that it would deploy to Korea by the first week of July. Vann, as part of the logistics team, was part of the advance party landing on Pusan on July 8, less than two weeks after the invasion.

By July 18 the entire 25th Infantry Division was in place in Korea. It had been a massive and herculean effort to move an entire Army division in only three weeks. The division was immediately put into combat as the North Korean Army was quickly sweeping across the whole of South Korea. The U.S. 24th Infantry Division and South Korean forces were falling back to form a defensive position around the critical deep port of Pusan and its essential port facilities in the southeastern part of South Korea.

Most of the 25th's soldiers were placed in blocking positions in the Hwaggan-Sangju-Hamchang area, where they were engaged in fierce battles beginning on July 24. Despite a valiant defense, the North Korean Army continued its relentless advance and the U.S. 24th Division, 25th Division, and South Korean ROK (Republic of Korea) forces fell back even further until the perimeter solidified. You can see in this map that by this time the North Koreans occupied more than 90 percent of South Korea.

The North Koreans, in their rush to essentially create a Dunkirk-like scenario, overran their resupply capabilities and left very few troops to protect their rear, probably reasoning that United Nations forces were in front of them, and nothing was behind them. But when the Pusan Perimeter held, it left North Korea with a glaring vulnerability which General Douglas MacArthur, commander in chief of United Nations ground forces organized to repel the North Korean invasion, would soon exploit.

Beyond Belief: True Stories of Civilian Heroes

Meanwhile, military commanders on the Pusan Perimeter realized they had their own vulnerabilities that were being exploited. North Korean agents began to infiltrate behind UN lines to attack military targets and cities. The UN units, untrained in combating guerrilla warfare and spread thinly along the Pusan Perimeter, were having difficulties repelling these North Korean infiltration units that were special forces troops like the North Korean 766th Independent Infantry Unit that had been successful in defeating ROK troops.

After World War II, elite U.S. Army Ranger units were disbanded as part of the general demobilization of the military, because they were too costly to maintain. But with the defeat of the ROK troops in the Battle of Pohang-dong, U.S. commanders felt that recreating Ranger-type units was essential to beginning a counteroffensive. This led Army Chief of Staff General J. Lawton Collins to order the creation of an elite force which could *"infiltrate through enemy lines and attack command posts, artillery, tank parks, and key communication centers and facilities."*

In early August, the EIGHTH U.S. Army ordered Lieutenant Colonel John H. McGee, the head of G-3 Operations Miscellaneous Division, to seek volunteers for a new experimental Army Ranger unit. McGee was given only seven weeks to organize and train the unit before it was sent into combat. Volunteers were solicited only from existing EIGHTH Army combat units in Korea. From the EIGHTH Army Replacement Pool McGee recruited Second Lieutenant Ralph Puckett, newly commissioned from West Point and with no combat experience, to serve as the company commander of the EIGHTH Army Ranger Company.

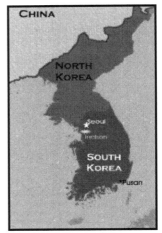

Back in Tokyo, General MacArthur and his staff were finalizing plans for a counteroffensive to exploit the vulnerabilities of the North Koreans. It would involve a daring amphibious landing far from Pusan at Inchon, which was a natural fortress port closer to the South Korean capital of Seoul. If successful, the UN forces would trap the enemy in a pincer attack.

Mr. John Paul Vann

Many Generals of MacArthur's staff thought the Inchon landing would be too risky but General MacArthur insisted it would work and plans were set in motion for the Counteroffensive. MacArthur viewed the plan for the landing as a great opportunity to change the course of the war. His advocacy shepherded the bold Inchon landing plan over the objection of the Joint Chiefs of Staff back at the Pentagon.

MacArthur activated the X Corps to take part in the landings. Led by Major General Edward Mallory "Ned" Almond, the X Corps was composed of the 7th Infantry Division, the 1st Marine Division and South Korean Army troops. On September 15, 1950, the soldiers, sailors and Marines of X Corps landed at Inchon. Even though the Inchon plans had been leaked in the media and throughout Japan, North Korea was still unprepared for the landing as most of their forces were fighting in the far South of Korea, concerned with breaking through the Pusan Perimeter. Key objectives in and around Inchon were taken with far fewer casualties than even the most optimistic estimates. MacArthur's big gamble was a success.

After the fall of Inchon, UN forces focused on the South Korean capital of Seoul—an objective twenty-five miles to the east of Pusan. The Han River and more than 20,000 North Korean troops occupying the city made capturing it more difficult. With the 7th Infantry Division on the 1st Marine Division's southern flank, the Marines were able to fight toward Seoul. By September 22, 1950, the X Corps reached Seoul's western edge. A hard fight for the city ensued. On September 29, 1950, the city fell to the UN forces. A brief ceremony gave control of the city to South Korean President Syngman Rhee.

Concurrently, back at the Pusan Perimeter, Second Lieutenant John Paul Vann was promoted to captain on September 13, 1950. As part of its counteroffensive, the U.S. 25th and 24th Divisions and South Korean troops were breaking out of their defensive positions on the Pusan Perimeter and advancing north.

The EIGHTH Army Ranger Company commanded by First Lieutenant Ralph Puckett joined the 25th Infantry Division at Taejon, as part of the U.S. IX Corps. Their first assignment was to

Beyond Belief: True Stories of Civilian Heroes

probe north to Poun, and begin a northward sweep to join up with U.S. X Corps. The troop rapidly moved 175 miles to Kaesong where they eliminated the last North Korean resistance south of the 38th parallel.

On November 23, the 25th Infantry Division rested in preparation for the final advance to the Yalu River in North Korea, while the EIGHTH Army Ranger Company scouted five kilometers north of the planned departure point, encountering no enemy troops. On November 25, the 25th Division and the attached EIGHTH Army Ranger Company ran into Chinese resistance. The resistance was light and they eventually captured their objective—Hill 205. The Rangers then established a perimeter on Hill 205 and spent the rest of the daylight hours fortifying their positions. Unknown at the time to the U.N. forces, the Chinese Second Phase Offensive would be launched that evening as 300,000 Chinese Communist troops had swarmed into Korea.

That night the first troops of the Chinese 39th Army moved against the Rangers on Hill 205. The first attack was mounted by a force estimated at only platoon size, and the well-entrenched Rangers were able to repulse the attack in less than an hour. Several Rangers were wounded including Company Commander Puckett. Puckett, however, refused evacuation, choosing to stay with his troops. At 11:00 p.m. a second attack, quickly followed by a third assault, struck the Rangers—this time the force was estimated to be company size. Thanks to their well-fortified defensive positions these attacks were repelled, but at the cost of dwindling ammunition supplies.

Although there was a platoon of American tanks at the foot of the hill opposite the Chinese attacks, they were not trained in night operations and could not be used effectively. At 11:30 p.m. the Chinese began attacking in greater numbers—this time an estimated two Chinese infantry companies were attacking and were able to move within hand grenade range. The beleaguered Rangers, their commander wounded a second time and unable to move, and with casualties mounting, turned back a fourth and fifth attack. With ammunition nearly depleted the Rangers were ordered to fix bayonets while awaiting the sixth attack.

At 2:45 a.m. the Chinese began a sixth and final attack with a heavy mortar barrage which inflicted a heavy toll on the remaining Rangers. It was mounted by a reinforced battalion of Chinese infantry, while other U.N. forces along the front were also being attacked, limiting the amount of artillery support for the Rangers. With their overwhelming numbers, Chinese forces quickly seized Hill 205. Puckett ordered his men to retreat from the hill to safety, imploring them to leave him behind as he felt he would be a burden to move. His men refused this order and three of them wrestled Puckett out of his foxhole and moved to the bottom of the hill. There, First Sergeant Charles L Pitts, the highest-ranking unwounded member of the company, withdrew from the battle.

The Rangers suffered over eighty percent casualties on Hill 205. Of the fifty-one who initially captured the hill, ten were killed or missing and thirty-one were wounded.[5] For his heroic efforts, Puckett was recommended for a Medal of Honor but that was downgraded to a Distinguished Service Cross. Seventy-one years later, however, after a review of military records, the Medal of Honor was finally approved, It was presented to ninety-five-year-old Ralph Puckett by President Joe Biden at the White House on May 21, 2021.

The President of the United States of America takes pleasure in presenting the Medal of Honor to First Lieutenant (Infantry) Ralph Puckett, Jr. (ASN: 0-59165), United States Army. First Lieutenant Puckett distinguished himself by acts of gallantry and intrepidity above and beyond the call of duty, while serving as the Commander, 8th U.S. Army Ranger Company during the period of 25 November 1950 through 26 November 1950, in Korea. As his

[5] "ARSOF in the Korean War, Part I and Part II" *Veritas: Journal of Army Special Operations History,* Fort Bragg, North Carolina: United states Army Special Operations Command, 2010

unit commenced a daylight attack on Hill 205, the enemy directed mortar, machine gun, and small arms fire against the advancing force. To obtain supporting fire, First Lieutenant Puckett mounted the closest tank, exposing himself to the deadly enemy fire. Leaping from the tank, he shouted words of encouragement to his men and began to lead the Rangers in the attack. Almost immediately, enemy fire threatened the success of the attack by pinning down one platoon. Leaving the safety of his position with full knowledge of the danger, First Lieutenant Puckett intentionally ran across an open area three times to draw enemy fire, thereby allowing the Rangers to locate and destroy the enemy positions and to seize Hill 205. During the night, the enemy launched a counterattack that lasted four hours. Over the course of the counterattack, the Rangers were inspired and motivated by the extraordinary leadership and courageous example exhibited by First Lieutenant Puckett. As a result, five human wave attacks by a battalion strength enemy element were repulsed. During the first attack, First Lieutenant Puckett was wounded by grenade fragments, but refused evacuation and continually directed artillery support that decimated attacking enemy formations, repeatedly abandoned positions of relative safety to make his way from foxhole to foxhole to check the company's perimeter, and distribute ammunition amongst the Rangers. When the enemy launched a sixth attack, it became clear to First Lieutenant Puckett that the position was untenable due to the unavailability of supporting artillery fire. During this attack, two enemy mortar rounds landed in his foxhole, inflicting grievous wounds which limited his mobility. Knowing his men were in a precarious situation, First Lieutenant Puckett commanded the Rangers to leave him behind and evacuate the area. Feeling a sense of duty to aid him, the Rangers refused the order and staged an effort to retrieve him from the foxhole while still under fire from the enemy. Ultimately, the Rangers succeeded in retrieving First Lieutenant Puckett and they moved to the bottom of the hill, where First Lieutenant Puckett called for devastating artillery fire on the top of the enemy controlled hill. First Lieutenant Puckett's extraordinary heroism and selflessness above and beyond the call of duty were in keeping with the highest traditions of military service and reflect great credit upon himself, his unit, and the United States Army.

Nine days after the retreat from Hill 205, on December 5, 1950, newly promoted Captain John Paul Vann assumed command of the EIGHTH Army Ranger Company. Because the ranks had been decimated from the Hill 205 fighting, the Rangers were only capable of being used to conduct routine patrols, or as a security force for divisional headquarters elements. With the company's casualties being replaced by regular soldiers with no Ranger training, it was nowhere close to being combat ready as a Ranger unit.

Under Captain Vann the company did participate in a few isolated missions from late 1950 into early 1951. They helped recapture Ganghwa Island from Chinese forces and joined the 25th Infantry Division in Operation **Killer** in late February as part of an effort to force Chinese troops north of the Han River.

In August 1950, Vann's wife, Mary Jane, gave birth to their son, Jesse Vann. Jesse had medical issues almost from the beginning of life. This resulted in Captain Vann being recalled from Korea on March 5, 1950, and sent home to care for his family's needs.

When Jesse recovered sufficiently, Vann was assigned to the 16th Infantry Regiment in Schweinfurt, West Germany, to command the regiment's Heavy Mortar Company. While there he received an evaluation from the Regimental Commander Colonel Bruce Palmer, Jr. as *"one of the few highly outstanding officers I know."* Palmer was later promoted to general, and he and Vann would reunite in Vietnam.

GARRISON DUTY

In 1955 Vann was promoted to major and reassigned to the U.S. Army Europe headquarters in Heidelberg, where he once again worked in Logistics. He returned to the United States in 1957 to attend the Command and General Staff College at Fort Leavenworth, Kansas. This assignment was deemed necessary to receive further promotions for a career officer like Vann—especially one who hoped to receive a general's stars on his shoulders. While working on his MBA and enrolled at Syracuse University in New York in May 1959, Vann was notified that he was being investigated of charges of having an affair with his underage babysitter.

When Vann completed his MBA at the end of July, he was assigned to Fort Jay, New York, rather than the Pentagon as his previous orders stated. Two weeks after graduation, the CID submitted an extensive report recommending that he be court-

Beyond Belief: True Stories of Civilian Heroes

martialed for adultery. The adultery charge was a misdemeanor charge included under the guise of *"conduct unbecoming an officer and a gentleman."* Vann's wife Mary Jane was listed as the victim in that charge. Although a misdemeanor, Conduct Unbecoming an Officer is a sufficiently serious charge that could lead to being dishonorably discharged from the military.

First Army headquarters appointed a Judge Advocate General attorney to conduct an Article 32 proceeding, the military equivalent of a grand jury. And, like a grand jury indictment, the burden of proof for an Article 32 does not require proof beyond a reasonable doubt, but only that the evidence is sufficient to go forth with a trial. Until his fate was adjudicated, Vann was assigned as deputy comptroller at Camp (later Fort) Drum, in upstate New York. Ultimately, the investigating officer recommended dropping the charges. First Army headquarters took until mid-December to concur with the investigating officer's recommendation. Nonetheless, it was a stigma that would hang like a cloud over the remainder of his military career.

Meanwhile, in the cold of the upstate New York winter, Mary Jane developed a bad cough and began to spit up blood. She went to the dispensary at Camp Drum and the results showed she had tuberculosis. Mary Jane had a friend in the Pentagon Personnel Section while they were still awaiting the results of the Article 32 investigation who asked if he could help. Mary Jane asked how the cold, damp weather was affecting her health, and asked if Vann could be dispatched to a warmer, drier climate. The friend, who understood the strains in the marriage, said her wish would be granted.

Vann won early promotion to lieutenant colonel in May 1961 and expected to become a "full bird" colonel before his contemporaries. But he knew no matter how superior he was, he would never receive the stars he so admired because even though the charges were dropped, they were on record, and the accusations themselves cast sufficient enough of a shadow over his career. Unlike the burden of proof in a trial, a promotion board for general officers would not have the same burden of proof as a court-martial. The General Promotion Board would look unkindly on the charges and invariably deny Vann the promotion he so badly wanted. With that in mind, he promised himself he would retire when he completed his twenty years in 1963.

But first a tour of duty in Vietnam was in order.

VIETNAM WAR (1962 – 1963)

When Vann arrived for duty in Saigon, he reported to Colonel David Porter, Senior U.S. Advisor to ARVN III Corps. MACV (Military Assistance Command, Vietnam) was headed by General Paul Harkins. MACV was newly formed and consisted of about 11,000 troops, mostly advisors.

From almost the minute he landed on South Vietnam's soil, John Paul Vann noticed the glaring difference between reality and the rosy and overinflated casualty reports coming from the desk jockeys back in Saigon. Vann was a leader who led from the front so when a battle was raging in his area of operations he would more often than not jump in a military spotter aircraft and begin to circle the battlefield. He knew what was *really* going on in the battlefield., and he saw disconnect between truth and "body count."

Author's Note:

I was an infantry squad leader in South Vietnam, and I could see how easily these numbers could become inflated. For instance, one time at a Fire Support Base I was at, the enemy tried to overrun our position. After we had successfully defended our position and stopped the attack there were parachute flares (it was nighttime) going off overhead to provide illumination. I was asked to provide a body count, so I looked out in front of my position and reported a good faith count. I don't remember the number but let's say it was 150. My superiors asked the same question of the squad leaders to my immediate left and right. They also said 150 each. So, with only three positions, the body count was 450. But here's where the inflated numbers come in. Tactics demand that defensive positions have overlapping "fields of fire." So the question becomes, how many of the 150 bodies were double counted since my peer squad leaders could see some of the same bodies I could see. Further, how many squad leaders would tell the Commanding Officer what he wanted to hear. Maybe they reported 200. The possibilities for error are endless. And by sunrise the next day, virtually all the bodies were gone – removed from the battlefield by the enemy. So, a body count is useless at that point except it eventually gets reported as fact.

Beyond Belief: True Stories of Civilian Heroes

Leaning on Vann's specialty in logistics, he was given responsibility to organize a supply system for the Army of the Republic of Vietnam (ARVN) forces. That system was hugely successful and soon supplies that once wallowed in red tape and took weeks and months to be delivered, were flowing to the proper units. After this success, Porter assigned Vann as the American adviser to Colonel Huynh Van Cao, commander of the ARVN 7th Division, who later became corps commander.

Lt. Col. John Paul Vann and General Huynh Van Cao, commander of the ARVN's Seventh Division

When Vann came to Vietnam, he was a strong proponent of the war, seeing the effort as necessary to stop the advance of communism in Asia. But he had an uncanny ability to see the big picture because he wanted to lead from the front, and he was not unafraid to fly a helicopter in to visit local tribal chiefs to get their view of the situation.

"The more Vann came to understand the political situation in Saigon, the more he became disenchanted with the way President Diem was running the country. It was an open secret in Saigon and Washington that the Diem government was rife with corruption. Vann witnessed firsthand how Diem refused to implement needed political and military reforms and how his corrupt brother, Ngo Dinh Nhu, rewarded friends in the military. Seeing how badly the Diem regime was responding to the ever-growing Communist threat, and the lack of military progress against the VC, Vann decided he had to tell his superior officers, and anyone else who would listen, just how badly things were going in Vietnam.

"It had become obvious to some of the Americans at MACV by late 1962 that the war on the ground was not going right.

Instead of learning from mistakes or correcting the situation, many of the senior officers around MACV's General Harkins had begun to rein in any officers who were deviating from the playbook. Vann, however, publicly called the January 1963 battle of Ap Bac a defeat for American and ARVN forces and "a miserable damn performance." Harkins almost fired him, giving him a severe tongue-lashing. From that day forward, Vann was persona non grata at MACV headquarters in Saigon."[6]

A major turning point in Vann's evolution from War Hawk to MACV and Pentagon critic came with the Battle of Ap Bac that commenced on January 2, 1963. Not really much bigger than a firefight, this battle involving several ARVN battalions with about 1,000 troops each that were unable to defeat a few hundred entrenched enemy troops. From his perch in a helicopter a few hundred feet above the battle, Vann watched with increasing frustration as ARVN commanders continuously hesitated and were reluctant to bring the battle to the enemy despite the superior numbers of the ARVN forces.

Compounding Vann's frustration was the fact that he drew up the battle plan and knew it to be sound. He felt the ARVN commanders and their troops did not have the initiative to counterattack a numerically inferior enemy. It was later said that a spy had leaked the attack to the enemy. Regardless, Vann felt the plan was still sound, but had not been executed properly because of hesitation on the part of the ARVN commanders.

"In his reports, Vann used statistical analysis methods to show that the South Vietnamese government was grossly inflating VC body counts, further infuriating his superiors. Vann also incurred the wrath of his superiors by stating openly that the ARVN troops would not risk conducting search-and-destroy missions but instead assumed defensive positions whenever possible. He further angered senior military leaders by his association and friendship with two young American reporters in Saigon, David Halberstam and Neil Sheehan. Vann shared his misgivings with them, and they in turn filed news reports of alleged

---

[6] Peter Kross, *John Paul Vann: Man and Legend,* History Net.com, February 20, 2007

Beyond Belief: True Stories of Civilian Heroes

ARVN ineptitude. Vann was also strident in his criticisms of the Strategic Hamlet Program, which he thought was a waste of time and energy, and he was critical of the way MACV ran counterintelligence operations.

"Harkins had finally had enough. In April 1963 Vann returned to America. When he arrived in Washington, he carried with him his final report as a senior adviser—a scathing critique of the way the war was being handled by the South Vietnamese armed forces. Few of the Pentagon's senior officials wanted to read his report, however.

"Vann's new assignment in the Pentagon involved managing the financial resources allocated to the Special Forces counterinsurgency program. He also interviewed many military officers who had been in Vietnam."[7]

Before leaving for Vietnam Vann realized his military career might be over, and started networking in the event he needed a career in civilian life. A mutual friend introduced Vann to recently retired Frank Brady, who had taken a job at Martin Marietta, a major defense contractor. While in El Paso, Texas, in early 1962, Brady and Vann met again and Vann reaffirmed his intention to retire after twenty years of service. Brady assured him that he could probably get him a job at Martin Marietta when he retired.

BETWEEN VIETNAM TOURS

Shortly after returning to the Pentagon, Vann flew to Denver, Colorado, to interview with Brady. Secure in the knowledge that he would be employed after retirement, he submitted his retirement papers to separate on July 31, 1963. Vann began working at Martin Marietta as an executive in charge of sales presentations. Shortly thereafter he realized what a mistake he had made. In his mind, the military career was far superior to anything he could achieve in civilian life. There were no stars given out in civilian life. Outwardly he was making a successful transition at Martin Marietta. Inwardly he was feeling crushed by both the monotony of the job and continuing problems at home. Mary Jane's issues had gotten worse.

---

[7]Ibid

210

Vann contacted some friends in the military in the hopes of getting his commission back. Major General Bob York wrote around Christmas 1963 that he was returning to the states to take command of the 82nd Airborne Division. York offered Vann command of a battalion and he jumped at the chance. The Army, however, was less than overjoyed and denied his request to return. When asked the reason, the general in charge of officer personnel at the Pentagon told General York that Vann's request to return to active status was denied because he knew that Chief of Staff General Maxwell Taylor and Defense Secretary Robert McNamara would disapprove. Vann then appealed to old friend Bruce Palmer, by then a major general and senior to York. General Palmer was unable to help either. It seems Vann's past marital indiscretions and/or abrasive, confrontational style led to this decision.

Vann was living with his civilian mentor Garland Hopkins, the Methodist minister who had saved Vann from poverty of his childhood. Hopkins had since been convicted of pedophilia. Distraught over having lost his family and ministerial career, and facing certain jail time, Hopkins took his own life. Vann found the body when he returned to the home one evening with a note containing burial instructions specifically meant for Vann to execute—particularly the obituary.

RETURN TO VIETNAM AS A CIVILIAN

Although Vann had a relatively successful career in two years at Martin Marietta, he longed to be back in Vietnam. He got his wish and returned to Vietnam in March 1965 as a civilian official of the Agency for International Development. After a brief assignment as province senior adviser, Vann was made Deputy for Civil Operations and Rural Development (CORDS) in the Third Corps Tactical Zone of Vietnam, which consisted of the twelve provinces north and west of Saigon—the part of South Vietnam most important to the United States. CORDS was an integrated group that consisted of USAID, U.S. Information Service, Central Intelligence Agency, and State Department, along with U.S. Army personnel to provide needed manpower. Among other undertakings, CORDS was responsible for the Phoenix Program, which targeted the assassination of Viet Cong leaders.

Beyond Belief: True Stories of Civilian Heroes

It was September 10, 1965, that Vann submitted a paper to his superiors on the problems and issues he saw with the war in Vietnam. Entitled *"Harnessing the Revolution in South Vietnam,"* the paper gave the first inkling of what a program of *"Vietnamization"* would look like.

In it, Vann noted that the existing Government of Vietnam (GVN, South Vietnam) was top heavy with wealthy Vietnamese, and operated from Saigon. He noted that these wealthy individuals were the ones with the "most to lose" should the communist National Liberation Front (NLF) run by North Vietnamese leader Ho Chi Minh, successfully gained control of the GVN. He further excoriated the GVN for paying "lip service" to the needs of the rural populace with whom the NLF seemed to be gaining substantial ground. Vann saw the rural populace as the key to the war and revolution and believed that the Viet Cong currently had the advantage there.

The paper was more of a concept paper but did propose setting up *"three or more test provinces"* with the goal of decentralizing authority from the ministries in Saigon to the test provinces. *"Fundamental to this proposal is the long-range objective of developing a political base from which a national government will emerge that is responsive to the dynamics of the social revolution now in progress. GVN has demonstration that it cannot establish stability, even with dictatorial powers, let alone achieve a popular base among the people. On the other hand, a representative type of government is not now possible that would be capable of dealing with the externally stimulated and backed aggression; indeed, over half the population is not even accessible without a military operation. We are therefore faced with the dichotomy of having to maintain an autocratic government while laying the foundation for a democratically oriented one. . . ." "Our current emphasis upon military action to strengthen GVN at all levels, but particularly at village and district levels."*[8]

It does not seem that this concept paper was ever implemented, even with the so-called test of three provinces. But

---

[8] John Paul Vann, *Harnessing the Revolution in South Vietnam* unpublished concept paper, September 10, 1965, South Vietnam

seven years before the United States withdrew its troops in favor of Vietnamization, the seeds of the plan to decentralize the war in order to gain support throughout the whole of Vietnam were first verbalized.

While the geopoliticians in Washington saw the conflict in Vietnam as democracy versus communism, from the very beginning John Paul Vann saw it as a social revolution occurring in real-time. He realized the United States was backing the wrong horse in supporting the corrupt, feudal South Vietnamese government. He realized that although the GVN could secure the bigger cities like Saigon, it was losing in the rural countryside. To win the war the Americans needed to win the hearts and minds of the people outside the cities—and you couldn't do that with a military strategy of attrition —a strategy that meant B-52 carpet bombing, and large-scale artillery bombardments in the rural countryside.

Vann, the paradox that he was, was too confrontational to his superiors and was viewed as a "hair shirt." To compensate for his inability to sway his military superiors, Vann began to leak information to the reporters who were covering the war in Vietnam for American newspapers. He befriended David Halberstam, Neil Sheehan, and Daniel Ellsberg. Ellsberg became famous, or infamous, for the anti-Vietnam War **Pentagon Papers**, published in the *New York Times*. For Vann, the problem was in Saigon—not the war itself. It was the corruption, and the nepotism, which was turning the Vietnamese populace away from the GVN. Winning the war while pursuing this strategy was hopeless.

Vann made numerous trips to Washington to brief superiors, sometimes even the Chiefs of Staff or their staffs. Shortly after the Tet offensive he penned a memo to his boss Leroy Wehrle, who at the time was Deputy Director—Vietnam Bureau for the Agency for International Development.

Regarding briefings with Undersecretary of State for East Asian Affairs Phillip

Beyond Belief: True Stories of Civilian Heroes

Habib, Chairman Joint Chiefs of Staff General Earle Wheeler, and U.S. Ambassador to South Vietnam Ellsworth Bunker in which Vann stated *"(They) received a considerably different evaluation of the events of the last five weeks than they had received through MACV channels. (They) seemed to accept that fact that the MACV reporting system had a built-in upgrading factor which makes military assessments far more optimistic than is justified.*

Despite this, he agreed with the assessment that the Viet Cong had strategically and militarily been terribly beaten and should be pursued but that the ARVN needed to come out of "their clenched up defensive positions."

They did not.

He felt the failures in Vietnam had been more than failures in the military. He was distressed that there did not seem to be any concentrated effort being made in the intelligence community to assess the reasons for the *"massive intelligence failures"* that occurred.

Finally, Vann *"found it strange that no significant responsible official on either the Vietnamese or the U.S. side is being relieved (of command) as a result of the VC Tet Offensive."*

But eventually Tet did catch up with American leaders. First, MACV General William Westmoreland's *"war of attrition"* strategy was discredited by the Tet Offensive. Eventually President Lyndon Johnson was the ultimate loser, deciding not to run for reelection for President in 1968.

Vann served as Deputy for Civil Operations and Rural Development Support CORDS III (i.e., commander of all civilian and military advisers in the Third Corps Tactical Zone) until November 1968, when was assigned to the same position in IV Corps, which consisted of the provinces south of Saigon in the Mekong Delta.

Vann was highly respected by a large segment of officers and civilians who were involved in the broader political aspects for the war because he favored small units performing aggressive patrolling instead of grandiose engagements by large units. Unlike many U.S. soldiers, he was respectful toward the ARVN soldiers notwithstanding their low morale, and was committed to training and strengthening their morale and commitment. He constantly briefed that the war in Vietnam must be envisaged as a long war at a lower level of engagement rather than a short war at a big-unit, high level of engagement.

After his assignment to IV Corps, Vann was assigned as the Senior American Advisor in II Corps Military Region in the early 1970's, when American involvement in the war was winding down and troops were being withdrawn. For that reason, his new job put him in charge of all United States personnel in this region, where he also advised the ARVN commander to the region and became the first American civilian to command U.S. regular troops in combat. His position was equivalent in

Brig. Gen. Nguyen Van Toan, ARVN II Corps Commander with Vann.

responsibilities to that of a major general in the U.S. Army. Vann didn't have the stars on his fatigues, but he was the commander of the troops.

VIETNAMIZATION

When Lyndon Johnson became president, he declared he would *"not be the first American President to lose a war."* While this statement may have been made from exasperation during his first days in office, it came to signify the "Americanization" of the war under Johnson.

When President Johnson took office Americans in Vietnam were only a few advisors, but by the election in 1968 more than 548,000 Americans were serving there, and already more than 30,000 Americans had died there. In the United States, protests over the war caused Johnson to rethink his position of American involvement in Vietnam. After the Tet Offensive in January 1968, he decided not to run for reelection. Despite a last-minute bombing halt in an effort to get Johnson's vice president Hubert Humphrey elected in November 1968, Richard Nixon won the election.

Beyond Belief: True Stories of Civilian Heroes

Nixon immediately saw the need to reduce American presence in Vietnam. The term *"Vietnamization"* was coined, according to Secretary of State Kissinger, during a January 28, 1969, meeting of National Security Council in the first week of the new Administration. General Andrew Goodpaster, deputy to MACV commander, General Creighton Abrams who had replaced Westmoreland, noted that the ARVN forces had been steadily increasing their competence and it might be time to de-Americanize the war. Secretary of Defense Melvin Laird agreed with the concept but not the term. Laird postulated *"What we need is a term like 'Vietnamizing' to put emphasis on the right issues."* Nixon was immediately drawn to Laird's suggestion.[9]

Vietnamization was a two-pronged policy. The first was strengthening the South Vietnamese forces supported with American equipment and supplies, and continuing to advise an enlarging ARVN force on the ground and with continued American air support above the ground. But the "feet on the ground" battles were to be borne of South Vietnamese forces.

The second part of the policy involved pacification. This was something that Vann had been advocating for since his 1965 paper on harnessing the social revolution in the countryside. Vann noted that we could not bomb the rural peasants into submitting to the South Vietnamese government but needed to win the peasantry's hearts and minds with pacification. Vann's ideas thus became part of official U.S. policy regarding the war in Vietnam.

After the Tet Offensive the North Vietnamese and the Viet Cong had pretty much expended all they had. As American troops withdrew, the ARVN took more responsibility for the conduct of the war. Save for the Cambodian invasion in 1970, the war had hit a lull as the North Vietnam's People's Army of Vietnam recovered from Tet and the ARVN tried to take over more of the war effort from the American military. In fact, with the Viet Cong cadre decimated, the war took on a more conventional tone, rather than the guerilla war that it had been. This was a benefit to the South Vietnam. However, in late 1971 and early 1972, the PAVN were victorious in Operation

---

[9] Kissinger, Henry (2003), *Ending the Vietnam War: a History of America's Involvement and extrication from the Vietnam War,* Simon and Schuster, pp. 81-82.

216

Lam Son 719. The PAVN decided that the time had come for large-scale conventional offensives that could end the war quickly. Hence, plans were drawn up for what would become known as the Easter Offensive.

Meanwhile, General Abrams finessed the military chain of command by making Vann a director and commander of the Second Regional Assistance Group (SRAG) with the equivalent rank of major general. Though technically still a civilian, in practical he was finally the commanding general of combat troops, in this case II Corps. And soon, he would be put to the test.

EASTER OFFENSIVE AND THE BATTLE OF KONTUM

The 1972 Easter Offensive Campaign began with a massive attack on the Demilitarized Zone in I Corps by 30,000 PAVN soldiers and more than 100 tanks. Two additional thrusts of equivalent size, one towards Saigon and a third to the Central Highlands and provincial capital of Kontum, began soon after. The North Vietnamese knew that if they could capture Kontum and the Central Highlands, they would cut South Vietnam in half..[10] The Battle for Kontum began on 13 May 1972 and pitted the ARVN 22nd and 23rd Divisions against the equivalent of three PAVN divisions, the 320th and 22nd Divisions, plus local Viet Cong forces.

North Vietnam had been using the Ho Chi Minh Trail along the Cambodian border as a logistical artery for years. The mountainous terrain and the jungle were natural shields against B-52 bombing. Vann had received intelligence that a major battle was coming and ordered increased B-52 strikes in February and March. Also, as a prelude to an impending attack on the Kontum fortress itself, several outlying Fire Support Bases in an area known as Rocket Ridge were attacked in early April. Since the start of the Easter Offensive the Kontum base area had come under increasing PAVN artillery and rocket fire, which had gone from thirty to fifty rounds per day in March, to up to 1000 per day by mid-April.

[10] Sheehan, Neil (1988) *A Bright Shining Lie: John Paul Vann and America in Vietnam*. New York. Random House, p. 754.

Beyond Belief: True Stories of Civilian Heroes

Two towns of significance stood between PAVN forces and Kontum: Tan Canh and Dak To. On the morning of April 23, the PAVN 2nd Division started their attack on Tan Canh by hitting ARVN tanks with AT-3 missiles. The regimental bunker took a direct hit injuring the senior U.S. advisor and several ARVN commanders. At 11:00 a.m. Vann landed to assess the situation and instructed the remaining U.S. advisors to prepare to escape and evade from the camp. At 7:00 p.m. PAVN rocket fire struck the ammunition dump, setting it on fire. At 9:00 p.m. a column of eighteen PAVN tanks was spotted in the area, and a U.S. Air Force C-130 gunship arrived at 11:00 p.m. to engage the North Vietnamese T-54 tanks with its 105-mm. cannon. Three T-54 tanks were disabled. At midnight the tank column turned towards Tan Canh and ARVN artillery commenced firing on the enemy tanks until stopped by PAVN counterbattery fire.

Just before 6:00 a.m. on April 24, the enemy attacked Tan Canh in two tank columns—one coming in the main gate and the other securing the airfield. Enemy artillery fire also successfully knocked out antennas at the command bunker. With the collapse of command and control on the base, American advisors abandoned the bunker and moved to new positions within the compound to attempt to call in airstrikes, but morning fog made that impossible.

An hour after the Tan Canh attack started, PAVN began their attack on Dak To. A Huey helicopter, attempting to evacuate American advisors was struck by anti-aircraft fire and crashed killing five of the 10 onboard. However, since the crash occurred outside the Dak To perimeter, the survivors had to evade capture with some not being repatriated until thirteen days later. Again, loss of command and control communications caused the U.S. advisors and ARVN troops to abandon the city to the south. As these troops attempted to cross the Dak Poko River they came under intense PAVN fire and senior U.S. Advisor Lieutenant Colonel Robert Brownlee disappeared and was listed as missing in action. With the loss of the main camps and remaining firebases along Rocket Ridge, the PAVN had clear sailing into Kontum.

After the loss of Dak To and Tan Canh, the PAVN had momentum on their side. But, whether because of logistical issues or just poor leadership that did not understand their advantage, the

PAVN waited three weeks before pressing on to Kontum. In the meantime, American forces dug in and fortified their positions. Outlying units were brought in to strengthen the defenses.

On May 13 the 1st Combat Aerial Team noticed signs of large troop movements to the north. At 10:30 p.m. that night, reports surfaced of lights moving down Route 14 toward Kontum. Captured documents stated that the attack would take place at 4:00 a.m. on May 14. It was suggested to Vann that he order an airstrike in preparation, but Vann noted that the artillery prep that had signaled previous attacks was absent. Another captured document indicated the attack had been moved back to 4:30 a.m. when suddenly the advisors realized the PAVN forces were operating on Hanoi time. Sure enough, the battle commenced at 5:30 a.m.—4:30 a.m. in Hanoi.

Attacking, for whatever reason, without the heavy artillery bombardment that had been used at Tan Canh and Dak To, the enemy drove straight down Route 14. Utilizing a pincer movement, PAVN Regiments attacked Kontum from the northwest, north and south. ARVN artillery began targeting the T-54 tanks moving down Route 14 and successfully destroyed two T-54 tanks with American supplied LAWs (Light, Anti-tank Weapons). The sky was overcast so jet fighter tactical air support was not available, but helicopters equipped with TOW anti-tank missiles were available and destroyed two more T-54 tanks before they could find cover in the jungle. By 9:00 a.m. the first PAVN attack had been thwarted.

For the next two weeks the battle see-sawed. PAVN advances were eventually thwarted and pushed back by ARVN forces augmented by U.S.-supplied artillery and tactical air support.

On May 28, PAVN occupied bunkers and buildings in sections of the city were too well fortified to be destroyed by air or artillery attacks. However, PAVN's ability to launch sustained attacks seemed to be spent. With U.S. and RVNAF air superiority, PAVN troops were not receiving adequate food and supplies from their bases in the jungle.

On June 6, PAVN mobilized their last reserve unit to cover the withdrawal of all remaining enemy troops within the town.

Beyond Belief: True Stories of Civilian Heroes

At this moment, and in these circumstances, Vietnamization *worked* in the Battle of Kontum, and in general it worked in putting down the Easter Offensive throughout Vietnam.

John Paul Vann one of the principal proponents of Vietnamization was basking in his success.

THE DEATH OF JOHN PAUL VANN

On June 9, 1972, the city of Kontum was officially declared safe and cleared of all NVA elements. It was a great victory for both the ARVN and Mr. Vann, senior advisor for II Corps. It was also the departure date for Brigadier General John Hill, deputy senior advisor to II Corps.

Mr. Vann was in Saigon that morning and scheduled to return to Pleiku in the evening to attend a party celebrating both the victory and Brigadier General Hill and Mrs. Hill's departure from Vietnam. After several toasts, Mr. Vann announced that he was going to depart Pleiku to spend the night in Kontum. Having visited the troops in Kontum every day during the battle, he did not want to forget them on the eve of their great victory.

The helicopter crew had been notified and First Lieutenant Ronald E. Doughtie, the pilot, was standing by the OH-58 helicopter at the team 21 helipad. Captain Robert A. Robertson, a passenger from Pleiku installation coordinator's office was also going along for the ride. No flight plan was prepared or filed with any known agency. First Lieutenant Doughtie did know that the weather enroute was marginal having commented on the fact to Captain Schwartz, U.S. Air Force pilot assigned to SRAG.

The aircraft departed Pleiku at approximately 8:50 p.m. and did not establish flight following with any known facility. At approximately 9:00 p.m. Mr. Vann contacted the advisors at Kontum and said he expected to land there in about fifteen minutes.

There is not much known from this point on − no distress call was heard by any of the aircraft operating in the vicinity. At approximately 9:30 p.m. it was reported by Task Force 14 that was clearing the highway to Kontum, that a helicopter had possibly crashed in the vicinity of Pao Mountain Pass. A check was conducted by 17th Group of all units having helicopters; none were flying. A check was made with SRAG and Mr. Vann's helicopter was reported out. A Search and Rescue (SAR) helicopter package of a Command and Control (C&C) aircraft, a lightship and a light fire team were launched in addition to an OV-10 Bronco reconnaissance airplane. U.S. Air Force SAR was notified, and a C-130 gunship was diverted to the scene as well.

Aerial flares proved ineffective due to the heavy trees and the lightship was put down to look for fires and wreckage. An aircraft fuselage was located in a stand of trees and ARVN soldiers vectored to the crash site.

Mr. Vann, whose body had been thrown clear of the wreckage, was put on board the C&C aircraft and flown to the 67th EVAC hospital. The other bodies were recovered the next morning, including those of First Lieutenant Doughtie and Captain Robertson.

POSTHUMOUS HONORS

President Nixon, whom Vann had briefed many times and who had great respect for Vann, awarded him the Presidential Medal of Freedom—the highest award this country gives to civilians. The citation reads:

> Soldier of peace and patriot of two nations, the name of John Paul Vann will be honored as long as free men remember the struggle to preserve the independence of South Vietnam. His military and civilian service in Vietnam spanned a decade, marked throughout by resourcefulness, professional excellence and unsurpassed courage, by supreme dedication and personal sacrifice. A truly noble American, a superb leader, he stands with Lafayette in that gallery of heroes who have made another brave people's cause their own.

For his heroism in battle, Vann also received the Distinguished Service Cross. As a civilian he was not eligible for the Medal of Honor and he became the only civilian since World War II to receive the Distinguished Service Cross.

Beyond Belief: True Stories of Civilian Heroes

The President of the United States of America, authorized by Act of Congress, July 9, 1918 (amended by act of July 25, 1963), takes pride in presenting the Distinguished Service Cross (Posthumously) to John Paul Vann, a United States Civilian, for extraordinary heroism and distinguished service as a U.S. civilian working with the Agency for International Development, United States State Department, in the Republic of Vietnam. Mr. Vann distinguished himself by extraordinary heroism in action during the period 23 April to 24 April 1972. During an intense enemy attack by mortar, artillery and guided missiles on the 22d Army of the Republic of Vietnam Division forward command post at Tan Canh, Mr. Vann chose to have his light helicopter land in order to assist the Command Group. After landing, he ordered his helicopter to begin evacuating civilian employees and the more than fifty wounded soldiers while he remained on the ground to assist in evacuating the wounded and provide direction to the demoralized troops. With total disregard for his own safety, Mr. Vann continuously exposed himself to enemy artillery and mortar fire. By personally assisting the wounded and giving them encouragement, he assured a calm and orderly evacuation. As the enemy fire increased in accuracy and tempo, he set the example by continuing to assist in carrying the wounded to the exposed helipad. His skillful command and control of the medical evacuation ships during the extremely intense enemy artillery fire enabled the maximum number of soldiers and civilians to be safely evacuated. On the following day the enemy launched a combined infantry tank team attack at the 22d Division Headquarters compound. Shortly thereafter, the Army of the Republic of Vietnam defense collapsed, enemy tanks penetrated the compound, and the enemy forces organized .51 caliber anti-aircraft positions in and around the compound area. To evade the enemy the United States advisors moved under heavy automatic weapons fire to an area approximately 500 meters away from the compound. Completely disregarding the intense small arms and .51 caliber anti-aircraft fire and the enemy tanks, Mr. Vann directed his helicopter toward the general location of the United States personnel, who were forced to remain in a concealed position. In searching for the advisors' location, his helicopter had to maintain an altitude and speed which made it extremely vulnerable to all forms of enemy fire. Undaunted, he continued his search until he located the advisors' position. Making an approach under minimal conditions he landed and quickly pulled three United States advisors into the aircraft. As the aircraft began to ascend, five Army of the Republic of Vietnam soldiers were clinging to the skids. Although the total weight far exceeded the maximum allowable for the light helicopter, Mr. Vann chose to save the Army of the Republic of Vietnam personnel holding on to the skids by having the helicopter maneuver without sharp evasive action. Consequently, the aircraft sustained numerous hits. In order to return to Tan Canh as soon as possible to save the remaining advisors and to save the soldiers clinging to the skids, Mr. Vann detoured his aircraft from Kontum to a nearby airfield. Throughout this time Mr. Vann was directing air strikes on enemy tanks and anti-aircraft positions. While en route back to Tam Canh, Mr. Vann's helicopter was struck by heavy anti-aircraft fire, which forced it to land. Throughout the day Mr. Vann assisted in extracting other advisors and soldiers in the Dak To area. On one such occasion another group of Army of the Republic of Vietnam soldiers attempted to cling to one side of his helicopter, caused it to crash. Undaunted by these occurrences, Mr. Vann continued directing air strikes and maneuvering friendly troops to safe areas. Because of his fearless and tireless efforts, Mr. Vann was directly responsible for saving hundreds of personnel from the enemy onslaught. His conspicuous gallantry and extraordinary heroic actions reflect great credit upon him and the United States of America

Mr. Joseph L. Galloway
War Correspondent—Bronze Star Recipient

By James G. Fausone

PROLIFIC

Reporter Joe Galloway was prolific, writing about what people needed to hear. Fate inserted him into Vietnam as a reporter at the start of the war. He saw firsthand the horrors and heroes of war and reported on the same. He chronicled American wars from Vietnam to Iraq prior to his retirement in 2010. He wrote with knowledge and passion. He often said he hated war but loved soldiers. He advised generals and wrote so mothers knew the challenges their boys faced. As Ernie Pyle, Pulitzer Prize war correspondent was to WWII reporting, Joe Galloway was to Vietnam war correspondents.

EARLY YEARS

Joe Galloway was born in Bryan, Texas, on November 13, 1941. Bryan had about 12,000 people in it when Joe was born. His father, Joseph L., fought in the U.S. Army during World War II. His mother was Marian Dewvall. His family relocated to Refugio, Texas, after his father was employed by Humble Oil upon his return from military service. Refugio had a population of 4,500; but after Hurricane Harvey hit in 2017 the population dropped to 2,700. This was the small Texas town from which grew a larger than life foreign war correspondent.

Joe explained his journalistic start on **Veterans Radio** in 2009. (Transcripts of the Veterans Radio's interviews of Galloway are used with permission. –Editors)

Beyond Belief: True Stories of Civilian Heroes

"I think I must have been born one. I worked on the school newspaper in high school. I helped start a competitive weekly in my hometown the summer I got out of high school and went off briefly to college. I was driven out of college by an early a.m. German language class taught by a portly lady with badly fitting dentures. In my view the class stood between me and joining the Army. I was seventeen. I had to browbeat my mother into agreeing to sign for me.

We were two blocks from the recruiting office in Victoria, Texas, when we passed the local newspaper. Mom said "Joe, what about your journalism?" I said, "Good call, Mom, stop the car." I had been their campus stringer for those few weeks and I walked in and asked if the editor had a job. He did and he hired me on the spot for $35 per week and a free subscription to the paper. I was on my way."

Thus started in 1958, a journalism career lasting until his retirement in 2010.

GOING TO THE ACTION

His start was humble at *The Victoria Advocate* in Victoria, Texas. However, Texas was not big enough to hold him. He moved to the United Press International (UPI) in Missouri and Kansas. UPI then sent him overseas as bureau chief and regional manager. He spent twenty-two years with UPI in locations such as Tokyo, Vietnam, Indonesia, India, Singapore, Moscow, and Los Angeles.

He arrived in Vietnam in 1965. This was a time of unbridled optimism that the United States would make a quick end to this war. General William Westmorland promised such to the American people.

In March 1965, the U.S. Air Force began to bomb North Vietnam—Operation **Rolling Thunder**. It began as over 100 American fighter-bombers attacked targets in North Vietnam. Scheduled to last eight weeks, **Rolling Thunder** would instead go on for three years.

This was also a time when the first U.S. air strikes also occurred against the Ho Chi Minh trail. Throughout the war the trail was heavily bombed by American jets with little actual success in halting the tremendous flow of soldiers and supplies from the North. 500 American jets were lost attacking the trail. After each attack, bomb damage along the trail was repaired.

During the entire war, the U.S. flew three million sorties and dropped nearly eight million tons of bombs, four times the tonnage dropped during World War II, in the largest display of firepower in the history of warfare. The majority of bombs were dropped in South Vietnam against Viet Cong and North Vietnamese Army positions. In North Vietnam, military targets included fuel depots and factories. The North Vietnamese reacted to the air strikes by decentralizing their factories and supply bases, thus minimizing their vulnerability to bomb damage.

BATTLE OF IA DRANG

In November 1965, the U.S. Army and North Vietnam's People's Army Vietnam (PAVN) met head-on for the first time in the Battle of Ia Drang. Both sides claimed victory; the Americans because of the heavy casualties inflicted on the enemy, and North Vietnamese leadership because it saw the strategic flaw in American tactical success—that its military could slowly grind down the U.S.'s commitment to the war.

Ia Drang is in the central highlands of Vietnam. The battle is notable for being the first large scale helicopter air assault and also the first use of Boeing B-52 Stratofortress strategic bombers in a tactical support role. Ia Drang set the blueprint for the Vietnam War with the Americans relying on air mobility, artillery fire, and

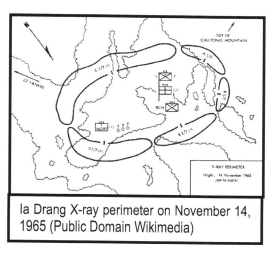

Ia Drang X-ray perimeter on November 14, 1965 (Public Domain Wikimedia)

close air support, while the PAVN neutralized that firepower by quickly engaging American forces at very close range.

Beyond Belief: True Stories of Civilian Heroes

Some 450 men of the First Battalion, Seventh Cavalry, under the command of then Lieutenant Colonel Harold Moore, were dropped into a small clearing in the Ia Drang Valley. They were immediately surrounded by 2,000 North Vietnamese soldiers. Three days later, only two and a half miles away, a sister battalion was brutally slaughtered. Together, these actions at the landing zones X-Ray and Albany constituted one of the most savage and significant battles of the Vietnam War.

This battle was seen as an opportunity to test a new theory of air mobility warfare by the U.S. Command. Air mobility called for battalion-sized forces to be delivered, supplied, and extracted from an area of action using helicopters. Since the heavy weapons of a normal combined-arms force could not follow, the infantry would be supported by coordinated close air support, artillery, and aerial rocket fire, arranged from a distance and directed by Forward Air Controllers (FACs) attached to ground units. The new tactics had been developed in the U.S. by the 11th Air Assault Division, which was renamed as the 1st Cavalry Division also known as *"Air Cav"* (Air Cavalry).

How these outnumbered Americans at Ia Drang persevered— sacrificing themselves for their comrades and never giving up against great odds —creates a vivid portrait of war at its most devastating and inspiring. Joseph L. Galloway was the only journalist with them on the ground throughout the fighting.

Joseph Galloway: (Todd J. Van Emst/Opelika-Auburn News via AP)

Thirty-three years later, in May 1998, Joe Galloway was awarded the Bronze Star with V device for helping to rescue a badly wounded soldier while under enemy fire on November 15, 1965, during the Battle of Ia Drang at Landing Zone X-Ray in Vietnam. His participation made him a beloved honorary member of **Air Cav.**

Mr. Joseph L. Galloway

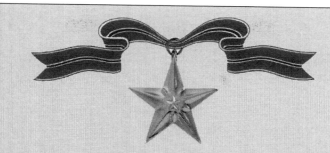

This is to certify that the President of the United States of America by Executive Order, 24 August 1962, has awarded the Bronze Star Medal with "V" device to Joseph L. Galloway for heroism while accompanying the 7th Cavalry Regiment. During the afternoon of 14 November 1965 a furious battle had been fought between the 1st Battalion, 7th Cavalry Regiment, and the 66th Regiment of the People's Army of Vietnam. Mr. Galloway voluntarily boarded a helicopter which landed at night on a hazardous resupply run into an active combat situation where he was determined to report to the world details of the first major battle of the Vietnam War. Early on 15 November 1965 in the fury of the action, an American fighter bomber dropped two napalm bombs on the Battalion Command Post and Aid Station area gravely wounding two soldiers. Mr. Galloway and a medical aid man rose, braving enemy fire, and ran to the aid of the injured soldiers. The medical aid man was immediately shot and killed. With assistance from another man, Mr. Galloway carried one of the injured soldiers to the medical aid station. He remained on the ground throughout the grueling three-day battle, frequently under fire, until the 1st Battalion, 7th Cavalry was replaced by other forces of the 1st Cavalry Division

Only a limited number of people are so noteworthy that their passing is memorialized in the *New York Times* or *Washington Post* obituaries. In the *Washington Post* obituary for Joe Galloway, the Battle of Ia Drang is recounted:

"In November 1965, journalist Joseph L. Galloway hitched a ride on an Army helicopter flying to the Ia Drang Valley, a rugged landscape of red dirt, brown elephant grass and truck-size termite mounds in the Central Highlands of South Vietnam.

Beyond Belief: True Stories of Civilian Heroes

Stepping off the chopper, he arrived at a battlefield that one Army pilot later called "hell on Earth, for a short period of time."

"Mr. Galloway, a 24-year-old reporter for United Press International, went on to witness and participate in the first major battle of the Vietnam War, in which an outmanned American battalion fought off three North Vietnamese army regiments while taking heavy casualties. He carried an M16 rifle alongside his notebook and cameras, and in the heat of battle, he charged into the fray to pull an Army private out of the flames of a napalm blast.

"At that time and that place, he was a soldier," Maj. Gen. Joseph K. Kellogg said more than three decades later, when the Army awarded Mr. Galloway the Bronze Star Medal for his efforts to save an injured private. "He was a soldier in spirit, he was a soldier in actions and he was a soldier in deeds."

Mr. Galloway later recounted the battle in a best-selling book, *We Were Soldiers Once ... and Young,* written with retired Lieutenant General. Harold G. Moore, the U.S. Army battalion commander at Ia Drang. The book was adapted into the movie "We Were Soldiers" starring Mel Gibson as Moore and Barry Pepper as Mr. Galloway. It was acclaimed for its unflinching account of one of the war's bloodiest battles.

"What I saw and wrote about broke my heart a thousand times, but it also gave me the best and most loyal friends of my life," Mr. Galloway said in an interview with the *Victoria Advocate*, the Texas daily where he had once worked as a cub reporter. "The soldiers accepted me as one of them, and I can think of no higher honor."

Joe Galloway explained to Lillie of **Veterans Radio** how a simple Texas boy ended up carrying a weapon in Vietnam:

Lillie: *"When you first got to Vietnam, you were also carrying a weapon. How did that happen?"*

Galloway: *"Not when I first got there, but not long after, there were battalion commanders who would tell you straight up, 'Look here, I don't have the spare bodies to give you your personal* *bodyguard. You have to take care of yourself. If you are not carrying a weapon, you can't march with my outfit.' Second of all, in spite of the fact that you carried a press card and it had real fine print on the back of it that said that you were to be treated with all the privileges afforded a major in the U.S. Army if you were captured by enemies of the United States. I didn't recall if they were very kind to anyone of any rank if you fell into the hands of the enemies. Besides, they were shooting at me. I felt obliged, on occasion, to shoot back."*

Lillie: *"After getting your first weapon, you went to Plei Me Camp, a Special Forces camp, and met up with Major Beckwith and got an even more powerful weapon. Can you tell us about that?"*

Galloway: *"It was the third week of October 1965 and Plei Me camp was under siege by a regiment of the North Vietnamese and they were holding the camp hostage as dangling bait to draw the South Vietnamese armored column up the road to rescue them and they had another regiment standing by to ambush them. I wanted to get in there, and the air space was closed. A couple of Huey helicopters had been shot down, a Skyraider and a bomber, the place had those .51 caliber Chinese anti-aircraft machine guns on tripods and they were looking down our throats.*

"I was stomping up and down the flight line at Camp Holloway saying rude words and things and I ran across an old Texas Aggie helicopter pilot, a Huey pilot with the 119th helicopter company. He said, 'What's the matter Joe?' I said, 'Well, I'm trying to get into Plei Me Camp and there is no way to go.' He said, 'Let me get the clipboard.' He took a look and said, 'The reason you can't get in there, is the air space is closed.' I said, 'I know that, dummy, but I still want in there.' He said, 'I wouldn't mind taking a look, so I will give you a ride.' Rayburns flew me in there. He hit the ground. I took a picture. We were corkscrewing to avoid those machine guns and dropping in as fast as he could and I shot a picture out the open doorway. You can see the triangular shaped camp filling that doorway in the picture. You can see the smoke from mortar bombs going off and that is where

we were headed. He brought that thing in and I bailed out. We threw some wounded aboard and off he went.

"This Master Sergeant Special Forces came up to me and said, 'Sir, I don't know who the heck you are, but Major Beckwith wants to speak to you right away.' I said, 'Which one is he?' He said, 'It's that big guy over there jumping up and down on his hat.' He said a lot of rude words we can't say on this network, but he said, 'Who are you?' I said, 'I'm a reporter.' He said, 'You know I need everything in the whole f*** world. I need medevac. I need food. I could use reinforcements. I need ammo. I need everything. I could use a bottle of Jim Bean, and a box of cigars. And what has the Army and its wisdom sent me but a f*** reporter? I got to tell you, son, I have no vacancy for a reporter, but I'm in desperate need of a corner machine gunner, and you're it!

"My mouth was hanging open by then. He hauled me over to a position and there was air-cooled .30 caliber machine gun sitting there and he showed me how to load it, how to clear a jam, and he gave me my instructions which was that I should shoot all the little brown men outside the wire but not the ones inside the wire, they belong to him. He said, 'While you are at it, keep one eye always on that machine gun positioned down in the other corner of the camp because it's manned by South Vietnamese CIDG. They're infiltrated, I don't trust them as far as I can throw them. If you see them turn that machine gun around, take them out.'

"I spent three days and three nights with that machine gun—it was what you call 'sporting times.' Finally, the armored column made it through the ambush, thanks to the 1st Cav hopscotching artillery batteries which were slung beneath Chinook helicopters. This was something new in this war and the North Vietnamese didn't know about it and when they snapped their ambush, they got hammered by precise artillery fire and they got hammered by a whole world of air."

Lillie: *"You did some more tours of Vietnam. After that first tour with LZ X-ray, were there other battles in that first tour that equaled it?"*

Mr. Joseph L. Galloway

Galloway: *"None that ever equaled it, not in that tour or three other tours that I pulled in Vietnam, not in a half dozen other wars I've covered. That was a high watermark and it was the bloodiest battles of the Vietnam War. Right then, right there—305 American boys killed in that campaign. Hundreds and hundreds wounded. Just a ferocious collision between the two finest light infantry outfits operating in the world. The North Vietnamese Army and the First Calvary Division.*

Reporter Joe Galloway is seen in Vietnam. (Courtesy of Joe Galloway)

"My impression of the American soldier in Vietnam in 1965, '71, '73, of the American soldier in the Gulf War, in Haiti, and two tours in Iraq, I have the highest respect for American soldiers.

"There is a difference between soldiers who fought in Vietnam in the draftee Army and those who fight today in Iraq and Afghanistan—the volunteer Army. These kids are more sophisticated. They are better educated, better trained and certainly better armed.

"Soldiering comes down to a matter of the heart. That is unchanging. I think it has never changed from the first day a guy picked up a rock to defend his cave and his wife and his kids, over 10,000 years ago. There is a sense about the soldier of selfless sacrifice. He isn't in it for the glory. There is no glory in combat. There is no glory in war. It's a hard, bloody task that will leave you carrying the burden of memories of things that no one should see, especially when you are eighteen or nineteen years old. The soldiers are the same. I've counted it a privilege to have been allowed to stand beside them then, to stand beside them today, and they are my brothers. What can I say?"

233

Beyond Belief: True Stories of Civilian Heroes

The casualties at Ia Drang were extensive. While both sides exaggerated death counts during the war, American casualties were seventy-nine killed in action (KIA) at *LZ* X-Ray and the U.S. claimed that the PAVN count was 634 KIA. It was the intensity of the air strikes and up-close killing on that hill that shocked the troops and the public when they ultimately read the truth.

The bravery and valor of men on the ground and in the air was recognized by the award of Medals of Honor and Distinguished Service Crosses, Silver Stars and Bronze Stars. Second Lieutenant Walter Marm, Company A, 1st Battalion, 7th Cavalry, received the Medal of Honor. Helicopter pilots Capt. Ed Freeman and Maj. Bruce Crandall were each awarded the Medal of Honor. Freeman flew fourteen flights and Crandall flew twenty-two volunteer flights in unarmed Hueys, called "Slicks," into LZ X-Ray while enemy fire was so heavy that medical evacuation helicopters refused to approach. With each flight, Crandall and Freeman delivered much needed water and ammunition and extracted wounded soldiers, saving countless lives.

POST-VIETNAM

The shocking exposure to the firefights at LZ X-Ray were not Galloway's last time in the war zone. He did four tours as a war correspondent in Vietnam between 1965 and the fall of Saigon in April 1975. He also covered the 1971 India-Pakistan War. Joe spent nearly twenty years as a senior editor and senior writer for *U.S. News & World Report* magazine.

He retired as a weekly columnist for McClatchy Newspapers in January 2010, writing, *"I have loved being a reporter; loved it when we got it right; understood it when we got it wrong . . . In the end, it all comes down to the people, both those you cover and those you work for, with or alongside, during 50 years."*

In retirement, he then had time to work on books, movies and other projects. Books such as, *Shock and Awe* (2017); *Home from the War* (2009); and *They Were Soldiers: The Sacrifice and Contribution of Our Vietnam Veterans* (2020).

Mr. Joseph L. Galloway

He was a guest on Veterans Radio three times. here are some additional taken from interviews conducted with him on Veterans Radio in 2009, 2017, and 2020:

When asked about his first seventy-two hours in-country Galloway explained:

"I landed about two weeks after the Marines. The 1st Battalion 9th Marines landed in Da Nang in March 1965. I landed in April, coming from Tokyo. I sort of made a stop there for six months. I got to Saigon on a flight where my seatmate was a little Buddhist monk in an orange robe. The closer we got to Saigon, the more he was talking about sticking to me like glue. I wondered what the heck was going on. We landed and they told everyone to remain in their seats and a squad of White Mice (the Saigon Police) got aboard and yanked that Buddhist monk out of his seat and dragged him down the aisle and down the stairs and he was one of those exiles who was trying to slip back in the country and he failed utterly. They put him on the next plane back out. That was my arrival in Vietnam.

"I reported in to the old United Press International Bureau and had a day or two in Saigon to get my press card from MACV. Then I got on the mail run, C-123 flight that ran from Saigon.

"It took forever to get there but eventually I made it to Da Nang and by then the Marines had taken over a former Merchant Marine brothel on the banks of the Da Nang river and turned it into a press center. I had a rented jeep and I lived in Da Nang for six or seven months. I would be up there for two or three months at a time before I would even get back to Saigon. I went on every operation the Marines made.

"When I was younger, I had read the collected works of Ernie Pyle and World War II and I decided then, if there was a war during my generation, I wanted to cover it. And if I covered it, I wanted to cover it like Pyle covered his generation. That's up front with the troops and that is precisely what I did. I didn't like Saigon and I didn't like the politics of the situation. I would get to Saigon once in a while and most of the 500-plus accredited

Beyond Belief: True Stories of Civilian Heroes

correspondents spent their time in Saigon. They went to the daily briefings, we called them the "Five O'clock Follies," and they would complain to me that they were lying to us. My answer was always the same, no one lies to you within the sound of the guns. You come out with me and people will tell you the truth.

"It was on the day I arrived. I got off that plane and a fellow ran up to me and said, 'I am Raua, I work for UPI, there is big trouble, come with me.' I was carrying a Samsonite suitcase and still wearing chinos and loafers. I hadn't even gotten a set of fatigues yet. I said, 'What about my suitcase?' and he said something rude about it and threw it in the 8th Aerial Transport Squadron hooch at Da Nang and dragged me on to a C-130 that was spinning up on the ramp. I didn't know where I was going or what was going on. We made a short flight and we landed in a place called Quang Ngai City. We got off and it was like someone had stirred an ant hill.

"They were under serious attack and serious pressure in that area. It was an early attempt by the Viet Cong to cut the country in half. I got off and there was confusion all around, planes and choppers coming and going, people running around. This photographer ran off to a Marine H-34, an old titanium magnesium-based helicopter, and he talked to the crew chief and then he waved at me and the next thing I know, I'm on this bird and we are flying out at a low level across the paddies.

"I still don't know where I am, and I still don't know where I'm going. This helicopter finally comes upon a hill that rises out of the rice paddies and it circled around this hill. I'm trying to look out the door and I can see there are a lot of people on top of this hill. We land there and they shut down, and there is dead silence. I got out of the bird and then I was told why they were giving us this ride. They needed our help.

"A battalion of South Vietnamese had been overrun and killed to the last man and we were there to help them find and bring back the bodies of the two American advisors. They had only time to sort of scratch out a little body depression in the ground and every man was lying where he had made his last stand, hands out like he was holding a rifle, but the rifle was gone. We went hole

236

to hole until we found the two Americans and carried them back to the helicopter. It was a very sobering welcome to Vietnam."

Lillie: *"That was on your first day?"*

Galloway: *"Yeah."*

Galloway worked on a project commemorating the 50th Anniversary of the Vietnam War and spoke to **Veterans Radio's** founder and host Dale Throneberry, a helicopter pilot in Vietnam, about it in 2017.

Throneberry: *"Joe is currently working as a special consultant on the Vietnam War 50th Anniversary Project that's run out of the Office of the Secretary Defense. He's also served as a consultant on the Ken Burns' production. He's done a lot. He's a veteran's veteran and he's never really been a veteran, except that he did get a Bronze Star for what he did in the Ia Drang Valley."*

Galloway: *"I first was asked by them to sit for an interview. It turned out to be eleven hours of interviews and two sessions in New York City six years ago. After the interviews, they asked that I come on as a permanent consultant. I've been helping out as best I could since then. Two years ago I went up to Ken's house in New Hampshire and, with the other advisors on this project, sat down and re-watched the roughs. I thought it was so good then, I was saying go ahead and broadcast it now. Ken's a perfectionist and they did it all exactly right and took their time and I've watched each of the episodes night by night like everybody else has and I've got to say that I think it was magnificent storytelling and history telling. Even if you count yourself an expert on Vietnam, if you served there, if you've read the books, still this eighteen hours [sic] in ten parts was great. I'm proud to have been associated with the production in even a small way.*

"I would say that no matter what we did, we would not win that war. Even if we sent in a million troops instead of half a million, the Vietnamese were never going to quit. General Moore, my co-author and I, sat down for three interviews with General Võ Nguyên Giá, the North Vietnamese commander. I said, 'General, they say that you've sent a million of your own countrymen to their

Beyond Belief: True Stories of Civilian Heroes

deaths in this war.' He looked at me and said, 'Yes, and I would have sent five million or ten million. We would have fought on for ten years, twenty years, fifty years if that's what it took to get the foreigners out of our country.'

"*I was left with no doubt that he would have done exactly that and we could still be there, we could still be fighting or rather our children and our grandchildren would still be fighting. What can I say? It broke my heart to watch this documentary night after night and see great young Americans who answered the country's call, either they were drafted or they enlisted, and they were sent halfway around the world to fight other young men in a war in which we really had no place.*"

After Galloway co-authored a follow up book, *We Are Soldiers Still: A Journey Back to the Battlefields of Vietnam*, he spoke with **Veterans Radio** for the last time in May 2020; fifteen months before his death.

Throneberry: *"Where did you come up with the idea to talk about the sacrifices and contributions of Vietnam Veterans?"*

Galloway: *"Marv Wolf and I have been friends for fifty-five years. When I first met him, he was a Spec 4 photographer in the 1st Cav Division Public Affairs Office at An Khe in 1965, and we've been friends ever since. He moved to North Carolina a couple of years ago, he lives about two hours' drive from me and we got our heads together and it's something both of us had been thinking about—and that is that so many Vietnam veterans came home to no welcome, no respect, the media, the movies portrayed Vietnam veterans as losers and Lieutenant Dan and a lot of bullshit like that and it's just wrong.*

"*That's not who I saw in four tours in Vietnam from the beginning of that war to the end of it. We wanted to focus on forty-eight Vietnam veterans—not so much about the war they fought, but about the lives that they have lived and the good that they have done for their communities and our country since that war. They came home and did good stuff and there are some famous people and there are some people you've never heard of but should have.*

238

Mr. Joseph L. Galloway

They are all successful and they are all giving individuals. And there ain't a loser among them."

A glimpse into Galloway's personal life and humanity was displayed in this 2017 conversation:

Throneberry: *"I want to talk about your wife—tell me a little bit about her."*

Galloway: *"Doc Gracie is a truly remarkable human being. Best thing that ever happened to me. They say third time's a charm and she's wife number three and we've been together . . . I met her fifty years ago in Indonesia, should have married her then, and kept track of her until about thirty years ago and saw her in D.C. Then she disappeared.*

"She turned up ten years ago and I said, 'Where the hell have you been?' She said, 'Well, I took my eight-year-old daughter and ran away and joined the circus.' Yes, she had signed on as a traveling nurse with Barnum & Bailey and a year later she and

Joe Galloway, Doc Gracie and Jacques. -(Photo by Doug Magruder via Facebook)

her little daughter were aerialists in the trapeze act in the Big Top. She did that for ten years and then she came back and got her nurse practitioner degree and license and then she got a PhD in public health and she turned back up.

"I said, 'You're not getting away this time. I'm going to marry you.' She's Singapore-Chinese, now an American citizen. She was first cousin of the old Singapore prime minister, Lee Kuan Yew, who founded modern Singapore and made it run like a Swiss watch . . . and she's nobody to mess with. She still works every day at the Community Free Clinic here in Concord. She doctor's people who have no insurance, people who are poor, people who

are homeless and a not inconsiderable number of homeless veterans who camp out in the woods behind the Harris Teeter grocery store. If they are too spooked to come to the clinic, she takes her black bag and goes out in the woods and treats them out there."

Throneberry: *"I wanted to bring her up because she was actually in Vietnam during the Tet Offensive."*

Galloway: *"She was, indeed, and was working with the street kids and war orphans in Saigon and a relative had a big house in Chợ Lớn, the Chinese section of Saigon. That house was burned down, so she went through some tough times."*

Throneberry: *"I wanted to get to that and how she continued on and just wanted to be a nurse and that's what she's doing forever."*

Galloway: *"That's what she's been going forever and she's going to keep doing it as long as she's drawing a breath."*

Throneberry: *"You're lucky that you found her again."*

Galloway: *"Absolutely. She says she's going to get another fifteen years out of me."*

Doc Gracie only got four more years with Joe when he passed in 2021. The measure of a man is the life he lived, the people he helped, and the body of work he left behind. Joe Galloway measures up in all regards. He proved himself in battle, in journalism and finally in his family life.

Mr. Rick Rescorla

A Hero named "Hard Core"

By Colin E. Kimball

The English town of Hayle, residing on an estuary of St. Ives Bay on Cornwall's western coast, is the birthplace of Cyril Richard *"Rick"* Rescorla. In 1943, when Rick was four years old, he became enamored with the American soldiers of the 175th Infantry Regiment headquartered in Hayle. The 175th Regiment was part of the famous 29th Infantry Division, the Blue/Grey Division, composed of men from Maryland and Virginia. These soldiers were the grandsons of men who fought against each other in the American Civil War just eighty years earlier and would help spearhead Normandy's liberation on Omaha Beach on D-day.

Raised by his mother and grandparents, Rick was a keen athlete known for his success in rugby, shot put, and boxing. He never knew his father. Growing up, he always thought that his grandparents were his actual parents. He did not know that his "older sister" was, in reality, his mother. and that his parents were his grandparents. This unconventional upbringing spared him from the indignities of the era as they pertained to the children of unwed mothers.

Beyond Belief: True Stories of Civilian Heroes

Soldierly duty and the adventure it could provide could not escape his attention. Book learning was not to his liking. So, in 1956, at the age of sixteen, he left school to serve in the British Army. He volunteered in the British Army as a paratrooper serving with the 1st Parachute Regiment and later transferring to an intelligence unit stationed on the isle of Cyprus.

During his early Army days, he abandoned his name of Cyril and began preferring to refer to himself as "Rick." During his stint in Cyprus, the local Greek Cypriots sought to gain their independence from Great Britain in what is known as the *Cyprus Emergency*. Communist influences were involved, which began Rescorla's mission of fighting communism. Finally, in 1959 the British ended the hostilities and relinquished their colonial rule uniting the Island of Cyprus as a republic independent from Greece.

Leaving the British Army in 1960 upon the conclusion of his enlistment, Rescorla joined the National Police Service in Rhodesia. Communist forces were at work behind the scenes helping foster troubles there.

He entered a three-year contract in Rhodesia and further exercised his passion for fighting communism. Toward the end of his three-year contract, the Rhodesian government began to exert its force on the white settlers. Not wanting to turn his guns on these people, Rescorla decided to leave Rhodesia and return to England. During this time in Rhodesia, he met an American named Dan Hill, who had served in various conflicts and was fighting communist forces in Rhodesia as a mercenary.

Rescorla returned to England and joined the Metropolitan Police in London. Compared to his experience in Cyprus and Rhodesia, London police work was too mundane. There was not enough conflict for a man with a taste for trouble. There were no communists to track down. Rescorla kept in touch with his American buddy, Dan Hill, who encouraged him to come to America and join the U.S. Army. Dan convinced Rescorla that there was a fight brewing against communism in Vietnam and joining the U.S. Army was an excellent way to get an opportunity to participate.

Rescorla took him up on the idea and, in 1963, joined the U.S. Army. After completing Basic Training, Officer Candidate School, and Jump Training, he was assigned to the 7th Cavalry Regiment, famous as the regiment Lieutenant Colonel George Armstrong Custer led at the Battle of the Little Big Horn.

In 1965 he was in Vietnam, a platoon leader serving under 7th Cavalry's commanding officer, Lieutenant Colonel Hal Moore. Moore recalled that Rescorla was *"the best platoon leader I ever saw."* Moore gave Rescorla the nickname *"Hard Core,"* and Rescorla reciprocated in kind by referring to his platoon as *"Hard Corps."*

In November 1965, 1/7 initiated the first-ever major helicopter assault in the Ia Drang Valley of South Vietnam in the Central Highlands near the Cambodian Border. The Battalion landed amid a large concentration of North Vietnamese Army (NVA) soldiers in several landing zones (LZs). Rescorla's Company landed in LZ X-Ray.

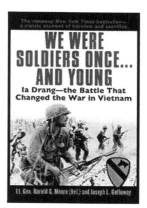

Once on the ground, Rescorla had his platoon dug in and then went on a brief reconnaissance patrol and came under fire. Coming back to the defensive position of his Hard Corps Platoon, Rescorla ordered his platoon to *"Fix bayonets."* A photographer took a photo of Rescorla, M-16 in hand, with its bayonet at the ready that was immortalized on the cover of Hal Moore's best-selling book, *We Were Soldiers Once . . . and Young.*

After the battle at Ia Drang, Rescorla would lead small scout teams to scout out enemy troop locations. In one daring mission composed of just four soldiers, they walked straight into a South Vietnamese village that was being lectured to by Viet Cong guerillas.

Beyond Belief: True Stories of Civilian Heroes

The four team members ran for their lives, being chased by the Viet Cong, young boys armed with AK-47s, and dogs that constantly gave away their positions. Along the way, some villagers tried to surrender to the safety they felt the Americans could provide. Ultimately, they found a sand bar on a river, flagged down a Huey helicopter flying overhead, and were retrieved and spared from the agony and death their capture would have wrought.

Rescorla was discharged from active duty in 1967. He remained in service in the U.S. Army Reserve, eventually reaching the rank of colonel. Using his GI Bill benefits, he entered the University of Oklahoma to study creative writing. He earned both a Bachelor of Arts and Master of Arts Degree in English, and then a Law Degree from the Oklahoma City University of Law. He also met his first wife, Betsy, the mother of his two children, and they were married in Dallas in 1972.

He wrote western stories for western magazines and began working on a novel. Rescorla then ventured into academia and taught Criminal Justice at the University of South Carolina and published a textbook on criminal justice.

Seeking an end to the modest income provided in academia, Rescorla moved to New York to take on a job in the security division of Dean Witter Reynolds, a brokerage firm in the South Tower of The World Trade Center in Manhattan, New York, in 1985.

Opened in 1973, the Twin Towers of the World Trade Center complex were symbolic of American wealth and power. The Cornish soldier known as Hard Core believed the towers represented a target to Islamic extremists and reached out to his army buddy, and friend, Dan Hill. Hill had spent years fighting communism and knew how devious minds thought. Rescorla asked Hill to come and assess the risks to the Twin Towers. Hill quickly determined that the lack of security in the underground parking garage made the buildings vulnerable to an attack by a truck bomb that could be easily placed next to one of the load-bearing columns. The New York Port Authority was responsible for building security at the complex. Rescorla and Hill took their study to the Port Authority, who politely told them that building security was none of their concern.

Mr. Rick Rescorla

In February 1993, a group of terrorists did what Hill predicted and brought an explosive-laden delivery truck into the basement of the North Tower and detonated a 1,300-pound device inside. The resulting blast killed six people and injured more than 1,000. Fortunately, the placement of the truck was such that when it exploded it didn't affect the structural integrity of the North Tower..

In the wake of the attack, Rescorla and Hill went to work. Often confused as a Nordic blue-eyed Muslim from the Nuristan province of Afghanistan, Hill immediately began frequenting the mosques in New York and New Jersey, trying to find the attack's ring leaders. Fluent in Arabic and devotion to the Islamic faith gave him cover, and his military skill gave him the covert skills he needed. Shortly after Hill began his undercover infiltration, his efforts began to pay off, and a network of terrorists led by a blind cleric was uncovered in New Jersey.

Meanwhile, Rescorla was promoted Chief of Security of Dean Witter in 1997. He became obsessed with protecting the operations spread over twenty floors of the South Tower following the merger with Morgan Stanley. Rescorla pled with the leadership to move company operations to a smaller complex in New Jersey because he believed the Twin Towers would be targeted again by Islamic extremists. Unfortunately, corporate executives' hands were tied as the company was locked into a long-term lease that wouldn't expire until 2006.

To compensate, Rescorla planned and drilled. To overcome the chaos of the mass exodus of people from a burning smoking building, he organized the employees in two-person teams that would descend the emergency exits two-by-two. This would help prevent logjams if one became injured as the other could assist.

Beyond Belief: True Stories of Civilian Heroes

He also insisted on mandatory fire drills every three months, demanding absolute adherence to the drills regardless of the business matters at hand. His leadership made him very unpopular with some of the high-level executives due to the disruption the drills caused. Rescorla reminded them that they were the largest tenant in the South Tower, and they could not wait for the New York City Fire Department and rescue personnel. Rescorla would direct the evacuations with a bull horn in hand with a strong, firm, and assuring voice.

In 1998, Rescorla divorced Betsy. He met Susan Greer while out on a morning jog. Running barefoot so that he could understand and describe the pain for a novel he was writing, the chance encounter blossomed into a romance that Rescorla said *"made his life."* They took up dancing while Rick was recovering from prostate cancer. They married in February 1999, in St Augustine, Florida, with Rescorla's best friend and fellow warrior, Dan Hill, serving as the Best Man.

It was a bright, beautiful sunny Tuesday morning and Rick Rescorla was at work at his desk on the 44th floor of the South Tower on September 11, 2001. At 8:46 a.m., Rescorla heard the booming explosion of United Airlines Flight 176 crashing into the North Tower. The Port Authority quickly came on the intercom alerting all employees to stay in place. Rescorla knew otherwise—he had spent the better part of a decade planning and drilling for such an eventuality. He grabbed his bullhorn and quickly alerted the entire staff of Morgan Stanley to begin the evacuations that they so often practiced.

Rescorla was able to keep people from crowding around the elevators and directed them two-by-two down the stairwells. He successfully guided 2,684 Morgan Stanley employees out of the South Tower even after it had been struck by the second airliner. As the building swayed back and forth, Rescorla sang "God Bless America" and Cornish folk songs that he belted out from his bullhorn. Just as it had done on LZ X-ray decades before, it distracted the people from their fears. While descending the stairs, he called his wife Susan, to reassure her of his love for her while reminding her of his duty to safely get all the employees out of the tower.

Once on the ground, Rescorla ignored requests to leave the area because he had four of his staff members remaining on the 44th floor. He remained faithful to his duty and he would not quit until everyone was safely evacuated. At 9:59 am, the South Tower collapsed. True to his nickname "Hard Core," Rick Rescorla was last seen climbing the stairs to aid the few staff members who remained behind. In total, only thirteen employees of Morgan Stanley, including Rescorla, lost their lives in the collapse of the Twin Towers of the World Trade Center. His proactive planning paid huge dividends. The scorn he had received from high-level executives turned to heroic admiration. He is celebrated as a hero of Morgan Stanley to this day.

Joe Galloway, who observed Second Lieutenant Rick "Hard Core" Rescorla in action on LZ X-ray, would write, *"You want a definition of a hero? In my book, it would simply say—Rick Rescorla."*

The National Infantry Museum at Fort Benning, Georgia, contains a full-size bronze statue of young Second Lieutenant Rescorla on its promenade in front of the building. He is immortalized as one of our nation's most accomplished warriors. His gallantry on the field of battle prepared him for his duty beyond his call to duty as an executive on Wall Street. His valor as he ascended the fire exit stairway with a team of New York firefighters knew no limits. He certainly knew the danger. But, true to his warrior spirit and call to duty, there were lives at stake. His job was unfinished.

In the poem *"If"* Rudyard Kipling, one of Rescorla's beloved writers, wrote about the virtues that are quickly recognizable in the life of Rick Rescorla. Several verses appear to apply directly to him.

If you can keep you head when all about you are losing theirs and blaming it on you . . .

If you can trust yourself when all men doubt you . . .

If you can wait and not be tired of waiting . . .

If you can meet with Triumph and Disaster and treat those two imposters just the same . . .

If you can force your heart and nerve and sinew to serve your turn long after they are gone,

And so hold on when there is nothing in you Except the will which says to them: Hold On . . .

If you can fill the unforgiving minute with sixty seconds worth of distance run

Yours is the earth and everything that is in it, and—which is more—you'll be a man my son!

Rick "Hard Core" Rescorla, an Englishman by birth, American by choice, is no longer with us on this earth, but his spirit influences a wide range of men from the "Legs" of the U.S. Army Infantry to the "white shirt and tie" executives on Wall Street. That wide range of humanity, figuratively representing the *"earth and everything in it."*

When I hear Kipling's words in his immortal poem *"If"* I think of Rick Rescorla, not just because he and Kipling shared the same accent and love for the written word, but because his life and call to duty imbodies those virtues that was so eloquently captured by Kipling. Rescorla's achievement was heroic. He saved many souls. May he Rest in Peace.

On September 11, 2019, in a ceremony posthumously awarding to Rick Rescorla the Presidential Citizen Medal, President Donald Trump presented it to Susan, his widow, stating, *"Rick earned the Silver Star and the Purple Heart for his service in Vietnam. He later became the vice president for security at Morgan Stanley in the World Trade Center. On the day of the attack, Rick died while leading countless others to safety. His selfless actions saved approximately 2,700 lives,"*

Mr. Bob Hope

America's Only Honorary Veteran

By Scott Baron

The name Bob Hope conjures up many different images for different people. For many, they immediately think of the seven "Road To" films he made with Bing Crosby, or perhaps they imagine him crooning *"Thanks for the Memories"* at the end of his numerous TV specials.

But for generations of American servicemen and servicewomen, and millions of other Americans, they instantly think of him entertaining soldiers and sailors in far-away places during peace and war for almost fifty years, during six wars, headlining fifty-seven United Service Operations (USO) shows.

Regardless of where he was sent or how high the risks, Hope was committed to supporting our nation's military and frequently insisted on traveling to the front lines, even if it placed him in harm's way, to put on a variety show of comedy, singing, and dancing for the troops.

His daughter Linda recalled *"A platoon in the South Pacific had marched to get to this base where Dad was doing some shows. They arrived late, and the show was over, and this one fellow was saying how disappointed he was. Dad heard that this platoon marched all this way and missed the show. He got a Jeep, enlisted (singer) Frances Langford and (comedian) Jerry Colonna, and found the platoon and did a half-hour show."* It wasn't an isolated occurrence as Hope was always willing to go the extra mile for the troops.

Bob Hope was born Leslie Townes Hope on May 29, 1903, in Eltham, County of London, now the Royal Borough of Greenwich, in a terraced house on Craigton Road. He was the fifth of seven sons born to William Henry Hope, a stonemason, and a Welsh mother, Avis (Townes) Hope, a light opera singer who later worked as a cleaner. William and Avis married in April 1891 and the family later emigrated to the United States, sailing aboard the *S.S. Philadelphia*. They passed through Ellis Island, New York, on March 30, 1908, before moving on to Cleveland, Ohio.

Working from the age of twelve, Hope earned pocket money by performing on streetcars, singing, dancing, and performing comedy. He entered numerous dancing and amateur talent contests as Lester Hope, and won a prize in 1915 for his impersonation of Charlie Chaplin. For a time, he attended the **Boys' Industrial School** in Lancaster, Ohio, and had a brief career as a boxer in 1919, fighting under the name **Packy East**. He had three wins and one loss.

Hope worked as a butcher's assistant and a lineman in his teens and early 20s. He also had a brief stint at Chandler Motor Car Company. In 1921, while helping his brother Jim clear trees for a power company, a tree he was in crashed to the ground, crushing his face. Hope underwent reconstructive surgery that contributed to his later distinctive appearance.

After deciding on a show business career, Hope and his girlfriend signed up for dancing lessons. Encouraged after they performed in a three-day engagement at a club, Hope formed a partnership with Lloyd Durbin, a friend from the dancing school. Silent film comedian Fatty Arbuckle saw them perform in 1925 and found them work with a touring troupe called **Hurley's Jolly Follies**.

Performing as a comedian and dancer on the vaudeville circuit, he later began acting on Broadway. His first film was a short titled **"Going Spanish"** in 1934. He also began performing on radio, mostly with NBC radio. He starred in his first feature film, "The Big Broadcast of 1938," performing the song *"Thanks for the Memories"* with Shirley Ross, which would later become his trademark tune. That same year, he began hosting "The Pepsodent Show" on radio.

By 1941, Hope had the top-rated radio show and was among the top-ten box office stars, but by this time, a large part of the world was at war. It could be said that Hope's first wartime performance was aboard the R.M.S. *Queen Mary* in September 1939, when he volunteered to perform a special show for the passengers.

As the "Commodore" of the *Queen Mary*, Everette Hoard recounted, *"On September 3, 1939, Bob and his wife, Dolores, were returning from Europe when war was declared. German U-boats were looking to sink it, so windows were covered, the portholes were painted, and many lights shut off. The ship's captain asked Bob to calm the nerves of the frightened passengers. Hope brought hope. He made them laugh, showing how hard it was to dance in a life preserver. Hope sang,* 'Thanks for the Memories' *with rewritten lyrics and quipped* 'Some folks slept on the floor; some in the corridor but I was more exclusive, my room had 'Gentleman' above the door.'"*

The USO was founded with the purpose of combining the efforts of the Salvation Army, Young Men's Christian Association (YMCA), Young Women's Christian Association (YWCA), National Catholic Community Service, National Travelers Aid Association, and the National Jewish Welfare Board, and focusing their joint efforts on helping members of the military. The USO brought entertainers, including singers, actors, comedians, and others, to perform shows for the men and women serving in the military.

When it opened its doors on February 4, 1941, the USO was a physical network of stateside club locations where service members

Beyond Belief: True Stories of Civilian Heroes

could go to relax, socialize and get a taste of the civilian world. In October 1941, the USO worked with entertainment executives to create a new branch of the organization called USO Camp Shows, Inc. which was organized into four circuits—the Victory Circuit, the Blue Circuit, the Hospital Circuit and the Foxhole Circuit. The Victory and Blue Circuit troupes entertained stateside military personnel, while the Hospital Circuit troupes were tasked with visiting the wounded and the Foxhole Circuit troupes headed overseas.

That month it sent its first overseas tour, featuring comedians Laurel and Hardy, Chico Marx, and Broadway tap dancer and film star Mitzi Mayfair, to the Caribbean to entertain troops.

An established comedian and actor at the onset of the war, Hope was one of the first major stars to join the USO in entertaining the troops during World War II, and soon became the organization's most iconic USO tour veteran. Bob Hope performed and broadcast his first USO show on the radio for service members on May 6, 1941, at March Field, an Army Air Corps Base at Riverside, California.

From that first show, Hope would go on to entertain the troops for nearly fifty years, through World War II, the Korean War, the Vietnam War, the Lebanon Civil War, the Iran-Iraq War and the Persian Gulf War. Just nine months after the United States entered World War II, in September 1942, Hope traveled to Alaska to entertain members of the armed forces stationed there.

His travel to Alaska, then a U.S. territory, required a special permit, and on September 16, 1942, Hope, comic Jerry Colonna, singer Frances Langford, and guitarist Tony Romano were flown in an Army Air Force twelve-passenger twin-engine Lockheed Lodestar west from Yakutat to Anchorage, Alaska, piloted by Lieutenant Bob Gates. Early on, he learned that entertaining the troops could be hazardous.

Gates, then a 22-year-old newly minted pilot, later recalled: *"Bob did a show at about three in the afternoon for about half of the 600 or so servicemen who were there unloading the ships. And we were just ready to leave when the commander said, 'Mr. Hope, only half of my troops got to see your show. Couldn't you do another one now?' And Bob said, 'Of course we can!'"'*

Mr. Bob Hope

Flying at night in Alaska was hazardous because there were no radio letdowns or navigational beacons except at Fairbanks and Anchorage, and at Elmendorf Air Force Base.

Gates protested *"Bob, no we can't. We can't fly at night up here. We can't go back tonight."*

To which Hope replied *"Oh, sure we can. It's only an hour and a half over there. We can do that."*

"So we did the show," Gates recalled, *"and got back to the airport at about 9 p.m., and it's raining. And the mountains are 12,000 feet high there. So we did a tight turn at 12,000 feet through the rain and started on course, and we got into the ice and one engine quit. And then the radio went out. So, there we were, the mountains higher than we were, losing altitude about 200 feet a minute, and how we got through is beyond me to tell you, other than God was looking out for us."*

After landing safely, Hope put his arm around Gates and said, *"Okay, now let's go to the barracks and change our drawers."* Although his film persona was playing a coward, Hope proved himself calm and courageous under fire.

Bob Hope performing at Noemfoor, off New Guinea, in world War II

Beyond Belief: True Stories of Civilian Heroes

Over the next months, Hope continued to host and perform in radio and USO performances at bases across the U.S. before embarking on overseas USO Camp Shows traveling overseas to visit troops in the European and Pacific Theatres in 1943. These shows were a brief but greatly appreciated distraction from the misery of war, a taste of home when they were deployed overseas, and a way to show that they and their efforts were not forgotten or taken for granted.

During the many WWII USO trips that followed, he hosted dozens of variety-style shows featuring some of the biggest names in Hollywood.

Accompanying him would be musicians, singers, and dancers, performing skits and monologues, as well as some of Hollywood's leading ladies from the time. Throughout the years, female stars like Elizabeth Taylor, Ann-Margret, Raquel Welch, Jayne Mansfield, and Brooke Shields accompanied Hope who said, *"If there's anything that gives our GIs a lift, it's the sight of a pretty girl, so I always take plenty along."*

Other stars that accompanied Hope on his USO tours included Bing Crosby, Jerry Colonna, Jill St. John, Les Brown and his band, Phyllis Diller, Redd Foxx, Neil Armstrong, Fred Astaire, Marilyn Monroe, James Stewart, Mickey Mantle, Zsa Zsa Gabor, Lucille Ball, Danny Kaye, among many others.

Hope's service was not without hazards. He endured air raids in Italy and Algeria during World War II. During a 1964 visit to Saigon, Hope and his crew were delayed by half an hour before returning to their hotel. When they eventually were able to leave the base, they were informed that a Viet Cong truck bomb intended for Hope exploded ten minutes before his troupe was scheduled to arrive at their hotel, one of many close calls for Hope, but it never dissuaded him from continuing.

"A funny thing happened as we arrived in Saigon," Hope later joked to the troops. *"I met my hotel going the other way."*

During one of his 1,000 shows, where bombs could be heard bursting nearby, he quipped: *"I understand the enemy is very close and with my act, they always have been."*

Mr. Bob Hope

Reflecting on Hope's USO shows in World War II, novelist John Steinbeck, who was working as a war correspondent, wrote in 1943:

"When the time for recognition of service to the nation in wartime comes to be considered, Bob Hope should be high on the list. This man drives himself and is driven. It is impossible to see how he can do so much, can cover so much ground, can work so hard, and can be so effective. He works month after month at a pace that would kill most people."

Along with his friend Bing Crosby, Hope was offered a commission in the United States Navy as a lieutenant commander, but President Franklin D. Roosevelt intervened, believing it would be more valuable for troop morale if they kept doing what they were doing by performing for all branches of military service.

Hope modestly downplayed his contributions, stating *"Believe me when I say that laughter up at the front lines is a very precious thing precious to those grand guys who are giving and taking the awful business that goes on there. There's a lump the size of Grant's Tomb in your throat when they come up to you and shake your hand and mumble 'Thanks.' Imagine those guys thanking me! Look what they're doin' for me. And for you."*

On top of putting on shows for the troops, Hope was a frequent visitor of military and veteran's hospitals, both when he was on a USO tour and when he was home on his own time. When on a tour overseas, beginning during WWII and continuing through the Vietnam War, Hope

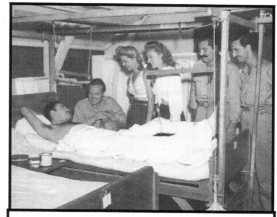

Bob Hope, Frances Langford, and Jerry Colonna visiting soldiers at a at a military hospital overseas during World War II.

visited military hospitals where young men lay injured or dying, to spend time with them. Of course, he was always there to give them a smile and a laugh to take their minds off of their situation, entering the wards and calling out *"Don't get up."*

His daughter, Linda, recalled, *"He would go to the hospitals all the time and just show up. Sometimes we would say, 'Where did dad go?' And my mom would go, 'Oh, he went to the VA hospital in Los Angeles to spend a few hours with the guys.' He would also do that if he was traveling someplace and there was a VA hospital there. He would make a visit and spend time with the different men while going through the different wards."*

But to many Americans, Bob Hope meant Christmas with the troops, although sources differ as to the first official Bob Hope Christmas Show. The National Archives records state that Hope hosted a special recording of the **"Pepsodent Show"** at the Sawtelle Veterans' Hospital on December 24, 1946. Navy records show that on December 23, 1947, Hope hosted a special recording of the **"Pepsodent Show"** at Corona Naval Hospital, California, in front of a military audience.

A year later, in December 1948, Hope and his USO troupe recorded a "Bob Hope Show" radio episode in front of troops stationed in Germany supporting the Berlin Airlift, at the request of the Pentagon. According to the Bob and Dolores Hope Foundation, it was this USO trip that inspired Hope to begin his tradition of entertaining the military community during the holiday season.

In December 1950, Hope recorded his first-ever holiday TV special for a New York studio audience after returning from a USO tour to Korea, where he recorded episodes of his show. A year later, in San Diego, Hope recorded a December 1951 episode of his show in front of service members returning home from Korea aboard the U.S.S. *Boxer*.

In 1954, Hope began traveling overseas to record the holiday USO shows and continued the annual tradition of filming a series of special holiday episodes of his show in front of military audiences serving overseas in places like Iceland, Greenland, Alaska, the Caribbean, the Mediterranean and the Western Pacific.

In 1964, Hope began the first of what would be nine USO trips to Vietnam to record special holiday episodes of his show. Hope left his own loved ones behind to be with the troops deployed to far-off and unfamiliar places who were able to enjoy a few hours of fun away from the battlefield.

At the same time, their families back home could watch the show on their television screens, hoping for the chance to see their deployed service member's face cross in front of the camera. Hope's dedication to the troops and his Vietnam Christmas shows became a tradition of holiday

Singer/Dancer Ann Margaret holds a special place in the heart of Vietnam veterans. She made two tours to Vietnam, first in 1966, and returned in 1968 with Bob Hope.

entertainment and endeared him in the hearts and minds of Americans for years to come. In an unpopular war Hope retained his popularity.

Hope subsequently filmed holiday tours overseas, hosted other USO trips and recorded non-holiday USO themed television specials. In 1983, he went to Beirut to spend Christmas with U.S. troops and in December 1988, Hope performed on bases and ships in the Persian Gulf. Two years later, in 1990, Hope and his

Beyond Belief: True Stories of Civilian Heroes

wife Dolores traveled to the Middle East during Operation **Desert Shield**, Hope's final USO tour.

Dolores Hope, Bob's wife of sixty-nine years and his partner in entertaining the troops from World War II until 1991, was the only woman allowed to perform for Americans in Saudi Arabia during the tour. The other women were only allowed to perform on aircraft carriers stationed offshore, and Dolores stole the show with her performance of *"White Christmas."* His final holiday special, "Hopes for the Holidays," aired in 1994.

During his career, Hope received numerous awards and honors, too many to list, and the Guinness Book of World Records lists his 1,500 awards as a record, including 50 honorary degrees, five honorary Academy Awards, two Golden Globes and four stars on the Hollywood Walk of Fame (Motion Picture, Radio, TV, and Live Theater.)

In October 1946, General Eisenhower awarded Hope the **Medal of Merit** for *"wartime contributions to Morale."* On September 11, 1962, President John F. Kennedy awarded Hope the **Congressional Gold Medal**, one of only three entertainers to be so honored, the other two being George M. Cohan and Irving Berlin. On January 20, 1969, President Lyndon Johnson presented Hope with the **Presidential Medal of Freedom**, and in 1986, on the 100th Anniversary of the Stature of Liberty, President Ronald Reagan presented Hope and eleven others with the Medal of Liberty. In 1995, President Bill Clinton conferred the **Medal of the Arts** to Hope.

Hope was inducted into the World Golf Hall of Fame in 1983 and the Television Hall of Fame in 1987. He received the **Kennedy Lifetime Achievement Award** in 1985, was knighted in 1998, being named a Knight Commander in the Order of the British Empire (OBE) and is the only civilian to be awarded the prestigious **West Point Sylvanus Thayer Award.**

The legendary entertainer and comedian would continue to perform, making his last television appearance in 1997. His last credited work was playing himself in a 1992 episode of "The Simpsons." He was a frequent visitor to the White House and friend to several Presidents, and he continued his charity work for veterans even after he stopped performing.

On October 29, 1997, by a Joint Resolution, the 105th Congress passed Public Law 105–67, conferring on Hope the first, and to date only, designation as an *"honorary veteran of the United States Armed Forces."*

The law stated in part:

> *"Whereas Leslie Townes (Bob) Hope is himself not a veteran, having attempted to enlist in the Armed Forces to serve his country during World War II, but being informed that the greatest service he could provide the Nation was as a civilian entertainer for the troops;*
>
> *"Whereas during, World War II, the Korean Conflict, the Vietnam War, and the Persian Gulf War and throughout the Cold War, Bob Hope traveled to visit and entertain millions of United States servicemembers in numerous countries, on ships at sea, and in combat zones ashore;*
>
> *"Whereas Bob Hope has given unselfishly of his time for over a half century to be with United States servicemembers on foreign shores, working tirelessly to bring a spirit of humor and cheer to millions of servicemembers during their loneliest moments, and thereby extending for the American people a touch of home away from home:*
>
> *"Now, therefore, be it Resolved by the Senate and House of Representatives of the United States of America in Congress assembled, That Congress extends its gratitude, on behalf of the American people, to Leslie Townes (Bob) Hope for his lifetime of accomplishments and service on behalf of United States military servicemembers."*

Said Hope of the honor *"I've been given many awards in my lifetime but to be numbered among the men and women I admire most is the greatest honor I have ever received."*

Beyond Belief: True Stories of Civilian Heroes

Bob Hope died at home from pneumonia on July 27, 2003 at the age of 100. While he never served in the armed forces, Hope dedicated the greater part of his career and personal life to serving the men and women in uniform all around the world.

MEET THE AUTHORS

SCOTT BARON

Scott Baron is the author of thirteen books on American military history including *They Also Served, Forged in Fire*, and *Forgotten No More*, and wrote a column for "Stars and Stripes" on celebrities who served in the military. He is a Vietnam-era veteran and former law enforcement officer who has spent the last twenty-one years as a U.S. history teacher. He has a master's degree in teaching and lives in California with Marisela, his wife of forty-three years.

MARIO BIRLOCHO

My name is Mario but I sign my work Birlocho, I am an Ecuadorian artist, born in a small city named Portoviejo. I love to draw sexy girls, adding a bit of humor in the process, and it has turned out into a full-time job. When I was a kid, I dreamed of drawing using nothing but computers. Grandma used to say I was "wasting my life." I like to see life through what I like to call "my vision." The main victims of that so-called vision are my characters "Mabú & Lorenzo," the topic of my stories are parodies of world class pop culture through the eyes of a girl from a small city in a coast province in a Sudamerican country . . . and her cat.

JIM FAUSONE

Jim Fausone has been a lawyer for four decades and a veteran advocate since going to law school on the GI Bill. He founded Legal Help for Veterans, PLLC; is a podcast host for VeteransRadio.net; and maintains HomeofHeroes.com a website dedicated to Medal of Honor recipients. He is a board member of Michigan Military and Veterans Hall of Honor. A former Lt.(j.g.) in NOAA Corps, he graduated from the University of Michigan College of Engineering and Gonzaga University School of Law. He has co-authored the books *How to Get into a Military Academy; Answers to Common Veteran Disability Questions*, and *Vietnam Stories - Best of Veterans Radio*. He has hosted the largest and longest Veterans Summit in SE Michigan for a dozen years getting information out to veterans about benefits and health care. He is married to his college sweetheart, a nurse and fellow veteran advocate, Brigadier General Carol Ann Fausone (ret.) USAF/Michigan ANG.

JIM FURLONG

James "Jim" Furlong was a combat infantryman in Vietnam. Serving with Company B, 2d Battalion, 14th Infantry Regiment, 25th Infantry Division. Jim was wounded and earned a Purple Heart and Distinguished Service Cross for extraordinary heroism. After the war, Jim returned home and continued his education receiving his master 's degree in Economics from the University of Denver. He started working in the private sector for large computer manufacturers selling integrated services to highly classified government installations. Now retired, Jim is frequently asked to speak about the war, focusing not on his personal experiences but giving voice "to those who will always be twenty-one" in our hearts.

COLIN KIMBALL

Colin Kimball of McKinney, Texas, served in the U.S. Air Force as a weather radar technician in the post-Vietnam era and used the GI Bill to attain a bachelor's and master's degree in Geology. Growing up as an Air Force brat, he became the "man of the house" when his father served in Vietnam in 1969 and 1970. He was haunted by the loss of the fathers of neighboring friends as well as his childhood best friend and older brother figure, PFC Franklin D. Lacey, USMC, who was killed in at Khe Sanh in 1968. Our nation's rush to forget the war and those who served in it disturbed him for decades. This experience, as well as the negative feelings from the public towards our military after Vietnam that he experienced when he served, inspired him to begin painting portraits of our nation's heroes so that their legacies would not be forgotten. Beginning with Frankie, whose portrait hangs in his mother's home and who has a local ballpark named after him, Colin founded the North Texas Fallen Warrior Portrait in 2013. To date it has placed seventy-nine portraits of local fallen warriors and law enforcement officers on permanent display in the Russell A. Steindam Courts Building in his home county of Collin County, Texas, north of Dallas. Kimball was also influential in persuading the local county commissioners to name their courthouse after 1st Lt Russell A. Steindam, a local hero who received a posthumous Medal of Honor in Vietnam. An avid historian, he uses his portraits as a vehicle to tell the stories of our military and law enforcement heroes. Colin has completed hundreds of portraits and his work is displayed in homes nationwide and at military and public institutions from Vicenza, Italy, Quantico, Virginia, to the University of Texas. He is currently working on a compendium of portraits of posthumous Medal of Honor recipients to preserve their legacies, and that their family names can be honored and remembered.

C. Douglas Sterner

Doug Sterner is a decorated, two-tour veteran of the Vietnam War. For the last thirty years he has compiled the largest and most complete database of U.S. Military Award citations, curates the *Military Times* HALL OF VALOR, and has become recognized as one of Americas foremost authorities of military awards and American military heroes. A life member of the Veterans of Foreign Wars, he is one of only two Americans in history to be granted Honorary, Lifetime Membership in the Legion of Valor. He has written scores of articles on U.S. military heroes for periodicals, contributed to *Chicken Soup for the Veteran's Soul*, and authored more than seventy-five reference books of award citations. His books can be found at www.herobooks.store. Doug makes his home in Pueblo, Colorado, a city he and his wife were instrumental in being officially designated as "America 's Home of Heroes."

Pamla M. Sterner

Pamla Sterner is an accomplished author, speaker, and public performer. As a ventriloquist, and stand-up comic, she has authored numerous books related to these arts. She started her own comedy company, Pueblo Pfunny, which she promotes on Facebook. With her husband she has written such non-fiction works as the couple's 500+ page treatise on Baby Boomers titled *The Defining Generation*. In 2004, as a political science student at Colorado State University-Pueblo, she wrote a paper for a class assignment that became the basis for the landmark Stolen Valor Act, passed by Congress in 2006, struck down by SCOTUS in 2012, and subsequently revised and nearly unanimously passed by Congress the following year. In her hometown of Pueblo, Colorado, she is best known for her efforts to honor and recognize Medal of Honor recipients, and as the driving force behind her city being named "America's Home of Heroes."

Dwight Jon Zimmerman

Dwight Jon Zimmerman is an award-winning, #1 *New York Times* bestselling author. In a career spanning more than forty years he has written everything from comic books (for Marvel Comics and DC Comics) to hundreds of military history articles and more than two dozen books. His book *First Command*, about the first commands of famous generals, was an award-winning documentary aired on the Military Channel. He co-authored *Uncommon Valor:*

The Medal of Honor and the Warriors Who Earned It in Afghanistan and Iraq which won the Military Writer Society of America's Founder 's Award, the organization 's highest honor, and was the first book to contain the complete history of the Medal of Honor. He lives in Brooklyn, New York.

Visit My Website

BEYOND BELIEF

Beyond Belief is a projected series of true, inspiring stories of some of America 's most unbelievable, but TRUE, stores of heroism. The stories are written by a team of authors all of them committed to our goal of providing readers with the stories that will leave them shaking their heads in wonder.

New volumes are planned for release twice each year, one on Memorial Day, and the other on Veterans Day.

True Stories of American Heroes That Defy Comprehension

True Stories of Navy Heroes That Defy Comprehension

True Stories of Military Chaplains That Defy Comprehension

Medal of Honor Books

Army (Civil War-WW I)

Army (WWII-GWOT)

Navy

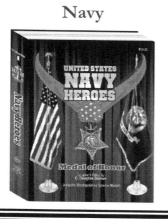

Marine Corps

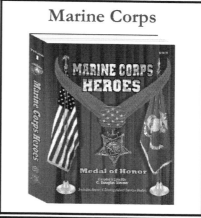

Air Force

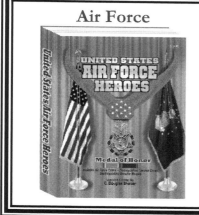

Coast Guard

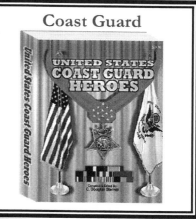

The following 24 volumes of **U.S. Military Heroes by Branch of Service** comprise the largest collection of award recipients ever published. Each 8 ½" x 11" book contains the names, citations, and often a photo and brief biography of the listed recipients. Often the last volume in any set (MOH, DSC, Navy Cross, Silver Star) and when broken down by war, includes informational appendixes analyzing awards by the rank of recipients, military occupational specialty, and unit, as well a list of recipients by how state and town. These represent more than 20,000 pages of detailed information on our most highly decorated heroes.

United States Navy Heroes

Volume II	Volume III	Volume IV
Navy Cross (1915 – WWII)	Navy Cross (WWII) "A"-"L"	Navy Cross (WWII) "M"-"Z"
Volume V	Volume VI	Volume VII
Navy Cross (Korea – Present)	Silver Star (WWII) "A"-"K"	Silver Star (WWII) "L"-"Z"
Naval Academy I	Naval Academy II	Corpsman & Chaplains
MOH, Navy Cross, DSC	Silver Star	MOH, Navy Cross DSC-SS

United States Army Heroes

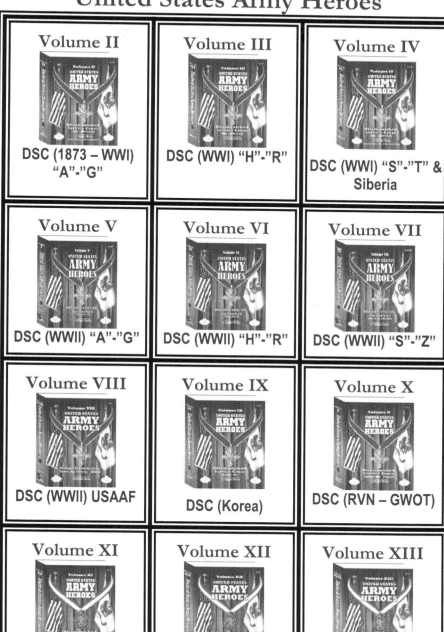

Volume II
DSC (1873 – WWI) "A"-"G"

Volume III
DSC (WWI) "H"-"R"

Volume IV
DSC (WWI) "S"-"T" & Siberia

Volume V
DSC (WWII) "A"-"G"

Volume VI
DSC (WWII) "H"-"R"

Volume VII
DSC (WWII) "S"-"Z"

Volume VIII
DSC (WWII) USAAF

Volume IX
DSC (Korea)

Volume X
DSC (RVN – GWOT)

Volume XI
DSM (1862 – 1941)

Volume XII
DSM (WWII – 1960)

Volume XIII
DSM (RVN – Present)

West Point Heroes

MOH, DSC, Navy Cross

Coming in 2022
West Point Heroes I
Silver Star

Coming in 2022
West Point Heroes I
Silver Star

United States Marine Corps Heroes

Volume II
Navy Cross (1915 – WWII)

Volume III
Navy Cross (Korea - Present

Volume IV
Silver Star (1900 – 1941)

Volume V
Silver Star (WWII) "A"-"K"

Volume VI
Silver Star (WWII) "L"-"Z"

Volume VII
Silver Star (1947 – Korea)

Volume VIII
Silver Star (RVN) "A"-""L"

Volume IX
Silver Star (RVN "M"-"Z" & GWOT

United States Air Force Heroes

Volume II

MOH, DSC, SS
USAAS (WWI)

Volume III

DSC USAAF (WWII)

Volume IV

Silver Star (WWII)
"A"-"C"

Volume V

Silver Star (WWII)
"D"-"H"

Volume VI

Silver Star (WWII)
"I"-"N"

Volume VII

Silver Star (WWII)
"O"-"S"

Volume VIII

Silver Star (WWII)
"T"-"Z"

Volume IX

MOH, DSC, SS
(Korea)

Volume X

DSM (1918-1965)

Coming in 2022

Volume X

Distinguished
Service Medals

Volume XI

Soldier's Medals
(WWII)

Volume XII

Soldier's Medals
(Korea)

SPECIAL COLLECTIONS

Vietnam War POWs		MOH at Arlington	CHAPLAINS

AIR FORCE	USA, USN, USMC, CIV	Citations, Photos, & More	MOH, DSC, NX, SS

WAR ON TERRORISM HEROES

Navy Heroes in the War on Terrorism

Citations for all awards of the Medal of Honor, Navy Cross, and the majority of Silver Star to members of the U.S. Navy in the wars in Iraq and Afghanistan. Appendixes provide analysis of recipients by unit, by specialty, by rank/rating, as well as a chronological analysis of these awards.

Marine Corps Heroes in the War on Terrorism

Citations for all awards of the Medal of Honor, Navy Cross, and Silver Star to U.S. Marines **and attached Navy Corpsmen** in the wars in Iraq and Afghanistan. Appendixes provide analysis of recipients by unit, by specialty, by rank/rating, as well as a chronological analysis of these awards.

Air Force Heroes in the War on Terrorism

Citations for all awards of the Air Force Cross and Silver Stars to members of the U.S. Air Force during the wars in Iraq and Afghanistan. Appendixes provide analysis of recipients by unit, by specialty, by rank, as well as a chronological analysis of these awards.

Army Heroes in the War on Terrorism (OIF)

Citations for all awards of the Medal of Honor, Distinguished Service Cross and Silver Stars to members of the U.S. Army during Operation ENDURING FREEDOM in Afghanistan. Appendixes provide analysis of recipients by unit, by specialty, by rank, as well as a chronological analysis of these awards.

Army Heroes in the War on Terrorism (OEF)

Citations for all awards of the Medal of Honor, Distinguished Service Cross and Silver Stars to members of the U.S. Army during Operation IRAQI FREEDOM in IRAQ. Appendixes provide analysis of recipients by unit, by specialty, by rank, as well as a chronological analysis of these awards.

U.S. ARMY HEROES BY DIVISION

This is the most comprehensive compilation of citations ever published. Each volume the names of the recipients of our highest military awards, and in many cases brief biographical information, a photo of the recipient, and personal data such as Date and Place of Birth, Home Town, Date of Death, and Burial Location. Appendixes break down the awards by rank, military specialty, unit, and more.

WORLD WAR I			
3D INFANTRY (WWI) VOLUME I	**3D INFANTRY (WWI) VOLUME II**	**82D AIRBORNE DIV.**	
MOH, DSC, SS "A"-"G"	SILVER STAR "H"-"Z"	(ALL WARS) MOH, DSC, SILVER STAR	
WORLD WAR II			
100/442 INF. JAPANESE-AMERICANS	**1ST INFANTRY DIV.**	**1ST INFANTRY DIV. VOLUME I**	**1ST INFANTRY DIV. VOLUME II**
MOH, DSC, SS "A"-"G"	(WWI – PRESENT) MOH, DSC, DSM	SILVER STAR "A"-"G"	SILVER STAR "H"-"Q"
1ST INF. DIV.	**7 & 8 ARMOR**	**35TH INF.**	**37TH INF.**

VOLUME II	DIV.	DIV.	DIV.

SILVER STAR "R"-"Z"	MOH, DSC, SILVER STAR	MOH, DSC, SILVER STAR	MOH, DSC, SILVER STAR
42D INF. DIV.	63D INF. DIV.	80TH INF. DIV.	82D ABN. DIV.

MOH, DSC, SILVER STAR	MOH, DSC, SILVER STAR	MOH, DSC, SILVER STAR	(WWI – PRESENT) MOH, DSC, SS

KOREAN WAR

2D INF. DIV. VOLUME I	2D INF. DIV. VOLUME II	3D INF. DIV. VOLUME I	3D INF. DIV. VOLUME II

MOH, DSC, SS "A"-"K"	SILVER STAR "L"-"Z"	MOH, DSC, SS "A"-"K"	MOH, DSC, SS "A"-"K"

24TH INF. DIV. MOH, DSC, SILVER STAR	**24TH INF. DIV.** MOH, DSC, SILVER STAR		
VIETNAM WAR			
11TH ARMORED CAV. MOH, DSC, SS, LOM, DFC, SM	**82D AIRBORNE DIV.** (WWI – PRESENT) MOH, DSC, SS		

WINGS OF VALOR

*A Projected 6-Volume History of
Army & Air Force Heroism in the Sky*

Volume I—The Birth of Military Aviation

Read the evolution of early combat aviation in World War II through the lives and actions of the 4 WWI Air Service Medal of Honor recipients. Follow the continuing efforts to establish a military air arm in the interim from 1918—1941.

Volume II—At War in the Pacific

From the attack on Pearl Harbor on December 7, 1941 until the close of 1943, the tide of war turned quickly in the Pacific. Through the lives, heroism, and in too many cased their death, the eight Pacific War Medal of Honor recipients from 1941 to 1943 reveal inspiring tales of the continuing evolution of combat aviation.

Volume III—Bombs Over Europe

The stories of 18 Medal of Honor recipients demonstrate how the United States Army Air Forces went head-to-head with the vaunted German Luftwaffe, and gained the aerial superiority necessary to enable the subsequent D-Day ground invasion.

THE DEFINING GENERATION

True Stories of a generation that challenged the traditions of the past, and in its search for meaning and purpose, redefined the world we live in today.

Fifteen years in development, "The Defining Generation" is a 600+ page tribute to the children of "The Greatest Generation." Baby boomers themselves, authors Doug and Pam Sterner weave personal vignettes, history, and the inspiring true stories of heroes and leaders of their generation. It is a positive portrayal of a generation in rebellion that rose up against traditions of the past, rejecting "the establishment" and its narrow views of life, equality, poverty and world need. The genesis of their thesis: "The Greatest Generation indeed saved our world (in World War II), but their children redefined it, making it better."

GO FOR BROKE:

The Nisei Warriors of World War II Who Conquered Germany, Japan, and American Bigotry

During World War II, Japanese-Americans were forcefully removed from their homes and businesses, and placed in "relocation" camps throughout the West. With countless instances of "Gestapo-like" tactics used against them, no one would have faulted them for being bitter or angry at the country that held them captive. Instead, the remarkable story of these Nisei (first generation Japanese born outside of Japan) warriors explains why they were eager to defend their American homeland, and how they became the most decorated fighting unit ever assembled in U.S. military history. Go For Broke is the incredible story of how these soldiers, known as the purple Heart Battalion," helped liberate Europe, the Pacific, and America from its pervasive and systemic bigotry.

A SPLENDID LITTLE WAR

"A Splendid Little War" recounts the chronology of events leading up to and during the fighting of the Spanish-American War. Perhaps no war in our history has been more popular at home or among those who fought it. American media played a significant role in instigating war, and fanning the patriotic fervor that made it so. In these pages you will meet the heroes of both sides and follow the chronology of battle through the actions of the aging Civil War heroes that commanded the American forces, and the young Soldiers, Sailors, Marines and Army Nurses who were conspicuous by their gallantry and devotion to duty and to each other.

DAY OF INFAMY

A Tribute to the Heroes of Pearl Harbor

The Japanese surprise attack on Pearl Harbor, Hawaii, on December 7, 1941 was perhaps the most cataclysmic event of the 20th Century. Within two hours the U.S. Navy 's Pacific Fleet was almost completely destroyed and Americas air forces at Hawaii and in the Far East were nearly annihilated. "Day of Infamy" takes the reader through the chronology of that fateful day through the actions of the 15 Sailors whose heroic actions in earned them the Medal of Honor. The little known stories of other heroes, and interesting snippets of human interest, enhance the narrative. Liberally illustrated with photos, maps, and pictures of individual heroes, this book is more than a history book—it is a look inside the human character of those who faced unbelievable odds in the most trying of times.

SHINMIYANGYO—THE OTHER KOREAN WAR

This book details the first American incursion in Korea in 1871, with narratives that are woven through the actions of the 14 Marines and Navy Bluejackets who received Medals of Honor for this first foreign war.

BOOKS BY AND ABOUT US

HOW PUEBLO BECAME THE HOME OF HEROES

Don't Fight City Hall - Entice them to Join You

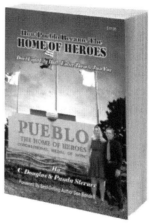

How Pueblo Became the Home of Heroes is much more than a fun read which is hard to put down. It is a memoir about the unique couple who spearheaded the drive to make Pueblo the Home of Heroes: Doug and Pamla Sterner. Doug and Pam are both magicians, singers, ventriloquists, but more important, patriots.

Pueblo, Colorado, the town they live in, at one time, was the only city in America which was the home of four living recipients of the Medal of Honor of Honor. It prompted a President of the nation to ask, "Is there something in the water out there?"

The stories of the celebrity-filled visits to Pueblo by celebrities, such as Wayne Newton and Adrian Cronauer (Good Morning, Vietnam!) and too many Medal of Honor recipients to share are neat and interesting.Few have done more to honor Medal of Honor recipients and other recipients of valorous military awards for all branches than the Sterners. It is great to read the story behind the stories.

Don Bendell (Best-Selling Author)

RESTORING VALOR

One Couple's Mission to Expose Fraudulent War Heroes and Protect Americas Military Awards System

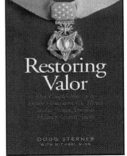

Stolen valor occurs when a person lies about receiving military decorations that he or she has in fact never earned. It has become a major societal problem that has been discussed numerous times in the news and, most recently, by the US Supreme Court. In Restoring Valor, Doug Sterner provides riveting case studies of the stolen valor imposters he has investigated and exposed, and the serious crimes—including murder—they have committed. He chronicles the evolution of stolen valor from the inception of the republic to today. Sterner demonstrates why the federal law he and his wife Pam helped to enact, called the Stolen Valor Act, is necessary.

JAMIE 'S STORY: GOD IS GOOD

A True Story of Friendship and Faith

Jaime Pacheco, one of the last Army Rangers killed in the Vietnam War, was the close friend of this author. In this small booklet, Doug Sterner details his own missions as a combat correspondent with Jamie 's Ranger Team, the impact on his life of Jamie 's death after Doug returned home, and the unexpected reunion with Jaime 's family decades later. Originally written as a personal memoir, this touching story set the stage for Doug 's subsequent work in his Home Of Heroes website, and much more.

Made in the USA
Columbia, SC
05 July 2022

62593035R00163